Praise for Many Ways, Middle Way, No Way

Hollywood Buddhism Sizzles! Michael Attie knows his dharma, and understands show-biz, and he puts the two together in this profound, lighthearted and often touching book. Attie will take you with him to visit the esteemed Zen master Sasaki Roshi or the Hindu saint Neem Karoli Baba, and then to meditate in his 'Don't Worry Zendo' or at the Playmates lingerie meditation hall. Can you find universal consciousness through the Feather Boa Dance? Read this book and find out! You'll have a good time on the way.

—Wes Nisker, author *Crazy Wisdom*, (Ten Speed Press)

Michael Attie's *Many Ways, Middle Way, No Way* examines Buddhism's many facets—its principles and practices, its lineages, and its consonance with other disciplines—all the time reminding us not to take *anything* too seriously. Attie's approach is encyclopedic, thoughtful, compassionate, and best of all, gently outrageous.

—Jeff Kane, author *The Healing Companion*, (HarperSanFrancisco)

A witty, compassionate, reverential and wise description of meditation and ordinary spiritual practice by a wandering pilgrim whose understanding matured immeasurably at midlife when he became the owner of "the world's largest lingerie store." Based upon his personal experiences, Attie describes an unconventional, self-authenticated, non-authoritarian spiritual practice drawn from Eastern devotional traditions and meditation techniques that embraces everyday life and promotes relationship and the collective experience. Attie's romp through Eastern mysticism and practice illuminates, instructs and celebrates life's juxtaposition of chaos, passion, music, poetry, art, travel and people with spiritual practice. His world is a warm place filled with love, humor and appreciation.

–Stan Madson, editor, The Bodhi Tree Book Review

In *Many Ways, Middle Way, No Way*, Michael Attie blends his clear and approachable Dharma interpretation with deep insight gained by living a joyful and attentive life. In so doing, he opens wider the path toward balance and clarity in our own lives. This manual is a true gift: an invigorating book filled with love, humor, wisdom, and a dose of invaluable anecdotes from poets, roshis, saints and sages.

–John Brandi, author, *Heartbeat Geography* (White Pine Press)

Michael Attie is passionate about meditation. With enchanting tales about his journey through the halls and temples of several Asian spiritual traditions and hilarious directions for breaking down staid concepts about meditation, Attie will entice even the most reluctant to find a cushion and begin a meditation practice. His life as a "Lingerie Monk," the richness of his experience as a meditator, and his earnest storytelling animate this personal and useful book.

–Susan Suntree, Editer, *Wisdom of the East: Stories of Compassion, Inspiration, and Love*(McGraw-Hill)

Many Ways, Middle Way, No Way is a unique, humorous and openhearted book which will delight the independent-minded spiritual seeker.

–Adelaide Donelley, author *Sorrow Mountain*(Kodansha)

MANY WAYS, MIDDLE WAY, NO WAY

A GUIDE TO MEDITATION, SPIRITUAL AWAKENING AND FUN

MICHAEL ATTIE

Many Ways, Middle Way, No Way

Stay open and quiet that is all.
What you seek is so near you
that there is no place for a way.

—Nisargadatta

Cover design:
Jake Freydont-Attie
& Noah Bardach

ISBN 0-9772538-0-5

Published by:
Neon Buddha Press
POB 46428
Los Angeles, CA 90046
info@dontworryzendo.com

TABLE OF CONTENTS

PREFACE

I wouldn't know whom to begin to acknowledge and thank for the inspirations and ideas in this book. I lay no claim to them being 'mine'; they come from here, there and everywhere. Writing this introduction, I realize why Milton Berle has always been my favorite comedian. Most of his humor usually centers around one topic—joke thievery. Meditators are sort of inspiration thieves. A line or concept from here or there—a lecture, interview or a book—sticks in your mind; insights from your sitting practice are confirmed and inspired. After a while it all fades in and you may not exactly recall where insights first came from.

Although we are all 'little Miltons,' meditators aren't possessive of wisdom, but believe that there is only one great teacher, whom we can all hear when we allow our usually busy minds to become quiet. Real understanding comes from this teacher and doesn't belong to anyone. So I don't feel too guilty for my omissions. Here and there I acknowledge a source, but I'm sure that many of the ideas and lines in this book I lifted right out of someone's talk or book without any credits. I can only thank and acknowledge many teachers and friends in dharma[*] who have inspired me along the way. A great blessing of my life has been to have met and studied with a number of deeply enlightened and inspired beings—all wonderful manifestations of the teaching. With gratitude I name the main ones who have shared their hearts, wisdom and inspiration: Joshu Sasaki Roshi[**] Shunryu Suzuki Roshi, Soen Nakagawa Roshi, Robert Aitken Roshi, Maezumi Roshi, Kalu Rimpoche**, H.H. The Dalai Lama, Neem Keroli Baba, Ramdass, Mother Krishna-bai, Jack Kornfield, Joko Beck, Steven Levine, Thich Nhat Hanh, Gary Snyder,

---

[*] Dharma is one of the most commonly used words in Eastern Mysticism—both Hindu and Buddhist. It means truth, reality, teachings—the truths about life, the universe, the human heart, mind and spirit, which we can learn through the practice of meditation and/or some spiritual discipline.

[**]. Roshi and Rimpoche, Japanese and Tibetan respectively, for teacher

Shinzen Young and my parents, Nanny and Eli. Thank you, Thank You, Thank You.

And deep gratitude to Marsha Berman, who acted as my remedial English IA teacher, often returning early chapters to me with more red crossouts and revisions than there were words in the original text; she transformed my barbaric English into an at least acceptable standard. And to Hal Ross, editor number two, who took over where Marsha left off with more red pencil, friendship, encouragement, and, I hope, may have further refined my English to occasional eloquence. And to Susan Goldberg, who studied the text and offered valuable insights and suggestions. To Ronnie Serr and Parvati Markus, who helped with the final editing and computer formatting.

Especial thanks to Lou Sitzer, Tom Surya, Nanny Attie, Silvana Behrens, Jeanne D'arcy, Diane Schainberg, Suzanne Taylor, Jeremy Tarcher, Laurie Savran, Pamala Machutt, Martha Bardach, Katherine Boyle, Ellen Kleiner and Daniel Flanaggan—all who looked at these chapters and offered valuable insights, feedback and encouragement.

Also my gratitude to my son Jake, who manned the store and offered invaluable computer and graphic aid. To Noah Bardach who helped with additional computer and graphic support. To Maria and Rebecca, catering for the belly; Esmerald and Anya, caring for the heart. To Stefanie and Gary, who kept an open refrigerator policy up the hill and provided psychological security by vowing to always feed me, even if I end up a penurious old man. To Jacquie and Steve, who kept an open refrigerator on the next hill over. To Bobji and Jean, who provided afternoon tea and gingersnap pick-up. To Niel, for walks around the block. To Carl Barks, the original title of the first versions of this book was 'Duck Dharma;' Barksists among my readers will understand. To the kind folks at Hollywood Certified Printers and Frank at Sharp Printers, both who helped through numerous printings of evolving manuscripts. To Phil who was always around with a helping hand and a saxophone duet. To Mary, calligrapher on the spot. And to Martha Duck Daughter, who—well how could I not thank her.

Most of these thoughts were organized and articulated trying to share dharma with people who came and sat in my living room—the

'Don't Worry Zendo.'* I thank the Don't Worriers for their patience, feedback, love and friendship and dedicate this book to; Silvana, Marsha, Ronni, Nava, Oscher, Meryl, David, Dee, Kathy, John, Jeanne, Cheryl, Tracy, Yonni, Fritz, Mark H., Ken, James, Fran, Phil, Susie, Sandra, Traci, Gigi, Mark Z., Mark M., Victor D., Ellie, Jan, Paul, Carol-Jean, Nina, Barbara, Robert and all other large and warm hearted Don't Worriers and Dharma friends everywhere.

* Zendo—Japanese for meditation hall.

PART ONE
INTRODUCTORY

INTRODUCTION

The Hindus typically divide life into three stages: the youth, the householder, and finally upon retirement from a busy family life, the spiritual seeker. My generation, in its enthusiastic discovery of eastern mysticism and meditation, often reversed this.

This was certainly true in my case. In my 20's I lived the life of a wandering pilgrim, staying at various monasteries and ashrams in India, Japan and in the U.S.A. In my 30's I retired from monkhood into the 'back to the land' lifestyle; I settled on a few acres in the California Sierras, built a house and grew my own vegetables, working at teaching and various odd jobs. At 40, my life took another turn: my father, who was getting on in years, offered me his business, 'Playmates of Hollywood.' If it was anything else I might have demurred, but I couldn't quite resist the prospect of owning "the world's largest lingerie store." I boarded up the cabin, headed down to L.A. and threw myself into a busy life.

I called on a Sufi Sheik I had met named Rashad. I asked him, "What does it mean? Why am I going into business?" Reshad looked deep into my eyes and poured more than words into my heart:

> You are going into business to give love to your customers. You may think that money and merchandise are changing hands, but that is not the important exchange. When someone leaves your store, they must feel absolutely content, like they have had a wonderful meal at the house of a most gracious host, as if they had been served hors d'oeuvres, wines, entrees, aperitifs, desserts—they should leave feeling that every possible consideration had been made to leave nothing unsatisfied.

I went to my old Zen teacher Sasaki Roshi and asked him the same question. I received a similar answer, "The store is your temple. It is the center of the universe. When you know this and love being there, the customer will also love being there."

My third guru in these matters was my father. Along with the keys to the store, he offered me a piece of unexpected advice; "The business of business is to forget business." Although he had never studied Buddhism, my father had a sort of natural Zen about him. Perhaps more from a simple desire for health and peace of mind than for any spiritual motivation, he recognized the challenge of being able to go home and get a good night's sleep, no matter how things were going at the store.

My respect for the Hindu view of life's stages continued to deepen the longer I studied meditation. I observed repeatedly that just going off into seclusion doesn't seem to help anyone too much in the long run. At least in the West, to help us grow into open, compassionate and wise people, meditation usually needs to be practiced as part of an engaged and active life in our society.

Non-separation is the bottom line and real challenge of meditation; continually letting go of our boundaries and experiencing everything and everyone as a part of ourselves. The broader we can extend our embrace of non-separation, the deeper our enlightenment. Of course, in a cave, because there is no one with us, the opportunities are limited. We might also finally feel limited living in some spiritual community where everyone is quiet, soft and pretty much has the same gentle aspirations as ourselves.

It seems that my whole generation is arriving at this conclusion. People are leaving their sequestered lives and moving out into the world. We can best realize the depths of our divinity by exploring the breadth of our humanity in numerous settings In my case, leaving the ashram and landing in a lingerie store, I had a few hard bumps, and more often, a few good laughs. It seemed a journey worth re-telling.

I have woven my personal tale throughout this book, often to illustrate points about the blessings and pitfalls of the spiritual path. Perhaps because the setting of much of my growth was in my father's and then my own lingerie and party-clothing store, I've always tried to avoid the solemnity that often plagues religion. Rather, a light and fun-loving heart has seemed to be the essential ingredient in studying and living the dharma. I have tried to infuse these pages with this same playful spirit. I hope you'll find it so.

WHY MEDITATE

For the past year, I've led a weekly afternoon meditation session, here in Hollywood, at a drop-in shelter for homeless teenagers. I've developed an introductory lesson about the ways that meditation can be helpful in one's life. Before the session, many of the kids are restless, bored, sleepy or plain disinterested. The speech, however, is effective. By the time I've finished I usually have their attention and most are eager to give meditation a try. It seems a good way to begin this book, so here is a condensed version of my talk.

Concentration. Whatever we wish to do in life, whether it is in business, sports, arts or whatever, we will succeed only to the degree that we have developed the power of concentration. At its most basic, meditation is an exercise in developing this power. As our concentration skills grow stronger, we can then apply them to whatever activities our lives are involved in.

Imagination and creativity. Meditation helps us to access the parts of our minds where creative leaps of the imagination occur. In the East, artistic creation and meditation almost always went hand in hand; most of the great artists and poets were meditators. And today, as interest in meditation grows in the West, its practice is similarly becoming widespread in our own artistic, musical and literary circles. Meditation is also an excellent stimulant for dreams. When I have time to go off and enter a period of intense sitting, my dream life is immeasurably enhanced. Often, months later I'll still be incorporating the dream inspirations into my art and my life.

Energy. You could say that a meditation session plugs you in for the day. Imperceptibly, beyond anything you can understand or describe, energy levels are charged and enhanced. To get you going and prepared for the day's work, a morning sitting is better than two or three cups of coffee. I often ride a stationary bike at the local gym in the morning. If for some reason I haven't meditated first, I'll look down to the control panel and notice that my pedaling is 10 or 15 RPMs slower than on meditation mornings. My whole energy charge hasn't been perked by the morning's plug-in.

Health. Almost any sort of healing is possible, once you have learned to open to the energy that can be experienced during meditation. When a meditator feels that their body is run down and vulnerable or the immune system is weak or that a cold is approaching, they'll often go off and do some intense sitting. The cold often disappears, the breath is stronger and more regular—vitality is restored.

People sometimes get back aches when they first take up meditation. Eventually they learn how to open to the energy currents that travel up and down the spine. At this point meditation is better than a chiropractor (and cheaper, too). The best thing for an aching, sore back is to sit up straight, stretch the spinal vertebrae apart and let the healing energy do its work.

Relaxation/stress relief. Meditation can teach us to access an inner peace where we know that things are okay no matter what the outer circumstances of our lives are. When I find myself restless in the middle of the night, I often sit up for ten or twenty minutes, then lie down, calmed and relaxed, and fall off into a peaceful slumber. Meditation is a proven tonic for a jagged nervous system.

Courage. For years I've kept an old fortune cookie saying tacked above my desk: "You will continue to take chances and be glad that you did so." Meditation can help us to find the positive energy, basic optimism, self-confidence, and perhaps fearlessness to take chances in life. We learn to experience a basic deep feeling that things will be OK no matter how they turn out. I can think of countless times in my life when I felt insecure about something: calling the girl for a date, proposing a project to someone who intimidated me, teaching classes. I think I can't do it. I sit to meditate for a few minutes and am soon laughing and telling myself, "Nothing to lose, may as well go for it."

We are all creating our personal myth—our vision and aspiration of the highest achievement we can realize in this life. Meditation practice is an invaluable aid, both in creating our vision for ourselves and in having the courage to do our best to realize it.

Perspective/patience. This is the compliment of courage. Sometimes it is important to step back and consider a situation before acting rashly. This can be especially important for young people. Often things get blown up; we get carried away and don't see the perspective of the complete picture. Taking a few breaths and contemplating the possible results of an action can save us a lot of trouble. Meditating on a proposed course of action may put a situation in a new and wiser light, and we can then act from a deeper wisdom.

Natural high. Meditation is learning how to really be here. I like to use the metaphor of a movie screen. When we are present and not wandering off somewhere in our minds, the screen of our life is ultra-wide seventy millimeter and lit-up in bright technicolor. The world is alive, fascinating, beautiful, mysterious. We don't need drugs.

The word 'Buddha' means 'awakened' in ancient *Pali* . When we meditate we are practicing moment after moment to keep our attention right here, not off somewhere in the past or future. We cultivate the habit of living fully awake – present for the people and events that we encounter in our lives.

Love. Basically we all want to be happy. The bottom line in finding happiness is having a life that is filled with love. Through meditation we can learn to experience enough inner fullness that we will begin to overflow – and then, we can be more open and generous. As we learn to give love, we receive it in kind.

Needless to say, most of the kids in the shelter have had difficult lives. Their injuries aren't too deeply hidden; many seem tough, defensive, cynical and often aggressive. Amazingly, when I raise this point, they all seem to pay attention, listen and hear me. However hardened their outward appearances, I hear few objections and a lot of agreement on this point. People know that love is the bottom line of life. Maybe these kids know it because they've missed it.

Honesty. We are usually unconsciously encumbered with defending the self-definitions that we are carrying around with us. Through meditation we begin to see and be less driven by the defensiveness that is pervading our personality. With less of a self-image to defend, our relationships are more honest and meaningful.

Wisdom/Enlightenment. All of the above points have dealt with our personal lives and with how meditation can improve and enrich them. This is natural and we mostly all begin here. But there is also something beyond this, which we can call wisdom or Enlightenment. Through deeper insights, we gradually learn to experience the truth that we don't exist as separate people. We are all creating each other and are a part of each other. All of the previous points dealt with how the dawning of this wisdom will effect our personal lives. At a certain point in our meditation practice, as this wisdom deepens, we sit as much to be helpful to others as to enhance our own lives.

Here we've arrived at the first of many paradoxes or complimentary dichotomies that one encounters on the spiritual path. Meditation will eventually take us to the impersonal level, but it can also be a great help at the personal level. In other words, we don't need to immediately eliminate all personal concerns from our sitting. Meditation will give us greater insight, perspective and positive energy to deal with whatever our life brings us with clarity and courage. Eventually, we'll be able to let go of our personal ruminations and move on to deeper levels of trans-personal energy.

Humor/playfulness. Our self-definitions are usually tightly bound by the success or failures of our personal endeavors. This is natural. Through meditation practice, we experience a spaciousness around our previously tight self-definition. There is no doubt I'm Mike, but I'm Mike and so much more.

We become less uptight and hobbled by an obsession to always be right or succeed. Real fun is not worrying too much about consequences. Having the space to see the humor in ourselves and others, we can be a little less serious and more playful in our relationships.

Sometime during my rap I also tell the kids at the shelter that actually no one can teach them how to meditate. The deeper one enters, the vaster, more mysterious and inexplicable it becomes. It would be like trying to tell a newborn baby how to live. At best a spiritual friend can point you in the right direction, but one must take the journey for oneself.

Words, words, words. For every minute devoted to them, in a book or talk, one should spend ten minutes in silent sitting. Here is where we find the real teacher. At this point, I light a stick of incense and invite the kids to breathe with me. You too. I hope you will put down this book many times, smile, breathe, let-go and invite the peaceful love-silence, that is the source of all these words, into your being.

THE PARADOXICAL WAY

The Buddha called the spiritual path “the middle way.” This might as easily be translated as “the balanced way,” “paradoxical way,” or “way of complementary dichotomies.” A life of spiritual practice often seems like a balancing act between seemingly opposed but actually complementary tendencies. As our life and practice unfolds, sometimes it is appropriate to emphasize one aspect, yet as conditions change over days or years, our practice may re-balance itself with more emphasis on the complementary approach. The re-balancing may occur many times in one’s lifetime.

Here is a brief survey of some of these complementary dichotomies. Most of them are elaborated on in later chapters.

<u>Doubt/Faith</u>—Some traditions, such as the Rinzai School of Zen, emphasize arousing a great sense of doubt — emptying our minds of its solidified certainties as to who we are and what the world is. In Tibetan Buddhism, a practice of great faith, the word for such radical doubt does not even exist. Actually, either way will bring us to the same truth—that we are not this little body that comes and goes, but are the illimitable and deathless source of all things. Some traditions emphasize a broad approach, Korean Zen Master Sung Sah Nimh says that the way requires "great faith, great doubt and great courage."

<u>Gradual/Sudden</u> Enlightenment—Zen Buddhists have been sparring over this issue for 1500 years and it’s one of the main fissures that have separated the Rinzai and Soto schools of Zen. Today, looking at the broad vista of the world’s mystical traditions, we can see that it’s a pointless debate. One may, in fact, have many gradually deepening sudden enlightenments. Beyond sudden or gradual is the endless realization of the fact that we are all already enlightened. Gradually and suddenly we realize this—over and over, deeper and deeper.

<u>Effort/Grace</u>—Sometimes, it seems that Grace is immediate; at other times it seems like our own great effort is required. With deepening practice, the line between the two becomes less certain. New understandings come to us easily, and we wonder if what seemed like effort may have been grace after all. Then, questions like “Who’s effort is it?” arise. Maybe, it’s all grace.

When he was a young Zen student, Robert Aitken became obsessed with the question, "Is effort necessary?" He spent two days searching Tokyo for his teacher, Soen-Nakagawa Roshi, who, when finally cornered and queried in a restaurant, would only respond back with wide eyes and mouth agape, "Effort? effort? effort?"

Bliss/Healing—Some teachers and traditions encourage us to experience bliss, and it is true that through meditation we will increasingly experience bliss as the nature of our consciousness and being. Other approaches, however, dwell more on healing—describing meditation as acknowledging, feeling and purifying our fears and psychological injuries. A balanced approach recognizes and embraces both our bliss and our contractions as they arise in the course of deepening practice.

Concentration/Observation—Some traditions encourage us to make great concentrated efforts—setting the mind up like a stone wall to block out all obstructive and distracting thoughts. In other approaches we just observe the body sensations, thoughts and feelings as they arise, without trying to change or exclude anything

Form/Formless—Some approaches emphasize meditation as mindful awareness of what we see in front of us in the world of form. Other ways emphasize experiencing our dissolution into the formless world of pure energy. These really go hand in hand. The deeper we learn to go into the formless, the more the world of form seems to manifest on a mysterious and sacred altar. We feel the fullness of the formless as the ocean/cradle that creates and blesses all form. And conversely, the more habitually we are awake to the world of form, the more we experience it as inseparable from the formless source-ocean.

Lovingkindness/Non-dualism—Generating feelings of lovingkindness towards self, other people and the whole world is emphasized in some practices. Pure non-dual approaches emphasize cutting thorough all dualistic concepts of separate self and others, in order to directly experience all-pervading non-dual consciousness. However, no one can stay in that state perpetually. As we learn to experience the non-dual, it is inevitable that feelings of loving-kindness begin to permeate our lives and meditations. Similarly, through cultivation of loving-kindness, we are led to an awareness of the interconnectedness of all things.

Devotional/Impersonal—Some people may be drawn to focus their meditations on a form of deity devotion (Jesus, Buddha, Mother Mary, Guru etc.) Others may be drawn to a formless meditation. I think most meditators eventually include some of both approaches in their practice. Either way, the embrace becomes more intimate as we let go of the past and future and allow the mind to rest in the present moment.

Feminine, receptive/ Masculine, arousing—The Buddha described meditation as similar to tuning a string: not too loose, not too tight. Sometimes we may need to be balanced towards being soft, quiet and receptive. Other times we may need a more arousing, energizing and masculine energy in our practice. Some pathways predominantly tilt toward one energy or another—i.e. Rinzai Zen is well known for its rather macho proto-samurai style, while the Soto Zen style is quiet and softer

Simplicity/Tantric activity—Some approaches promote a life-style that is rather reclusive and removed from activities. Others are more Tantric—they believe that we grow through throwing ourselves into the distractions and difficulties of an active life in the world. We all have periods of our life that are lived on one side or another of this divide. We slowly learn the level of simplicity or complexity best suited to our gifts and needs.

Indulgence/Asceticism—When the Buddha used the phrase 'middle way,' he was usually referring to a spiritual life that was well balanced between these two extremes. This is one of the most difficult paradoxes that people on the spiritual path are always trying to understand and resolve.

Some teachers recommend total indulgence. The underlying idea is that one cannot find complete liberation unless one has used up one's karma, —i.e. lived out and satisfied all of one's latent desires. Of course, the ascetics would claim that a life lived as a total hedonistic spree, rather than eliminating karma, will just create more of it—and a very self-centered sort of spiritual aspirant. Which way is correct? As we learn to quiet our minds, we will hear the guiding voice of our intuition.

Withdrawal/Engagement—Sometimes we are full of energy, overflowing with the fruits of spiritual practice. In these times we can devote our life to engaged good works— spiritual, social, political, environmental causes. For many, this life of service is a way of practice and of fullfillment. At other times, though, we may need to withdraw from society in order to recharge.

Enthusiasm/Resistance— Sometimes our practice is full of joy, openness and grace; the divine presence is immediate and imminent. We naturally have great enthusiasm for meditation. At other times we're just not in the mood—tired, restless, afraid or grouchy. As our sitting matures we give in less to our mood swings and judgments of good or bad. We just do it. We come to understand that we are surrendering to a process that is infinitely greater than what our limited intellect can understand. Who knows? Periods of difficult practice may be more beneficial than easy ones.

Aachan Cha, a great Thai master, described meditation practice as like going down a road with ditches off the shoulder on either side: "Sometimes I see a student going way off to the left—I say, 'watch out, head right.' Other times they're far to the right; I give a warning—'head left.'" At times, as our lives and practices unfold, it is necessary and appropriate to go off for a while to the left or right. It is also helpful to know that there is a balanced middle to which we may return.

A SHORT SPIRITUAL AUTOBIOGRAPHY

Over the last one hundred years, what started as a trickle has become a veritable flood of Eastern spiritual traditions transplanting themselves to the West. In meditation circles, people wonder how these ancient traditions will transform and coalesce as styles and approaches particularly suited to Western culture evolve. In the scale of such cultural diffusions, one hundred years is actually a very short time. In China, it took many centuries after the initial introduction of Buddhism for Chan, the particularly Chinese form of Buddhism, to arise. Although we still have no idea what a particularly Western form of Dharma practice will look like, certain tendencies are unmistakable. Here are a few:

Gender equality. By and large the history of Eastern spirituality has been blatantly sexist. The Hindu, Buddhist and Sufi traditions have largely reflected the patriarchal cultures in which they flourished; the women, for the most part, were kept in the kitchen. Although there have been some notable exceptions, dharma has largely been a man's game. Throughout India, Southeast Asia, China and Japan, the great teachers, as well as most of the people that the society allowed the time and leisure for serious practice, have usually been men.

Reflecting the growing gender equality of our culture, for the first time in history this has changed. Many of the most inspiring and influential Dharma teachers in the West are women. Looking at various Dharma centers, woman also comprise an equal share of practitioners, officers, board members. The salubrious effects of this gentle and nurturing feminine influence is reflected in many ways.

Democratic and informal. Dharma centers that are run in an autocratic and hierarchical style don't seem to survive as well as centers where the final authority, even above that of the teacher, is vested in a board of directors, elected by the committed practitioners. The courage, honesty and outspokenness required in the give and take of group decision- making may be as important as any strictly "spiritual" practice.

In the melting-pot world that we inhabit today, it is hard to take the rigid social roles and distinctions of traditional societies too seriously. Dharma centers reflect this; the ones that are flourishing are usually notable for a friendly, informal and open style of social intercourse.

Ecumenical. In the late forties, Aldous Huxley, one of the first great Western mystics, wrote his pioneering book, *The Perennial Philosophy*. He claimed that the various religions might differ in their rituals, prayers and outer beliefs—but in their essential core, they are identical. He showed that the perennial essence is only taught in the particular religion's inner or esoteric school: Islam's Sufi sect, Kabbalistic Judaism, esoteric Christianity, Advaitic Vedanta.

This understanding has set a wonderful ecumenical tone to our spiritual renaissance. Some people may feel most deeply rooted in the practices of one tradition or another, but they usually don't have the narrow-minded and self-righteousness belief that theirs is the only or the best path. Other people, like myself, are sort of spiritual butterflies, who love to taste and incorporate the practices of many traditions in their lives, and yet know the ultimate truth is unspeakable and beyond any one of them.

Beginning in the sixties, ecumenical conferences have become a hallmark of our times. Zen roshis, swamis, rabbis and Sufi sheiks all sit together on the podium. I've attended a number of such gatherings. And it doesn't take a genius to see that they are all essentially saying the same thing.

Engaged. While there is a quietist streak in eastern spirituality, westerners, probably due to the influence of the Judeo-Christian ethic, tend to want to bring their understanding into the world. After a while we find that it is not so difficult to experience our true nature; when we sit quietly it will shine through all things. The next challenge is to express it through some enlightened activity.

Earth Based. As our planet is endangered, a spirituality that is not grounded on a love and commitment to its health seems self-centered and frivolous. The truth be told, we are not separate from the Earth; the children cannot flourish if the mother is unhealthy. In these times, at least living lightly and responsibly on the planet, or better, being an environmental activist of some sort, seems inseparable from the spiritual path.

Mostly all urban meditation centers hope to or have acquired a country retreat center. Many groups have back packing retreats. One way or another, all recognize that being in community with unspoiled nature is among the greatest of teachers.

Egalitarian and Sangha oriented. Telling "your story" is a tradition that is emerging at many Western dharma centers. After meditation meetings someone may volunteer to tell their story: how they came to find the dharma and meditation practice in their life. This practice reflects our egalitarian tendencies: everyone's story is precious and equally important.

Likewise, I find that when people come to meditate with me, a commonly asked question is, "How and why did you take up meditation in your life?" Western people don't mind being direct and personal. As my journey has been typical of America's pilgrimage to encounter eastern mysticism, taking up this question might be an interesting way to begin this book. True, my story is precious and important, but no more so than yours or anyone else's. We are all walking on this path of life, hopefully learning to be mindful, compassionate, and happy. Our paths may look different at times and similar at others, but they do all point to the same direction. So here is my short spiritual autobiography.

Almost everyone who explores meditation practice is motivated by some balance of two forces—personal suffering and an intimation that real peace and even rapture is possible. If life were an endless Club Med, there would be no reason to change it or try something new. However, most people's lives contain a shadow of some pain and feelings of incompleteness. Yet, also here and there, through nature, art, relationships, mind-expanding drugs, or travel (to name a few), we know that our true nature is one of great joy. And more, we may intuit that we may learn how to experience it more deeply and regularly.

This 'carrot and stick' effect was no different in my case than in many others. The stick was not too remarkable or different than that of the common lot—general feelings of social insecurity, inadequacy and loneliness. Through shyness, ineptitude or feelings of unworthiness, I was usually without a girlfriend in grade school and through most of college. I had some deep feeling of doom that this was my destined lot in life.

Fortunately, I also found a carrot that saved me from total despair. My first religion was music. Through junior and senior high school I was something of a Schroeder and felt a personal identity with Beethoven. A primary pursuit of my after school hours was reading biographies and listening to his (and other classical) music. I would feel empowered by the promethian side of Beethoven to "grab destiny by the throat." Of course it would all fade away by the next day when I would be too terror stricken to approach whatever girl was the object of that semester's secret crush.

This all culminated late one evening when listening to a recording of the late quartet op. 132. I experienced what was probably the first 'spiritual awakening' of my life. Mystics often describe the spiritual experience as similar to an onion being peeled away layer by layer. With the unpeeling of each layer, one enters more deeply into a core of vulnerable gentleness and delicious intimacy with the source of life. Something like this happened. I felt the embrace of an affirmation beyond all the pains and joys of life and death. I guess people thought I was crazy when I went around telling them that I had met the spirit of Beethoven. Maybe I was. But I knew I had touched something that was my most real self. I wanted to learn how to open into it again.

My religious upbringing was that of a typical fifties middle-class Jewish household. Several days a week, after grade school I would go off to Hebrew School for Bar-Mitzvah preparation. Unfortunately, the Judaism of the fifties didn't have much of a spiritual or intellectual content to challenge a young and curious mind. Most of the teachers seemed to be neurotic, the lessons were rote and the Rabbi let you choose between three prepared Bar-Mitzvah speeches. I sometimes jokingly say that he was my first Zen Roshi, as I eventually turned East to fill the spiritual vacuum that if felt. Fortunately, Judaism has recently gone deeper into its roots and found a more spiritually relevant content.

By the time of my Bar Mitzvah, I considered myself an agnostic. Through the services of my father, I had discovered the written lectures of Robert Ingersoll, the nineteenth century humanist and 'great agnostic.' In grandiose oratory, Ingersoll thoroughly debunked revealed religions as unscientific superstition and proclaimed that the only real religion was what one could find for oneself in the human heart.

I first came across Buddhism and Zen in the early sixties, after my freshman year in college. Someone gave me the book *Zen Flesh, Zen Bones,* a translation of dialogues from the early Chinese Tang dynasty

Zen eccentrics. I was utterly captivated by these stories and, of all the people attending UCLA summer school, happened to ask just the right one if she had ever heard of Zen. She not only had heard of it but gave me directions to a suburban house where a Zen master who had just arrived from Japan was in residence. I anticipated that Zen would be having tea and enigmatic conversations; the thought of meditating had never entered my mind. Sasaki Roshi did serve me tea, but then set he set me on a cushion and gave me my first meditation lesson. Roshi was never lacking in a keen sense of humor. He would point his finger at me, say “Pow, Pow,” laugh and then say in his few words of English, “Now show me Zen.” I certainly wasn’t ready for such subtle teachings. However, the idea of ‘being in the moment’ stuck. I remember walking around UCLA talking about and trying to practice it. Sometimes, things seemed to light up and come alive; I think I was having my first taste of walking meditation.

The closest I got to a real Zen encounter was one afternoon during meditation when a door-to-door salesman rang. He was offering a free treatment at a local beauty parlor as an inducement to try out a vacuum cleaner. Since the Roshi was bald and spent about half of the day obsessively mopping and dusting his tiny cottage, I would say the pesky salesman was knocking at the wrong door. The concept of a Zen monk seemed to be unknown to him; he persisted in asking for the ‘lady of the house’ and in trying to get in to demonstrate the vacuum cleaner. Roshi rubbed his bald head repeatedly and laughingly insisted, “No hair, No dirt.” I think he was enjoying some Zen symbolism. The salesman finally gave up his efforts to meet the lady of the house. I doubt if he ever got the symbolism.

I went back to visit Roshi a few more times that summer and then transferred to Berkeley where, although the seeds of meditation practice had been planted, exams, papers and protests quickly took over my life. However, sometimes when I had a few spare moments, and especially during a summer spent wandering around Europe, I would find myself staring at blank walls and trying to empty my mind.

One day in my senior year, I noticed a tall, lanky long- haired fellow dressed in Franciscan robes wandering across campus. I introduced myself and learned that he wasn’t an official Franciscan, but just liked their robes. (These were psychedelic years, people dressed up in archetypal garb.) Sri Christos taught a yoga and meditation class on the top floor of the Student Union every Wednesday afternoon. I became a regular and made the very gentle and kind Sri Christos into my second meditation teacher. Sri Christos was a fan of the great Hindu sage, Sri Ramana Maharshi (1880-1950), and he shared with us Ramana's writings and teachings on non-duality This was a turning point. I quickly became a devotee and began to devour the teachings of Sri Ramana.

I graduated with a degree in history and decided, before applying to grad school, to take a year off to explore and read on my own. That year stretched to two, and then to three, as I realized that studying meditation and Eastern spirituality was what I really wanted to do with my life, rather than teach history. About a year after graduation, a real transformation occurred in my life. I started to set my alarm early to get up for a few hours of early morning sitting. I gave up my occasional pot smoking. I spent my free days reading extensively on Hinduism and Buddhism, often at the excellent library of the Berkeley Theological Seminary. Living in an inexpensive off- campus room, it was easy to support myself working a day or two a week at odd jobs. I would also go down to L.A periodically, where my father would always offer me temporary work in one of his clothing stores.

Living in the mid-sixties Bay Area, I was definitely positioned in the best place in the Western World for a life of investigating Eastern spirituality. The first Eastern teachers were arriving in the West and a wave of excitement would pass through spiritual circles as each would visit town. About that time in Berkeley I joined the 'Floating Lotus Magical Opera Company,' a group of people who were interested in Eastern Spirituality and had banded together and created a theater ritual based on an amalgam of Balinese, Chinese, Hindu and Tibetan spiritual dramas. We would travel around the Bay Area and Northern California, meditating, chanting and performing the Opera. I remember one evening there was an incredible excitement in the troupe because a real Tibetan Lama was in the audience. This was Tarthang Tulku, the first Tibetan teacher to show up in America. Of course, today there are Tibetan Buddhist Centers almost everywhere, and a new Tibetan Rinpoche shows up in town almost every week.

About this time I discovered the San Francisco Zen Center and Shunru Suzuki Roshi. I started attending lectures and sort of fell in love with Suzuki Roshi. He was a man of unusual grace, transparency and gentle humor. I remember the first time I went to a lecture. Being a young romantic would-be mystic, I cried while looking at Suzuki Roshi's beautiful eyes and repeating to myself the last lines of Yeats' poem 'Lapis Lazuli':

> Two Chinamen, behind them a third
> Are carved in Lapis Lazuli...
> Their eyes, mid many wrinkles, their eyes,
> Their ancient glittering eyes are gay.

About this time a book was published that influenced and inspired many people: *The Three Pilars of Zen.* This was something of an revelation; it was the first book that actually described the details of Zen practice, rather than just the philosophy. Although the book came from a samurai-like and rather hysterical Zen tradition, it inspired a generation of future meditators, myself included, with a great enthusiasm to go off and do intensive Zen retreats.

Also at that time, the rigors of life in a traveling theater troupe started to wear on me. I felt the need for a settled life in which to pursue a more diligent and uninterrupted meditation practice. My father, who owned a chain of clothing stores in LA, offered me the management of a store. So I resettled in L.A., took over the store and became a full time student of old Sasaki Roshi.

My stay in L.A. lasted for several years, during which time I probably mismanaged more than managed the store. I was lucky not to have fomented a strike by making the employees meditate with me in the mornings before the store opened. Although I always remained fond of Sasaki Roshi, I gradually became disillusioned with his approach to Zen. The Rinzai Zen practiced at his center was something like being in the army. I came to realize that I wanted to practice at a place that emphasized compassion and caring about other people's growth as much as your own.

Sasaki also seemed to me to be something of a spiritual egoist. His basic mindset seemed to be that he was the only person with a true understanding. If another teacher was mentioned, his usual reply was, "Not a real Roshi." Having wandered the spiritual circuit a great deal since then, I now realize that this sort of subtle spiritual ego among supposedly egoless teachers is, unfortunately, almost more common than uncommon. I was especially upset one day when a friend tried to show Roshi a book of Ramana Maharshi's teachings. Without really looking at the book, he spent the good part of a lecture putting it down. This was the last straw for me. (I have heard through friends that Sasaki Roshi has become much more open-minded in recent years.)

So I gave the store back to my dad, (by that time he was probably relieved that I hadn't bankrupted him through the neglect of my going off to endless Zen retreats,) and I shipped off to Japan to find a Zen monastery. As my luck would have it, I ended up at Ryutakuji, a picture book monastery on the slopes of Mt. Fuji. The abbott, Soen-Nakagawa Roshi, is undoubtedly one of great legends of 20th Century Zen. He ran Ryutakuji in a soft and gentle style that was perfectly suited to my tastes: no stick, no yelling, people being kind to each other.

I actually can remember very few of Soen Roshi's words. The lectures were in Japanese, so my main memory is that they went on forever. About all I can remember of the interviews is that he gave me almost the same koan* as Sasaki Roshi; "Show me mu (emptiness) when you are dead." (I doubt if they conspired.) Soen's presence, however, was infectious and unforgettable. Although he was a little man, he seemed to have the huge broad smile and deep booming voice of a giant. I still remember his handshake and the warm glow I would carry with me for a few days after receiving it. Soen Roshi still periodically shows up in my dreams; I inevitably wake-up filled with love and a warm happiness that is sometimes mixed with a little longing to see him again. I would have stayed on at Ryutakuji, except for one problem; the sitting periods were interminable. By the end of my first three month training season there, I had torn the ligaments in my knee. Hobbling on a cane, I landed in L.A., resigned that this body was not designed for intense Zen sitting, at least not Japanese monastic style. So I gave up on organized group sitting for a while.

Visiting in the Bay Area, a friend took me to a Sufi meeting. This was the heyday of Sufi Dancing in Marin county. Three or four hundred people would pack the big meetings on Wednesday nights. The

---

* Koan—Rationally unsolvable Zen riddle

Sufi Choir would sing while drummers and musicians played; everyone would chant mantras and move in concentric circle mandalas. I felt as if I had been waiting for this all my life. What a revelation and relief from the sober and restrained world of Zen! Since I couldn't sit cross-legged, I would enter a path that emphasized singing and dancing. I moved to Marin county, enrolled in music school and became a Sufi.

But disillusionment gradually crept in. I loved all of the joyous exaltation, but to my judgmental mind, it started to look like a lot of frosting with no cake. Personally, I also kept a diligent meditation practice, though just in my room on a chair. But it seemed that many of the Sufis lacked that commitment and just went for the hoopla. It didn't seem that a strong practice was pushing the people to confront and grow through their fears, delusions and sharp edges. Perhaps they were, and I just could not see it.

Also, my Hindu side was feeling undernourished. From the beginnings of my spiritual life I had always been sort of an ecumenical Hindu/Buddhist—feeling an equal interest and enthusiasm for both pathways. For these years I had been reading the works and feeling devotion for Ramana Maharshi and a few of the other great Hindu Gurus. And now, through a number of friends who had visited India and returned, word was spreading of Neem Keroli Baba, an old man usually wrapped in a blanket who Ramdas (Richard Alpert) was eventually to make famous in the West. I had already done the Zen pilgrimage, now it was time for the complement; I packed my bags, went to L.A. for a few months and worked for my dad, saved a few dollars and bought a ticket to India.

My expectations of meeting the 'Great Guru' were largely formed by reading accounts of people's encounters with Ramana Maharshi. Typically, at a certain point the Maharshi would initiate them: as he would look intently at them, all conceptions of separation, time and space would melt away. The person's questions would be answered and doubts dissolved; in a timeless flow of blissful grace they would feel 'taken up' into a guru/disciple relationship.

It often didn't work out quite that way with Neem Keroli Baba. But first a little background. Baba, when he was a young man, entered a cave to meditate on Hanuman—the Hindu monkey deity. People in Northern India believe that when he emerged, three years later, he had become an Avatar (incarnation) of Hanuman himself in human form. And he did live a monkey-like life. Besides having a big ape's body and limbs, in my short three weeks with him (right before his maha-samadhi—i.e. death of the body), he mostly laughed, played, made jokes and threw fruit at people.

I quickly learned to forget my expectations about meeting the Guru, or anything else for that matter. If there is one word to describe someone who incarnates a monkey spirit, it is anarchy. Baba didn't seem to have any operating principle except unpredictability; in my case at least, he certainly didn't seem to operate in the "direct line to bliss" style. It seemed that everyone who was around him encountered just the right circumstances that enabled them to experience their own personal chaos that could lead to their deepest purification and healing..

The second or third day I was at Neem Karoli Baba's ashram, I fell completely in love – not with the guru, but with a woman. After some brief flirtations with each other, her previously estranged boyfriend returned and the reconciled couple moved in across a curtain divide from me. This situation released a flood of unresolved emotions and images from my unconscious. For days I lived in some sort of heaven/hell state. The little bit I did sleep would be accompanied by endless dreams of abandonment, despair and loneliness. So I would sit up and meditate through the night, feeling united with Baba in ever deeper states of blissful grace. During the day Baba would look at me, laugh and say something like "Strange dreams last night," or "You live in the White House." (I had moved outside of my room and spent the nights on the porch of what was called the White House.) I felt wrenched apart but Baba was telling me that he was with me and guiding this process that I was going through.

The point is that in a few very intense weeks, a tremendous amount of deep karma was purified and released. Since then I've never felt anywhere near that sort of despair or emotional turmoil around a relationship or lack of one. When one finds a great teacher to hang out with, this sort of cleansing can happen. They are a fire which can quickly draw out and burn up a tremendous amount of old injuries, fears and unnecessary baggage.

Neem Keroli Baba somehow established a unique and wildly unpredictable relation with everyone who showed up at the ashram. One never knew when or how this would happen, but almost everyone has their special story. In my case it was potatoes. The ashram seemed to be run in a sort of arbitrary and chaotic way, designed I suspect to bring everyone's insecurities and petty jealousies to the surface. Some were allowed to stay later in the day, others had to leave early, there were various grades of accommodations, from quite nice to primitive. You never knew where you stood for long. One day, in a back corner of the ashram, I was talking with someone about how to improve my status when out of the blue Baba was standing there watching us. He called her over and inquired about what we were talking about. After a few moments consultation he called over the ashram cook and gave special instructions; I was to be cooked for special and eat by myself—only potatoes. For the remainder of my stay I sat apart from everyone on the verandah, eating my all-potato diet.

I have no idea what this meant except that for the twenty-five years since that day potatoes have been my sacrament and fetish. If I'm ill I go on the potato diet and recover quickly. Hungry, a bite or two does the job. Anyone who visits me for a meal or invites me to a potluck knows what they'll get. One of these days I'm going to do pilgrimage high in the Andes to the potato birthplace. I can only guess that Baba must have seen deep into my body and detected that it has some sort of extreme potato requirements.

Neem Keroli Baba had a deep spiritual power and psychic gift that many people who met him can attest to. One day, after I had been there for a week or two, the friend with whom I had come to India suddenly asked Baba, "What should I do?" Baba laughed and replied, "Go on pilgrimage. Go to Dakshineswar, Varanasi, Rishikesh, Ramanashram, Ananda Ashram, see Anandamayama. And take Gita's brother (my name at the time) with you." There followed a day of endless discussions with various advisers: I must go immediately, postpone departure, appeal the "Jao" (go away) order, etc. Finally the next day I cried out, "Baba, I don't want to go." Baba laughed, "Then don't go, you'll go soon enough."

One morning, a week or two after this incident, orders came suddenly: everyone (40 or 50 Westerners who were resident in the ashram and a few houses in the surrounding Himalayan valley) must leave within a half-hour and not come back for one month.

Pandemonium ensued as people were throwing things in bags and running to the bus stop. Every few minutes some ashram worker would come running up to the house, "Baba says everyone must be out of here in five minutes."

That was the last I ever saw of Neem Keroli Baba in the body; two weeks after the Jao order, he did likewise. Before dying Baba said, "The love is too great, this body cannot contain it any longer." He also said many times, "I am coming to America." I believe that he has come to America – through the deep love that he has inspired in the lives of many devotees here. The three weeks that I spent with Neem Keroli Baba were the intense beginning of a connection, through dreams and meditations, that has deepened and grown more intimate through the years.

And as Baba predicted, after his passing I remained in India for another eight months and went on pilgrimage, pretty much to all of the places he mentioned. Then I returned to America, worked at this and that, did a back-to-the land stint and built a house in the Sierra foothills, raised a son, inherited my father's business and founded the Don't Worry Zendo in Los Angeles. All the while I went on studying and practicing with various teachers and groups—Zen, Vipassana, Tibetan and Advaita. This has been a long pilgrimage and I'm only part way through it. I don't think it is necessary to complete the story right here but we should pause and consider some lessons gained by taking you through it this far with me.

BHAKTI AND JNANA/GURUS AND TEACHERS

> There are two ways, one is inquiry
> the other is surrender.
> —Ramana Maharshi

Most spiritual paths are a blending of some combination of two elements: the way of the head and the way of the heart. In India the way of the head is called *jnana*, which could be translated alternatively as wisdom, discrimination or inquiry. The way of the heart is called *bhakti*, which means love, devotion, surrender. Just as individuals vary in their psychological and emotional makeup, various teachers and practices often tend towards one or the other. As one's spiritual practice matures and ripens, it often becomes broad and well-balanced enough to deeply incorporate both the way of the head and of the heart.

The way of the head is the more rational, scientific or even agnostic approach. The jnani rejects all beliefs in anything that is not experienced as certain and real, right here and now. There are no intervening deities, guides, heavenly realms—because there is no past and no other place. There is only being: just this mind/moment, and the inquiry into its nature.

Some element of bhakti, however, can be found in almost all spiritual pathways. For most people, a pure jnana approach is too abstract, dry and difficult. They also need the emotional fervor of love and devotion to fuel their spiritual pursuit. If so, they can direct themselves toward a guru—(a person inhabiting a material body) or toward a primeval deity such as Buddha, Kwannon, Avalokitishvara, Jesus, Mother Mary, Rama, Krishna or Hanuman.

Sometimes a guru is conceived of as an incarnation of one of these deities, or bhakti energy might be directed towards an all-encompassing idea of the divine: God, Allah or a concept such as Buddha-Mind. Through fascination, love and faith we all can learn to empty ourselves and experience the truth that everything we see is the guru/deity. When one's practice is enlivened by the heart element of devotion, one might want to sing and dance, as well as sit and contemplate.

People often need to make a distinction between a guru and a master/teacher. Traditionally, the guru is thought of as a divine incarnation of God, who has taken a human body to help humanity. The guru is perceived as being infallible; his or her every action is in harmony with all of creation and embodies the perfect teaching for devotees.

Guru reverence is found in some of the meditation traditions of India as well as in Tibetan Buddhism. In contrast, in the Vipassana of Southeast Asia and in the Zen of China, Korea and Japan, the teacher is not usually regarded in such avataric, super-human terms, but rather as a gifted but very human person who has worked hard and realized a deep understanding.

Are the Indians and Tibetans just more gullible or psychologically immature and in need of projecting God-like qualities onto some sort of substitute mother or father figures? Or is it that the very highest beings, people you can think of in Guru like terms (Ramakrishna in the ninteenth century, Ramana Maharshi—regarded as an incarnation of Shiva, Neem Keroli Baba in the twentieth century) only take their incarnations in India? These are good questions to ponder; I've never figured it out myself and they may be unanswerable anyway.

In whatever way it is conceived, guru devotion is a way of bhakti and surrender; it is among the most subtle, deep and powerful paths. If you are fortunate enough to encounter a teacher (or an archetypal deity) whom you can love and regard in such guru-like terms, this may be a great blessing to you. What counts is developing the love and faith that allows you to regard the Guru as everything. The boundries between yourself and all things will dissolve within this love.

For the bhakti anything that could ever exist or happen is part of the guru. Anything one could ever think or feel, the very consciousness to whom any thought or feeling is occurring, the very concepts of time and space: all are the guru/deity. The deeper that this faith and devotion become part of one's meditation, the less room is left for anything – except to endlessly open, let-go, surrender and affirm that it is not even one's meditation, but it all belongs to the guru. All things and the guru/deity are one in an unspeakable vast and spacious love that creates all being.

Before continuing to extol the benefits of guru-devotion, I must raise a big red flag of caution. I may have been lucky that my guru, Neem Keroli Baba, died five weeks after I met him—longer exposure might have resulted in some disillusionment. (Although I've never met or heard of anyone who was disillusioned with Neem Keroli Baba.) Certainly with Western Gurus disappointment is often the end result.

Recently, I came across a book entitled *Enlightened Masters*, a survey of Westerners who conceive of themselves as realized beings. Some were described by their devotees (or themselves) in guru-like terms. I found these parts of the book to be a frightening study of spiritual self-deception—how many World Avatars can be incarnated in the West? The historical record is a sad account of crises and disappointment; somehow in the West, high pedestals have almost invariably led to cataclysmic falls. An eighty page excerpt from the book would be excellent and sobering reading for potentially naive novitiates on the spiritual path; it might save many from future disillusionment.

Prescribing the qualities of a good dharma teacher is one of the most important and difficult tasks in writing a book on the spiritual path. Every rule has exceptions and qualifications. My personal advice is to regard dharma guides as teachers and be wary of anyone who claims to be more than that. As a matter of fact, a main criterion in looking for a dharma teacher is that they <u>not</u> claim to be a guru. Be very cautious of any teacher who claims to be superhuman, or who tries to control you or tell you how to live your life, rather than empower you to think for yourself.

Look for a teacher who is not stuck in one role, but can adapt themselves to the student and situation. Some students, who are fragile and insecure, need encouragement, support and spacious and unconditional acceptance. Others, who are arrogant and too self-assured, may need a strong kick in the pants—the original teaching device of classical Zen training.

A teacher, like a psychologist, is often the receptacle of endless projections and transference from the student. The teacher must be beyond all needs of approval from their students. They must be absolutely centered in the wisdom that both they and the student are not only this incarnated body and personality but also are vast undifferentiated being, untouched by the conditions of their incarnation in time and space.

I once asked Rick Fields why he was loyal to his teacher, Chogyam Trungpa, for so many years. Rick replied that Trungpa was the one teacher he met who was consistently hard on him. This is a most important function of the teacher. After one begins spiritual practice, it often does not take long until one begins to have deep and powerful experiences. The ego is usually quick to expropriate them; delusions of spiritual grandeur are all too common. The teacher's job is to continually pull out the rug and let the student know that these experiences are just the beginning of the spiritual path rather than the end. Some of the self-proclaimed avatars in *Enlightened Masters* could probably have benefited from a few hard knocks from a worthy and watchful teacher.

This raises the issue of lineage and successorship. Generally speaking, your best bet is to find a teacher who is an acknowledged successor in a recognized tradition. However, like everything else, this is not a hard and fast rule; with Dharma coming west, it sometimes seems that "spiritual transmission" has broken down. There have been a number of transmissions that have failed; the dharma heir has been notable for spiritual arrogance and sexual misconduct. Also, excellent teachers who appear out of the blue are not uncommon

Look for a teacher whose life exhibits the qualities you would want dharma practice to bring to your own life—courage, freedom, joy, peace, humor, gratitude, humility, gentleness, and a warm, open and compassionate heart. Look for someone who is not grim and uptight about dharma practice, but playful and fun-loving; someone who is not arrogant and aloof, but humble and human. I'm always skeptical of teachers who emerge from a back room to teach and then disappear into it afterward, rather than mixing and being friendly with everyone; in short, look for someone who is warm-hearted and grounded enough to function well on the ordinary, material and social plane, as well as on the spiritual. Of course, all of these qualities can be faked—and unfortunately they often are. There is no easy answer except to learn to trust your heart and intuition, which fortunately become more perceptive with experience.

If this book ever becomes a best seller, I sometimes wonder if I'll be able to maintain my own spiritual humility. I'm counting on the devise of the greeting monitor. This is someone who stays by the front door to welcome any new people who might wander into the Don't Worry Zendo. Among the orientations are severe warnings that the alleged teacher (me) is actually quite stupid, usually doesn't know what he is talking about, nobody pays to much attention to him and everyone usually does the opposite of whatever he says. So far I think this has worked, at least no one has accused me of suffering from a hugely inflated spiritual ego—although it may limit the number of new recruits who stick around the Don't Worry Zendo.

Now back to the Guru question. Some readers may feel that I've short-changed them in this chapter. I have my Guru and now I'm telling them to forget it and go look for a teacher. So here is the advertisement part of this book wherein I promote my own Guru and lineage; if you feel no particular devotional affinity or direction and would like one, I am glad to share mine with you. The Hanuman/ Neem Keroli Baba love is there for any one who wants to partake of it. Write to me for a picture of Baba, put it and/or a Hanuman icon on your altar. Hanuman Baba will begin to permeate your meditations and dreams. Also, read Ramdas' wonderful book, 'Miracle of Love,' which tells the story of Neem Keroli Baba.

I cannot begin to think about, explain or understand this phenomenon. All I know is that it's beyond me and even beginning to try to understand it blows my fuses and induces rapid mental and heart meltdown. Guru devotion is a direct short cut to a vast openness where you know, somehow beyond your understanding or judging, that any and everything that ever did or could happen is one and perfect. In some incomprehensible, mysterious way, my life is not mine but is an unfolding of Hanuman's play. It's mostly a comedy, filled with love, tenderness, service, compassion and humor. This book's advertisement is now completed.

After an absence of twenty-five years I recently made a month long pilgrimage to India. I spent a few days in Bombay. In the mornings I would go to discourses of Ramesh Balsakar, a highly respected Jnana Sage. The subject was the very nature of awareness, being and the self. The bhakti element was mostly absent.

I spent my evenings wandering through the Bomganga district. This has been called the Varanasi of Bombay; it is sort of a secret jewel, located right in the middle of the big city. Surrounding a sacred tank of water, it is a little village of many temples on narrow lanes that lead down to the shores of the Arabian Sea. In the evenings the sounds of conches, bells, harmoniums and devotional singing fill the darkening narrow lanes of the neighborhood. Priests and devotees offer incense, flowers, fruits and sweets at numerous shrines to Shiva, Lakshmi, Rama Sita, Hanuman and other Hindu Deities. Beautiful, powerful, playful and mysterious sculptures of the Dieties preside over the inner sanctums of each temple. Wandering from temple to temple, one becomes a Bhakti inebriate, intoxicated with the fervor of divine love. Devotion inundates you from all sides.

For the more sophisticated Hindu and, fortunately, for myself there is no conflict between my mornings and evenings, between Jnana and Bhakti. Each helps to deepen the other. The Hindu knows that all of the deities are really one. And there is also room for the Jnana realization that ultimately all of the Deities do not exist at all: they are just as much of a delusion as the separate limited ego-self.

At another level, however, they are very real archetypes produced by the human unconscious over millennia. Devotion to these Deities generates feelings of love, devotion, service, compassion, gentleness, gratitude and courage. These feelings can act like an energy dynamo for spiritual practice and catapult us into pure non-dual realms, where neither devotee, nor Deities, nor anything that can be described in words or forms exists.

Sri Ramana Maharshi is the best study case for this merging of Bhakti and Jnana. He is usually considered to be the great Jnani of this past century. It is sometimes forgotten that he was also one of its greatest Bhaktis. Sri Ramana's devotion was towards Arunachala, the holy mountain which Indians consider to be an incarnation of Lord Shiva. The 'Marital Garland of Letters to Arunachala' a long poem that he wrote, comprises one of the most beautiful and fervent devotional poems I have ever encountered. Although Sri Ramana was completely realized, to help the devotees most of the verses are written from the point of view of the seeker. To share the flavor of the union of Bhakti and Jhana, I will end this chapter with a sampling of a few of the verses.

Arunachala! Thou dost root out the ego of those who meditate on Thee in the heart, Oh Arunachala!

Unmoving Hill, melting into a Sea of Grace, have mercy I pray, Oh Arunachala!

Fiery Gem, shining in all directions, do Thou burn up my dross, Oh Arunachala!

Shine as my Guru, making me free from faults and worthy of Thy Grace, Oh Arunachala!

Unasked Thou givest; this is Thy imperishable fame. Do not belie Thy name, Oh Arunachala!

Sweet fruit within my hands, let me be mad with ecstasy, drunk with the Bliss of Thy Essence, Oh Arunachala!

Blazoned as the Devourer of Thy votaries, how can I survive who have embraced Thee, Oh Arunachala!

Tear off these robes, expose me naked, then robe me with Thy Love, Oh Arunachala!

With madness for Thee hast Thou freed me of madness for the world; grant me now the cure of all madness, Oh Arunachala!

Show me the abundance of Thy Grace, in the Open Field where there is no coming and going. Oh Arunachala!

I am a fool who prays only when overwhelmed by misery, yet disappoint me not, Oh Arunachala!

Weak though my effort was, by Thy Grace I gained the Self, Oh Arunachala!

Unite with me to destroy our separate identities as Thou and I, and bless me with the state of ever vibrant joy, Oh Arunachala!

When I melted away and entered Thee, my Refuge, I found Thee standing naked, Oh Arunachala!

In my unloving self Thou didst create a passion for Thee, therefore forsake me not, Oh Arunachala!

Thou didst take aim at me with darts of Love and then devoured me alive, Oh Arunachala!

As snow in water, let me melt as Love in Thee, Who art Love itself, Oh Arunachala!

Let me be the votary of the votaries of those who hear Thy name with love, Oh Arunachala!

Shine Thou for ever as the loving Saviour of helpless suppliants like myself, Oh Arunachala!

Familiar to Thine ears are the sweet songs of votaries who melt to the very bones with love for Thee, yet let my poor strains also be acceptable, Oh Arunachala!

Hill of Patience, bear with my foolish words, regarding them as hymns of joy or as Thou please, Oh Arunachala!

Oh Arunachala! My Loving Lord! Throw Thy garland about my shoulders, wearing Thyself this one strung by me, Arunachala!

YOUR WAY

There are generally two views regarding the panoply of spiritual traditions available to us today—the purists and the potpourris. Purists maintain that each tradition should scrupulously preserve the purity of the practices that make it distinct; people should not mix traditions and teachers, but should find one path, one teacher, one practice, one place and stay with it all for a long time. Purists believe that mixing creates a homogeneous and indistinct mush, both in the practitioner and in the practice.

The potpourris take the opposite view: that we have the opportunity to approach the spiritual path unencumbered, and to create something fresh, new and uniquely suitable for our time and place. Further, if an individual does not have some broad exposure in the spiritual world, there is the danger of falling into a cult. Some experience of various traditions and practices enables one to discriminate between the genuine and the bogus, and it will ultimately allow one to be rooted in a true spiritual home that is absolutely and uniquely one's own—free of reliance on any particular practice, path or circumstances.

At the left wing of the potpourris are the spiritual anarchists, who beyond picking and choosing among established traditions feel free to create their own practices, rites and liturgies from scratch. You could call them the spiritual artists.

There is something to be said for all these views. It is actually wonderful that there are purists, potpourris and spiritual anarchists. Since my instincts, however, have always led me in the latter directions, in this chapter I'm going to take up the their positions. Most books on meditation speak from the point of view of one tradition and (at least implicitly) propose a purist approach. Here I will make an appeal for the mixers, innovators and anarchists.

The history of Hinduism is a good case study for the potpourri cause and a precedent for what is happening today on a broader scale in the West. At one time what is now considered to be Hinduism consisted of numerous and sometimes conflicting cults of various deities. Over the millennia all of these cults have largely fused into one religion, now called Hinduism. Although the most worthwhile aspects of the various streams have maintained their distinct characteristics, they all exist within a sophisticated and over-arching understanding that there is no conflict between the various streams; they all complement each other and are all contained within one vast view of reality.

Here in the West, where all of the world's religious traditions are inevitably mixing and being exposed to each other, a similar process is occurring. The potpourris would maintain that this is a natural process and is not to be regretted. Despite the world's rampant tribalism that sometimes makes it seem otherwise, people increasingly realize that our similarities and common interests outweigh our perceived differences and potential conflicts.

Our individual lives often are a reflection of this fusion occuring within the larger society. In my own case, over the years I pursued spiritual practices with a number of dharma teachers at various centers. Each re-balanced and refined my practices and understandings in some new way. Each opened doorways to deeper insights and subtler energies. However, even though I grew and learned, I always knew that my ultimate commitment was to spiritual growth, and not to any particular path or place. A practice really serves its purpose when it takes you beyond itself and frees you—even of itself.

The miracle, magic and mystery of the spiritual path is that the next teacher, teaching and practice always seems to arrive exactly on schedule. If we begin the process with some dedication and honesty, it soon seems like the universe takes over; we may not know if we are doing the spiritual path or it is doing us. We increasingly feel that an intelligence that is infinitely wiser than ours is guiding the whole process, down to the minute details of our lives. We just step aside and watch it unfold.

Everything, however, may not always seem to fit like a glove. Teachings often arrive disguised as difficulties and conflicts. In my case, I suffer from chronic cynicism; wherever I went, I always found plenty to gripe about. Robert Aitkin Roshi's lectures were too scholarly. Zen Center of LA was too ritualistic. At Vipassana retreats, everyone was too deliberate; I felt like I was locked up with a bunch of slow motion robots. Joko Beck's approach was too severe. Etc. etc. and on and on.

Although I may have had some misgivings in all of these settings, I didn't necessarily run for the closest door. I may not have stayed forever, but I did remain at each of these places, often for prolonged periods of study and practice. And I learned a great deal from each of these teachers.

The main point is to find a group that you at least don't find totally unpleasant or offensive and that isn't too far from your home. Taking up meditation with a group may not be worth it if you have to go running all over town and it makes you too busy. With the dedication and effort of regular sitting, along with receiving some basic dharma instructions and group encouragement, the process of spiritual opening will inevitably begin to unfold. Your true inner teacher will manifest in your heart and in all the circumstances of your life.

You don't need to be totally thrilled with a practice place. It may even be helpful if everything is not just the way you would have it. We then have the opportunity to watch how our mind always wants things to be exactly our way and then to let go of our judgments and opinions. Accepting things that seem less than perfect to our picking-and-choosing mind may be the deepest practice of all.

People who decide to take up meditation and go to a center are often at first disappointed by what they find. With enthusiasm fired by a friend, a lecture or a book, they anticipated walking into a field of bright and shining Bodhisattvas. Instead, they find a motley crowd, some of whom seem as troubled and depressed as many of the people in their usual work and social circles. Or even more so, because it is usually when suffering and difficulties surface in people's lives that they are motivated to take up a spiritual practice.

And even though things don't seem so great at the start, they may get even worse. Meditation is a purification process that brings latent emotions and injuries to the surface of consciousness. Both people and spiritual centers grow and evolve through recurrent crises.

I have been at more than a few centers that have gone through such catharses. People who have only practiced at one place and have put their absolute trust in a now compromised teacher are usually the hardest hit. They often suffer deep disillusionment and may become cynical towards meditation practice for a long period of their life. On the other hand, the potential hazards are not as great for people who have had some broader exposure to the spiritual path. Once they have tasted the fruits of meditation, faith in the value of spiritual practice is unshakable, regardless of all external circumstances.

Spiritual truth is both absolutely obvious and confoundingly evanescent, evasive and ungraspable. We get it and then it slips away, countless times. We need to be re-reminded endlessly, through both practice and teachings, until our nervous system and mental loops are rearranged and it is inseparable from our being.

Joshu was one of the most celebrated of the classic Tang Dynasty Zen masters. He did not settle down in one spot to teach until he had reached the age of eighty. Before that, he spent twenty years wandering around China, visiting most of the notable masters of his day. Before embarking on his years of pilgrimage he said: "Even with a seven-year-old child, if he is superior to me, I shall follow him and beg for his teaching. Even with a hundred-year-old man, if he is inferior to me, I shall follow him and teach him."

I try to remember Joshu's words and be ready to learn from anyone. Some people may like fashion shows or soccer games, but I love to go to teachings to hear some good dharma. For fun, inspiration, and mental dexterity, it's the best hobby, art form and sport that I've ever found.

Sometimes someone may say to me, "Don't you get tired of hearing the same thing over and over again." Often, I agree. If a teacher is talking from the head and not the heart, I would rather take a walk. If they use the same tired old spiritual clichés, the talk will quickly become wilted and unendurable; I'm usually out the door in about thirty seconds. A good teacher, however, is a poet. As there are innumerable doors to the spiritual experience, they will have their own unique expression of dharma. For me the teacher transcends the path. If he/she is deeply enlightened, I don't care if he/she is a Roshi, a Rishi or a Rabbi; the teaching will transcend any particular approach and speak to the universal human experience.

A good teacher is also a dharma athlete. This is where the fun comes in; if you think a teacher is out of their element, challenge them. If they seem off on an abstract cloud of ideas, ask them what kind of tree is outside the window over their shoulder, or the color of their socks. Make up your own or use any one of endless Zen testing questions. "The hungry guest didn't touch the food but left full; what did he eat?" "Does a dog have Buddha –Nature?" Dharma debates are one of the major forms of entertainment in Tibetan society and an integral part of the Zen tradition.

There are two other criteria by which I judge a teacher. First, he/she pulls the rational rug out from under us. Rather than filling our heads with more ideas, he/she takes away our given definitions; as our rational concepts collapse, we are pushed beyond our known limits into a deeper embrace of the blessing of this very moment.

Second, a real teaching is not just words, but a transmission of blessing/energy. I always feel this way when the Dalai Lama comes to town. His body and words seem just a tiny tip of an immense energy universe. They are a joke and a pretext; only the excuse to get us into the room. What is really being transmitted has almost nothing to do with them. A few years ago he gave a talk at UCLA. The sound system was terrible; nobody could understand a word he said. I thought this was the best talk I ever heard. I gave up trying to understand and just felt the vast presence that appears to the outer senses as His Holiness' body and speech.

Potpourri and non-denominational meditation groups are springing up in cities all over the US. As often as not, they are started by people who have tried the more traditional approaches and want to reinvest them with fresh energy, and who also wish to experiment and improvise with new forms. In the potpourri stream, anything anyone has found meaningful in their spiritual life and growth fits. Rote traditions and rituals can easily become empty and spiritless formulas. On the other hand, ceremonies are more likely to be alive with spirit and heart when they are spontaneous and created on the spot.

A few years ago, I took the furniture out of my living room and founded the Don't Worry Zendo. From the start, I placed it in the middle of the potpourri stream. First, since Neem Keroli Baba is the person who told me to teach Dharma, it is mixed-up right from the name itself; it is not a Zendo at all—it is actually a Hanuman Temple. This may technically make me a Hindu and not a Buddhist. I don't know and care even less. But as Zen is the most recognizable buzz word for all Eastern mysticism, 'Zendo' has come to mean any meditation place. Also, at the time of its founding, I had a girlfriend who thought that 'Don't Worry Zendo' had a cute ring to it.

At the DWZ we have done Sufi dancing and celebrate Shabbos meals. We occasionally do full moon, late-night walking meditations around the quiet side streets of West Hollywood. This is especially peaceful in the spring months, when the mockingbirds start serenading the neighborhood after midnight. Silence is observed, except for poems or ceremonies that are created on the spot and celebrate the very moment. At 2 am, we do a ritual meal at Cantor's deli. Potato knishes are actually an excellent communion wafer.

After sitting we read from a sutra or some other sacred text. Why be limited? Hindu, Buddhist, Sufi, Taoist, Christian or Jewish sources—they are all variations on the same themes of love, emptiness and the limitless human heart. Or we may read poetry: Rilke, Yeats, Rumi, Allen Ginsberg, Gary Snyder, Jack Kerouac. Some Irving Berlin songs are exquisite dharma expositions. Or we read from contemporary sources; selections from Zippy the Pinhead or Calvin and Hobbes are sublime dharma sutras. There is also the occasional pandemonium reading. Everyone reads a different text, at the same time. This may sound confusing but chaos can be a doorway to quiet mind.

And occasionally, we break up the sitting periods by doing the Feather Boa Dance. Of every innovation of the Don't Worry Zendo, this is the one that I am proudest of and that I believe to be the most worthy of emulation and dissemination to other Dharma centers. In a way, the Feather Boa Dance seems as inevitable as the wheel or silicon chip. I'm amazed that it waited for the Don't Worry Zendo to be discovered.

Basically the Feather Boa Dance is the best practice I've ever found to combine sub-atomic nuclear scientific theory with the esoteric teachings of the ancient Sufi mystery schools. Recent science has shown the string to be the minutest ingredient of the universe: the building block out of which even quarks and anti-quarks are made. The Sufi symbol for the enraptured soul in divine communion is the feathered-winged heart.

Put them together and what do we have? The boa is the feathered string, the lighter-than-air, love-melting backbone. In a room full of dancing people, with a rainbow of brightly colored boas flying through the air, the truth is evident and immediate; there is only one backbone that we all share; it is infinitely vast, intimate and it is made out of love.

This is not just talk. Please get a few friends and boas together and try it. Mostly we play Philip Glass (especially scores from 'In the Upper Room' or 'Mishima'), but any wild, expansive and open-hearted music will do. Try Slavonic dances, Fellini soundtracks, Rossini overtures, Beethoven or circus music.

In the depths of the Boa Dance, as in meditation, the universal unconscious takes over; you are no longer doing it, it is doing you. The dance allows the easiest and most immediate access to the experience of non-doing. It may only be a matter of time before the Boa Dance makes meditation obsolete.

PART TWO
THE BASICS

THE KNOT: BREATHING

An old master said that Zen practice was "sitting in the knot till it dissolves and sweeping the garden—no matter what size." The knot is our ego's delusion of being a separate self. We usually live our life so lost in this delusion that we are not only oblivious that we are in the knot, but we are exerting all our efforts to draw it tighter.

We are each made of the universe and we are not a separate finite self. The universe wants us to know this. It is always knocking at the door and pushing at the walls, but we are too busy holding them up to hear it. If we devote some time to sitting still, we will start to hear the knocking of our vast and true self.

So how do we begin to untie the knot? First we sort the knot out into its components—breath, body, feelings, perceptions, memories, thoughts. Uninvestigated, each sphere just confirms the ego's obsession—'I am my breath, my thoughts, my feelings, my body. I exist as a separate entity.' However, a thorough study and investigation of any one of these spheres will reveal the delusional nature of the 'I as a separate self' obsession. We experience that all of these spheres actually originate and have their substance in the boundless source that is beyond any fixed notion of who or what we individually are. When we understand this the knot collapses and all of the separate spheres return to and then arise again from the same boundless source.

Over the millennia, different schools and traditions of meditation have often emphasized working with one particular sphere of investigation over others. Today we can see that the investigation of these different spheres are complementary and equally valid ways of untying the knot and experiencing the reality of the boundless self. We can approach meditation as a broad inquiry into all of the realms in which our seeming separation manifests or we can give special emphasis to one or several areas.

If there is, however, a common thread among almost all approaches to meditation, it is some emphasis on the awareness of breath. In some traditions this is the only technique that there is: just to be aware of the breath. If you don't go any deeper into meditation instructions than just breath-awareness—that's okay. You will save yourself a lot of time reading endless books on various styles of meditation.

The most common instructions are to loosen the belt and breathe naturally from the belly—neither especially fast, slow, deep, shallow, strong or weak. Let the breath do what it wants to do naturally—just be aware of it. No matter how many times the mind wanders off, gently bring it back to being aware of in-breath, out-breath, in-breath, out-breath.

Our minds are usually awash in the stormy seas of our agitated thought forms—the turbulent world of planning and attachment, fear and hope, past and future. Breath-awareness is the surest means of programming our mind to let go of its wanderings and live more in the peaceful waters of the present moment. As conscious breathing becomes habitual, at pre-cognitive levels within our nervous system, we naturally and spontaneously let go of tightness, contraction and tension. At the cognitive level, with each breath we let go of our wandering mind and bring it back to the present moment. We're all addicted to our planning minds and go off on our projections a thousand times a day. A thousand and one times the breath will bring us back to being right here, in the present moment.

When meditating with breath-awareness we naturally begin to inquire, who is breathing? What is aware of the breath? What is the shape of the breath, the space in which it occurs? What is the breath made of? Whose breath is this?—mine or the trees, the meadows, the city's, the planet Earth's, nature's, the universe's? Breath by breath, do I have the power to make myself breathe, have a breath, or is it given to me by some power, some source-mystery greater than me? The preposterousness of the notion 'I', 'mine', or 'my breath' soon becomes apparent.

When we are working with the spheres of body sensations, feelings, memories, thoughts and perceptions, it is often difficult to separate out the notion of 'I' from the phenomena; they are more deeply entwined with the ego identity. Breath-awareness most easily allows us to see that the 'I' has nothing to do with it—it's all a gift from some greater power. For this reason awareness of breath is the most fundamental and universally practiced meditation technique.

The ripened meditator does not need to hold onto any particular technique all of the time. Every technique, including breath awareness, is a devise for allowing us to experience the energy of the universe, which we and all things are made of. Eventually, just opening to the energy itself becomes the fuel and focus of meditation; the particular technique uses itself up and can be dropped – at least for awhile. Almost inevitably, however, mind-wandering creeps back in. And so, as we feel the need, we can return to breath awareness. Our breath is always there like a safe harbor that we re-enter, in order to re-center and re-focus our meditation.

Breath-awareness is an invaluable tool in both sitting and walking meditation, and also as an aid to help us be more mindful during the course of our everyday life. However, we need not be 100% concentrated on and absorbed in the breath as we walk around town. This would certainly be dangerous and probably quickly result in broken noses (from walking into walls) and worse injuries. The mind can also be focused on whatever it is that we've got to do. There is, however, a background of breath- awareness going on at the same time. Sogyal Rimpoche, a contemporary Tibetan Lama, says that if just 25% of our mind stays with the breath, that is adequate and will help to keep our awareness in the present moment.

Thich Nhat Hanh, a contemporary Vietnamese Buddhist Master, teaches walking meditation techniques that combine awareness of the breath with body awareness, with mantras for staying in the present moment, smiling, and being one with whatever is encountered—be it flowers, trees, sky, seashore, busy streets or whatever. The most fundamental is the awareness of breath. Thich Nhat Hanh says, "If you see a beautiful tree branch, stop and admire it, but maintain some awareness of the breath or your mind will almost inevitably wander off from the present moment." His motto is "present moment...wonderful moment." Breath-awareness is the lifeline to make this kind of awareness habitual.

When the breath becomes a focus of our meditation, whether we are sitting or walking, with each breath we take a more delicious sip of our intimacy with all things. Each breath wants to clean us out, let our separation-walls collapse and allow us to experience the source-ocean flooding us at our deepest level. Each breath is an opportunity to experience a more radiant facet of our heart jewel.

We only think a breath is ours because of the past and future. When we've quieted our minds, each breath only exists alone, not connected to the previous or next breath. Then we are no longer breathing. Perhaps space is breathing, mind is breathing, the whole universe is breathing. Wes Niskar once said, "When space is breathing, space is blessing." A good mantra for breath meditation.

An old hermit in a cave high in the Himalayas, when asked about the ultimate wisdom, replied, "The universe is all breathing, it's all just breathing itself." Another old hermit said, "The breath of the mystery is breathing you." Conscious breathing allows us to realize the truth that our individual breath is not ours, but that it is rather an inseparable part of the one great breath. Our real lungs are not the little sacks in our chest, but are the vast space that surrounds us. They inhale and exhale our very being into a flow of radiant aliveness and intimate connection with all things.

> Prayer is nothing but inhaling and exhaling of the one breath of the universe.
>
> —Hildegard of Bingen

RESISTANCE—SANGHA

Yesterday's the past, tomorrow's the future,
but today is a gift. That's why it's called the present.
—Caption from a 'Family Circus' cartoon.

Practicing letting-go in the present, holding on to nothing, just being with this right-now-moment, is the way to find true peace in this life. At first, however, living in the present moment is a totally foreign idea to most of us. Until our practice is well established, we'd prefer to live in our fantasies, memories, projections and planning— i.e. in the past and future.

Here we encounter one of the fundamental paradoxes of the spiritual path. It is through living in the present moment that we can learn to experience the deep peace that is our true nature. Unfortunately, at first letting go in the present moment is also the place where we encounter our greatest fear and insecurity. We have been living in the tight grip of our obsessive thinking mind—our ego's attempt to structure our life based on its memories of the past and hopes for the future. As the thinking mind to loosens its grip, we often feel a panic. The thinking mind is all that we have known; letting go of it is a little bit like dying. In the West, this is known as the 'dark night of the soul,' or the 'valley of the shadow of death.' These phrases sound foreboding and overwhelming, and sometimes this sort of experience may be so. More often, however, it's like the panic of a little dying that happens over and over.

If we let go of our obsessive mind and experience our natural spaciousness, the universe will fill us up with grace. This is inevitable, as grace is always present and imminent. Often, however, especially in the earlier stages of practice, there is a gap between the letting go and the grace. In the gap appears the little panic.

And resistance. The mind will revolt in a million ways, with a million excuses to keep us from continuing our practice: too tired, too restless and agitated, too busy with a million more important things that have to be done, too upset over something or angry at someone, too sad or depressed about something, and on and on. At this point in our practice we need spiritual friends.

The Buddha said there are three great treasures for deepening our understanding: Buddha, Dharma and Sangha, translated as teacher, teachings and community. Although all are essential, in many ways the last, community, is the most helpful for dealing with resistance. In other words, don't always meditate alone, but find yourself a group of friends to sit with. If you can't find a congenial group in your neighborhood, then start one. Put up some notices on local bulletin boards. The benefits are numerous.

Several mornings a week, a few friends come over to my house early in the morning for a group sitting. The truth is that I am naturally lazy; I know that if I sat alone I would often turn off the alarm and roll back under the warm covers. I've been smart enough to set up a situation where that is not possible. I've got get up, unlock the door, light the incense and join in. For lazy people like myself, there is nothing better than group pressure to help encourage a diligent meditation practice.

Even if you are part of a sangha that meets just one night or morning a week, this responsibility and commitment will be like an anchor of regularity and strength in your practice. Often, if you are sitting alone when the inevitable difficulties or resistances arise, you might just get up and wander, lie down or escape to a book or a cup of tea. In a group you know you've made a commitment to stick it out until the timekeeper rings the bell. When you've sat through the difficulties — with patience, equanimity and courage – that is when you'll often experience deeper resources of energy and peace. Rewiring the habitual patterns of our minds is hard work. Sitting with a group inevitably makes this easier.

Multi-day retreats are where group sitting really comes into its own. Here, especially during the early years of practice, it is all but essential. Quite simply, one absolutely needs the encouragement of group support to find the strength, endurance and commitment to experience the deep openings that are possible on retreat. Sitting by oneself this is almost impossible; with a group it becomes much easier and even likely.

Besides the commitment of 'seeing it through,' and the advantages of peer pressure, group sitting helps in other ways. A group can sort of act like an energy dynamo. In some sessions one person may be stronger and more centered, other times it may be a different person. With time it all evens out and all contribute and are benefited by the developing group energy.

Some people approach meditation from the idea that they just want to sit alone and avoid groups. There is nothing wrong with this—some of the time. But it's good to balance solitary practice with group sitting.

Joshu Sasaki Roshi, a revered old Zen master, said that experiencing enlightenment was relatively easy but living correctly with people was much more difficult. We do lead our lives with each other, so it won't do much good to not practice meditation with each other as well. Another revered old Zen teacher, Robert Aitken Roshi, compared sangha practice to cleaning potatoes. The most efficient way to clean the potatoes is to put them all in a tub of water then turn them with a stick. They get cleaned rubbing against each other. Sangha potatoes are similar. The rubbing brings out the difficulties — our ideas and our boundaries of who we think we are and what we want. Through experiencing the inevitable difficulties of practicing with other people, we are presented with wonderful opportunities to understand and soften our sharp edges.

There was once a meeting of Zen teachers. They had a discussion of the best ways to teach westerners meditation. Some argued for meditation on emptiness, others for koans, observation, strong concentration, or just sitting with breath, body and mind awareness. Then one teacher, Kobun Chino Roshi, got up and said that none of this mattered. The only important thing is just to have "gratitude that we can all sit together." The arguing Roshis were immediately silenced.

When grace starts to flow one experiences, "Ah, I am sacred through and through." A deeper stage of practice is, "Ah, all beings are sacred through and through." Group sitting can make this broader embrace more accessible. You discover that you are not just an individual meditator, but you are the whole room and all of the meditators. Or, to quote an old Zen master, "There is only one person meditating."

An indescribable magic happens in group practice. Like wanting to really be present with a lover, we begin to feel responsibility for the whole group's practice as much as for our own. As our commitment to help maintain the group's energy deepens, we don't as readily let ourselves succumb to the mind's or body's restlessness.

A ripened and broad meditation practice is filled with loving kindness. As we learn to experience the blissful nature of pure awareness, we inevitably wish it to our sangha friends and all beings. As our breaths become more subtle, the air becomes an ocean of sacred energy that we are all sharing, being sustained by and being part of together. As our minds become quieter, the bird sounds, the wind in the trees and the passing autos become sacred music that is part of our collective experience. The music is made more delicious by our knowing that we are helping each other share it together.

At the Don't Worry Zendo, we sometimes do a smiling communion meditation. Please try this with a group of meditation friends. Sit in a circle with your eyes open. Look at each other and smile. You can hold hands if you like. You can call it a smiling contest and all try to out-smile each other. This may start out as a joke, but before you know it you will all feel it and the smiles will be very real. There is no more powerful medicine to bring us out of our constricted little worlds then just appreciating that we are all here, alive and able to appreciate this sacred moment together. This very space that we are in is alive with the one life that we are all a part of.

At some Zen temples, meditators take turns monitoring the hall in late night sessions—walking the aisles correcting slumping postures and waking drowsers. There is no more inspiring and humbling experience than observing the work and effort that intense meditation retreats demand. Sitters have to summon the strength and courage to sit through restlessness, sleepiness, and physical and psychological pain. Just the witnessing of our sharing this difficult work, as well as the beatitude that fills the hall, arouses deep feelings of compassion and Sangha caring.

Zen Center Los Angeles
Sesshin,
Good-Humor man
passing at Normandy Ave.
Fifty-seven minds
becoming one mind,
Ah! How delicious.

JUST SIT HERE

If you have time to chatter
Read books
If you have time to read
Walk into mountain, desert and ocean
If you have time to walk
sing songs and dance
If you have time to dance
Sit quietly, you Happy Lucky Idiot
—Nanao Sasaki

Dear faithful reader, if you've persevered this far, I hope by now that you are interested in giving meditation a try. So it's time to talk shop, about the nuts and bolts of sitting: exactly what to do with your eyes, mouth, bones, etc.

Eyes

When you are really sitting you won't know or care if your eyes are open, closed or half-closed.
—Maezumi Roshi

Most Zen teachers recommend keeping the eyes half-open during meditation. Hindu yogis and Vipassana practicioners usually meditate with the eyes closed. Dzogchen and a few Zen sects recommend meditating with the eyes wide open. Looking at the plethora of prescriptions, one reaches the same conclusion as Maezumi Roshi: it's nothing to get too concerned about one way or the other.

Experienced meditators do, however, find some advantages in learning to adjust the eyes at various stages of practice. As meditation ripens one may sometimes experience waves of bliss-energy spontaneously rising up into the head. When this happens, the eyes will want to naturally close; it's fine to let them do this. At other times, however, when meditating with the eyes closed one may experience excessive mind-wandering, sluggishness and sleepiness; then it is good to sit with the eyes wide open . Also if one is feeling physical or psychological pain, fear or panic, sitting with the eyes open is often calming. If one is in a busy place with a lot of distracting movement, of course it's good to close the eyes.

I have found that experienced meditators often sit with their eyes open or half-opened. As one's meditation matures, it become broad, expansive and all inclusive—everything in the world becomes part of the meditation. Eyes open sitting may help promote this vast meditation. Remember, it is always best not to be too rigid: try all of the different eye-positions, and eventually you will like to meditate in all of them.

Mouth—Rinzai Zen students usually sit with a determined and strong sort of grimace. Thich Nhat Hanh teaches that one should meditate with a half-smile. Other schools say just relax. Some say tongue against the upper palate, others softly against the teeth, etc. The same plethora of prescriptions leads us to a similar conclusion—just do what comes naturally and don't worry or think about it too much. Really, innumerable moods come over one in meditation—perhaps the mouth should just reflect these moods.

A few Dzogchen teachers recommend meditating with the mouth wide open. I like this style and often sit this way. Combined with wide open and bulging eyes, it's the stunned and in a state of shock approach: you are too full to know much of anything or to do much thinking. The balloon of nothingness has blown you up.

With each breath,
the 'you can't understand' balloon
is blowing you up,
the breath of mystery
is breathing you.

Please try this sometimes. But keep in mind that the open- mouth style developed in the mosquito and insect free Tibetan highlands. You wouldn't want to try it at a swampy Japanese Zen temple.

Hands—We find the same rampant variations of style. Zen adepts rest the left palm on the right: with the thumbs lightly touching each other, the hands form a big circle. At some Zen temples the meditation instructions are just to put your mind in that big circle and to become it. This is an excellent approach to meditation. Vipassaniis usually just rest one palm lightly on the other. Hindus often rest the hands on the knees. Again, the point is to understand that none of these ways are essential for good meditation. Find something that feels comfortable to you and then forget your hands.

Legs—Unfortunately for the beginning meditator, legs are often not so easily forgotten. This is the body part that often takes some stretching and adjusting, especially for westerners.

There is of course the option of meditating in a chair. This might be fine; many a famous meditator, because of various bodily injuries, was never able to sit cross-legged. The most notable was Hui-Neng, the founder of Zen. He was a peasant wood-cutter, who attained a spontaneous deep enlightenment when he happened to pass someone who was reciting a Buddhist Sutra. Because of a bad knee he was never able to sit cross-legged. He joined a monastery, got a job working in the kitchen and went on to become the famous Sixth Chinese Patriarch. The Hui-Nengs, however, are the great exceptions.

It really depends on one's aspiration and needs: if they are not more than sitting an occasional short period for some relaxation and stress relief, then sitting in a chair is fine. But for the serious and committed, where meditation is conceived of as a means for the transformation of one's whole life, learning to sit in a comfortable cross-legged position is extremely helpful. At this level of commitment, one will also want to sit periodic multi-day retreats. Here is where cross-legged sitting has a great advantage; it is much easier on the back. Sitting for a few days in a chair is likely to result in chronic back-ache and fatigue. Also, meditators almost inevitably find that deep concentration, focus and power comes most easily with cross-legged sitting.

If you can stretch your legs to a good half-lotus position—one foot resting on the opposite thigh—this is best; it will give you excellent stability and support. The 'Burmese' style, with one leg tucked into the crotch and the other leg tucked right in front of it on the mat, is also fine. The most important point for cross-legged sitting is to have your knees resting on the mat, i.e. not up in the air ala American Indian style. Again, there is nothing wrong with the knees up for a period or two, but for long-haul meditation your back will become sore and tired. To get the knees on the ground, you'll want to sit with your butt raised up on some cushions. The height of the cushions varies with different bodies and leg positions. Usually sitting in the Burmese style requires a higher cushion than necessary in a half-lotus position.

Another excellent option is 'seiza' style, kneeling with the butt resting on the ankles. A bench or cushions are often used to aide sitting seiza. At Japanese Zen temples, the women usually sit seiza style, while the men rarely do. This may be do to the fact that sitting seiza will occasionally cause the penis to fall asleep, a rather unpleasant non-sensation, even for Zen monks. However this is rare and no reason to avoid sitting seiza; maybe it's happened to me a couple of times in hundreds or thousands of seiza sitting periods. And just as with any other limb, mercifully, complete circulation quickly returns.

Back—Back-aches are a major problem for beginning meditators. Yet, the experienced meditator often finds that a good sit can cure a tired and aching back. It is important to find a balance between keeping the back erect and straight and yet not too rigid and stiff. One sits as if a string is pulling one up at the top and rear of the skull, right above the spinal column, so that the chin is tucked in a little. There should be some tension, power and strength in the lower torso. Although erect and with the spine comfortably stretched out, the upper body, chest, neck, shoulders and head should be relaxed and soft. Stretching out the spine in this way acts as a relief for tight and pinched nerves and muscles. Eventually one may experience healing sensations, what the Hindus call Kundalini energy, circulating up and down the spine during meditation. At this point back aches often just get wiped out completely.

Learning how to sit with a comfortable back usually requires some experimentation and fine-tuning. If the back is aching, try sticking out the chest or letting it sink in a little, leaning foreword or back, rounding or lengthening the lower back, etc. With time, each meditator finds the comfortable positions that will work best for him or her.

Find Your Seat—It often takes up to a year or two for new meditators to 'find their seat'—i.e. be able to sit for moderate periods, say a few days retreat, in relative comfort. This takes endless resilience and experimentation—trying various leg positions, cushion sizes, etc. Many new meditators take up hatha-yoga. This is an excellent aid to opening up the legs and pelvis and preparing the body for comfortable meditation. Gradually one learns what works and can just forget the body for increasing periods of time.

Lying Down—Since the Don't Worry Zendo is run in a rather easy-going and informal style, people sometimes show up who want to meditate while lying down. I always have to convince them that lying down really won't get them very far. Meditation is a balance between the receptive, relaxing, softening and opening feminine energies and the active, asserting and penetrating masculine energies. Both are necessary and require their compliment.

There is a strength of will-power and concentration that arises while sitting that just does not develop while lying down. If one has sat up for a few good meditation periods, than it might be okay to take a break with some lying down meditation and one might then experience a deep peace and letting go. However, if someone exclusively does lying down meditation, usually they'll just fall asleep or float off into day-dreams and mind wandering. (There are, of course, exceptions to every rule. In this case, sick people often have very profound lying-down meditation.)

When, Where, How Long—In most schools and traditions, early morning is the preferred time for meditation. The mind and the environment are clearest then and most free of distractions. When I lived in a Japanese Zen monastery, there might or might not have been a few periods of evening meditation, depending on whether the day's work in the fields or on the alms rounds had been over-exhausting. But regardless, there was always a few hours of morning meditation.

Looking at different traditions, one can find everything from twenty minutes to an hour for the average or prescribed meditation period length. There is no rule; experiment and find a sitting period that feels appropriate for you. If your sitting is always easy and you never come up against any psychological or emotional pain, panic or resistance, then try sitting for a longer period. It does not hurt to push your limits a little, but not so much that you become discouraged. You don't want to get stuck in a macho, samurai mentality because; short periods can be equally valuable.

There is also the 'keep them guessing style.' At Ryutakuji, the Japanese Zen monastery that I practiced at, the sitting periods were usually about 35 or 40 minutes. During sesshins however, once a day there would be a period where the time-keeper would pretty much throw away his watch. It might last up to an hour and a half. Talk about panic! Ironically, Ryutakuji translates as 'temple of the swamp-dragon;' when there was no bell after forty or so minutes, I could palpably feel that the dragon was on the loose—prowling in my panic-stricken belly.

For a meditation timer, I recommend a watch with an on-the-hour time signal. They are reliable, portable and relatively cheap. Usually whenever I start, I just sit till the beep. Sometimes the periods are short and sometimes longer; I don't get attached to any particular length. If I have the time for more meditation, I take a break and then sit until the next beep.

There are many possibilities for how to spend the breaks between sitting periods. At home I often like to do ten or fifteen minutes of yoga stretches. One can also have a cup of tea, read a text, lie down, take a short nap, dance, step outside for a walk and some fresh air. I've always had a love-hate feeling towards kinhin, the formal single-file walking meditation that is done in Zen temples between sitting periods. Part of me really enjoys kinhin and finds it very peaceful. My anarchistic half rebels at its seemingly regimented style. Knowing something of the history of the relation between Japanese militarism and the Zen establishment, one might especially feel this way. Basically, the Zen monks got into step in the kinhin line and kept marching—right up to the waiting kamikaze planes. Not a great advertisement for overly organized and regimented practice.

It is helpful to have a special place for practice: a room, a niche, or corner of a room that is put aside for meditation and study. Keep this place scrupulously clean and dusted. Set up a little altar with a candle, incense, a plant, fruit or fresh flowers, some sacred objects and images. If there is room, set up cushions for a few people: voila—you have a zendo. This space will acquire a purified vibration that can really help your practice. Just going there will calm and focus an agitated mind. On the other hand, if your quarters are tight, don't let a lack of space discourage your practice. It will just be more cozy and intimate. Innumerable well-known yogis and roshis just get up in the morning and sit on their beds.

In my life, I often feel that I'm living a balance between being a monk and being an artist and poet. If I go too far in one direction, I usually re-balance it by retreating back the other way. On the one hand, I value the persistent routine of a regular schedule. I know this is essential for deepening practice and I usually live my life in this manner. I also, however, guard against getting in a rut. I like to leave room for the unknown, the unexpected and spontaneous. Sometimes people that go off the deep-end become meditation nerds: rather narrow-minded, claustrophobic and uninterested in life. This is a big mistake; we grow through living a full and involved life, as well as through sitting. Rather than always going to bed at a regular hour so that I can get up for early sitting, some evenings I stay up late— for a long nighttime walk, or to read, write, talk, see a movie, play, music, or whatever.

Often I set up a little mini-schedule for myself. I put three or four days aside for early morning practice. I try to make it fun, playful and challenging. Sometimes each morning I get up an hour earlier, till by the last morning I'm up by three and really have a morning mini-retreat. Sometimes I coordinate the final day with the full or new moon. If I get lazy or distracted half-way through, it's not the end of the world. I just start on a new mini-schedule—maybe altered a bit. Then I might take a few days and stay up late.

Work, family and living situations change. I can think back to periods of my life when I sat in the mid-mornings, afternoons, evenings or would get up in the middle of the night. The main thing is to be resilient and relentless; if one schedule gets stale or the conditions of your life change, then alter it to something else. Try anything and everything; but be like a tough and scrappy fighter, who keeps coming back over and over. There need be no hard and fast rule, except that through all the vagaries of life to keep a commitment to some sitting, at some time and place, no matter where or when.

> Come, come, whoever you are.
> Wanderer, worshipper, lover of leaving,
> It doesn't matter,

Ours is not a caravan of despair.
Come, come even if you have broken
Your vows a thousand times.
Come, come yet again, come.
—Rumi

Sometimes people claim that they don't need to do sitting meditation because they are "meditating all the time throughout their daily lives." This sounds good and there may be something to it. Continual mindfulness is certainly the ideal of practice. But there is a fallacy that such claims overlook. For most of us, in order to touch that deepest place of stillness and silence it is necessary to put some time aside that is free of all the usual distractions of our busy and active lives. We can then carry that still center with us through the day.

Through the book I use many words to describe the indescribable reality that we are all made of. A perennial favorite of mystics of all stripes is —'silence.' At the core of our being and of all being is a place of deeply peaceful silence and stillness. The consciousness to which all thoughts are occurring and which is hearing all sounds is actually this one delicious melting love-silence.

The great classical composers have a way of expressing the utter stillness and simplicity that we can find through meditation. Some of my favorite musical moments are in theme and variation movements; towards the end of the variations the composer suddenly eliminates all ornamentation and complexity and reduces the theme to its simplest harmonic structure, returning to an even deeper simplicity than the opening theme. Listen to the second movement of the Schumann A Major string quartet, the last movement of the Brahms B flat Major quartet. In bare-boned simplicity and unadorned stillness time stands still, the heart breaks open and melts.

Our minds are usually like the embellished and ornamented earlier variations. The feverish brain never lets things be, but is always adding something. We can't sit and experience the silence of a room, but we are always filling it with our inner dialogue. When we learn to turn off the inner dialogue and really experience silence, we are amazed. For the first time we really see the room we are sitting in; it is utterly peaceful, alive, beautiful and part of us.

> All the evil in men comes from one thing and one thing alone, their inability to rest in a room.
>
> —Blaise Pascal

As our practice ripens, this peaceful silence grows deeper and vaster; the world appears from it and disappears into it. When we learn to turn down the volume, we experience that our mind is like a huge and awe-inspiring cathedral. Its silence is not an absence, but is alive and breathing. It radiates the love that creates all things.

> No particular thought can be mind's natural state, only silence. Not the idea of silence, but silence itself. When the mind is in its natural state, it reverts to silence spontaneously after every experience or, rather, every experience happens against the background of silence...If you do not disturb this quiet and stay in it, you find that it is permeated with a light and a love you have never known; and yet you recognize it at once as your own nature.
>
> —Nisargadatta

> One of the signs of God-realization is joy. There is absolutely no hesitancy in such a person, who is like an ocean in joyous waves. But deep beneath the surface, there is profound silence and peace....Consider the honeybee, which at first buzzes loudly while circling a flower, but finally settles in silence deep within the core of the fragrant blossom.
>
> —Ramakrishna

All the changes of our life become a celebration when we have stilled our minds and touched our hidden treasure—-the depth of silence that creates us and everything.

DIFFICULTIES, OBSTRUCTIONS, DISTRACTIONS

One of the Buddha's great contributions to history was the development of monasticism. He was the first person to widely promulgate the idea of 'dropping-out.' The idea caught on like wild- fire; for several hundreds of years following his death, Buddhist monks and nuns proliferated in Northern India. They lived simple lives: meditating, wandering the roads and living on donated plots of land on the outskirts of the towns in which they preached the dharma and begged for their one daily meal.

About four hundred years after the Buddha, Mahayana Buddhism developed out of this simpler and monastically-oriented earlier Buddhism. The emphasis shifted from dropping-out to living an active life in the world. The 'enlightened layman' became the ideal. Mahayana granted that if one lived a simple, reclusive life, some sort of enlightenment might be attained without too much difficulty. But, if one lived a more active life, fully in the world, a deeper and broader enlightenment was possible, an enlightenment that could help not only oneself , but many other people as well. Mahayana adherents held that it is through the complications, problems and conflicts that arise in a more engaged life that one will find both deeper challenges and lessons, as well as deeper realizations.

We probably should recognize and accept that for most of us in today's world, living anything but a Mahayana approach and life style is unlikely. As our society's distribution of affluence and social generosity is rapidly shrinking, we usually have to be somewhat engaged just to feed, cloth and shelter ourselves. (The India of the Buddha's time was far different from today's India. It was actually a society of great affluence and abundance, that could easily afford to supply the monastics with shelter and a daily meal.) Besides this, our world is smaller and more complex, the interconnectedness of everything more obvious and communication more invasive. For a stretch of time it is still wonderful to isolate oneself, but it is usually neither possible nor desirable to do it for a lifetime.

> Hindrances spontaneously self-liberate.
>
> —A Tantric manual

This is one of the key sayings of the Mahayana. It tells us that the difficulties which arise in our lives and practice are our best teachers. At the beginning of practice, people often want to keep their meditation pure and separate from the rest of their lives. They try to push their problems and difficulties out of their minds. Later, they learn to see things more holistically—i.e. to accept things with less picking and choosing. We come to appreciate that our lives and practices are one inseparable path and our difficulties arise just on schedule to teach us valuable lessons. It is better to embrace our problems than to try to separate ourselves from them; they are an inseperable part of our life and our meditation. The same source that has blessed us with exposure to dharma and some leisure to practice it, has also brought us our trials and tribulations.

> When you come to a place in your life where there's a bind or something in your way, just take a gentle indrawn breath and give it a blessing.
>
> —Joe Miller

It's strange, but if nothing comes up very strongly in our meditation, it is easy to just go on sitting with a sort of half-wandering, half-conscious vapid mind — floating among the endless little wavelets of scattered planning, day-dreamings and half-formulated fears and hopes that are our usual mental horizon. However, when some recurrent obsession, difficulty or distraction arises, this presents the opportunity to awaken. Our mind becomes focused on something and just this strong fixation reminds us that we had been mindlessly wandering in a stupor.

A strong obsession or difficulty can also give us the energy needed to continue on with our meditation. It does not matter what the content of the hindrance is; it is a difficulty and obsession essentially because we attach so much energy to it. The energy is ours. The particular circumstances are just bringing it to the surface. The experienced and skillful meditator learns the art of detaching the energy quota from the circumstances and letting the circumstances pass while the energy stays and nourishes practice.

This process of detachment and sublimation has three steps.

Analysis—You are obsessed by particular difficulties because of attachments and the desire to control. You want certain outcomes and people and the world are not easily complying. Sort out and consider what the desires and attachments really are. They may be very real problems—work , family and relations, the sad state of the world, etc.—that cannot and should not be so easily dismissed. Or they may be more of our endless personal ruminations— can I achieve my goals, am I appreciated or abused, understood, etc. Even if we are dealing with real problems concerning ourselves or the world, at a certain point, the mental loops are unproductive and it's better to drop them. You'll do your best but

Feeling—Our attachment to obsessive thought patterns stems from fear—of not getting what we think we want and need, of not being loved, etc. Usually, our attempts to avoid feeling our fears are the half-conscious motivations that are behind most of our actions. Just bringing awareness to our recurrent thoughts' underlying fear is a big step towards our liberation.

Softening, Letting-Go—There is no timetable for this step. But, if we open and let ourselves feel it, the fear will use itself up and transform itself. This is nothing we can try to make happen. It will happen on its own and in its own time.

Most of us start our practice with a busy, complicated and chaotic mind. We may not be aware of this until we make our first attempts at meditation. Then we are amazed to discover the thinking mind's unruly, random and uncontrollable nature. We may think that taking up meditation has caused this mental mess; with time we come to realize that we are just becoming aware of the usual habits of the thinking mind. Recognizing the stormy seas of our normal mental processes is definitely a first step.

Once they see this, however, people are prone to give it up as hopeless. "My mind was running wild all over the place." "I was at work, fixing my car, paying bills, out on a hot date—but rarely here." "I stayed with it for a few breaths—then ten minutes later woke up and was visiting my aunt in Tuskaloosa." A thousand times the mind goes off somewhere. A thousand and one times we catch it, become aware of it, let go of the mental wanderings and come back to here and now.

People are often too hard on themselves; they become angry and frustrated at the futility of their attempts to stay in the moment. Its important to avoid this trap; meditation is best approached with infinite lightness, patience and self-forgiveness. Being upset and angry only adds one more level to our already over-dense mental overlay. There is enough regret and self-blaming in our lives already; we don't need to take up meditation to add to our feelings of inadequacy. As we mature in practice, we don't fight the mind, but, with good humor, we accept the wanderings as parts of it's the mind's nature. As we stop fighting, we get a little more proficient at letting go of the wanderings before they carry us away.

> If something comes into your mind, let it come in and let it go out. It will not stay long. When you try to stop your thinking, it means you are bothered by it. Do not be bothered by anything.
>
> —Shunryu Suzuki Roshi

This applies to all of our recurrent mental distractions. When we investigate them, understand them and realize their true content, rather than try to push them away, their power over us slowly diminishes. When we can say, "Oh, here is jealousy for the 100,000th time, no big deal," we can let go of it easier. Be it anger, lust, fear, self-pity, inadequacy: when they are familiar old friends and we know them inside out, they lose their power to take us away from the here and now.

> Have a friendly attitude towards your thoughts. Rather than trying to push them away, invite them to tea.
>
> —Allen Ginsberg

Meditators often use the metaphor of the mind being a bright limitless sky with a radiant sun shining through it. As we come to know the wondrous vastness of the sky/mind, we also come to understand that anything that keeps us from appreciating it—the passing thought/clouds that temporarily block out the full sky view—must be very important to us and necessary for us to experience, or we would not let them block out the full radiant vastness. They must have lessons for us. Moreover, we stop fighting the clouds, because we know that ultimately, even if we don't always experience it, the clouds are also made out of the sun. It's OK if they block it out for awhile. They will pass, like all things.

> Those who despise samsara and seek nirvana only lengthen the way to full enlightenment.
>
> —Tibetan Saying

You can think of meditation as similar to planting a young sapling. For the first year or two, to protect it from wild winds, you may need to shelter and stake it. As it gets older and more mature, the winds are good for it and make it strong. The oldest trees on earth are the gnarled and twisted four thousand year old Bristlecone Pines that grow high on the exposed hillsides in California's White Mountains. These trees have become super-resilient just because they are subjected to the wild elements.

During the summer, the Hollywood Blvd. branch of the Don't Worry Zendo sits up on the roof. This is sometimes known as the 'Distraction Zendo.' It may be for those meditators who have gone beyond the first stake the tree phase and are willing to try taking a leap to the 'wild windy hillside' phase. Around us swirls the turmoil and cares of the city: sirens, ghetto blasters, traffic, police helicopters, yelling, occasional gunshots. At first, sitting in this chaotic setting may seem distracting and difficult; the mind of the seasoned meditator is an open door. The heart that can accept and hold everything is vast and limitless

> Open to beauty, open to pain, open to love.
> Just open heart, dear God
> Open heart open.

In a mature meditation practice, the mind becomes something like a big spider web with the spider in the middle. Distractions keep arising in the mind, they get caught in the web and are fed on by the spider. Its okay for things to arise in the mind—the more outlandish, bizarre and derelict the better— because everything is food for the spider. And the more food the spider has, the more it becomes enormous, agile, voracious and all- consuming. That's okay also, because this is not a frightening or scary spider, but actually a guardian ally-angel, a love being; it is, ultimately, our pure mind, God and the universe. As our practice deepens, whatever comes up—in external circumstances or in our minds—won't bother us too much; we have a growing confidence, experience and certitude that it will all be devoured by the vast mind/spider. Everything will be OK.

> Actually, it is easier for those who have difficulties in sitting to arouse the true way seeking mind than for those who can sit easily....Be grateful for the weeds you have in your mind because eventually they will enrich your practice....In continuous practice, under a succession of agreeable and disagreeable situations, you will realize the marrow of Zen and acquire its true strength.
>
> —Shunryu Suzuki Roshi

GRIEVING, HEALING, BLISSING

Whoever walks into the fire appears suddenly in the stream.
A head goes under on that water surface,
that head pokes out of the fire.
Most people guard against going into the fire,
and so end up in it.
The voice of the fire tells the truth saying,
"I am no fire, I am fountainhead,
come into me and don't mind the sparks."
—Rumi

This poem points to one of the fundamental paradoxes of the spiritual path. The water symbolizes our true nature, which is union, love, peace—whatever you wish too call it. However, if we seek the water exclusively, we may taste it now and then, but we will never experience it on any permanent basis. To become deeply-rooted in the bliss nature, we have to investigate the shadow side of our fears, pain, delusions and anger.

People often discover this after they've done a few intense meditation retreats. They work very hard, push themselves to the limits of their endurance and then they may get a few tastes of 'true nature.' The question inevitably comes up—"Why did I have to exhaust myself just to experience what I already am and always have been?" At this point a deeper and more subtle level of practice becomes likely. To be easily, spontaneously and deeply-rooted in that 'self-nature,' it is essential to study why one is not naturally in it all the time.

Just get rid of the unreal and the real will shine of its own.
—Nisargadatta

To 'get rid of the unreal,' we have to make friends with it, be open to it, understand it and feel it. This is as important as trying to push through it by means of a strong concentration or focusing practice. If we allow negative energy to work its way out through our body, minds and feelings then the 'real' that remains is that which we have always been, are and ever shall be.

Some people don't want to take up meditation because they think that if they do, they're supposed to get into some sort of airy-fairy, lovey-floating feeling. And the truth is, they feel bad and grumpy and angry, and they don't want to be dishonest to themselves and be any different than they actually are. Here is good news for these people; the most important thing in meditation is to be honest and feel what you actually feel. They can meditate and go on being irritable, angry grouches. BUT, eventually they'll get tired of it. In between their emotional funk, they'll start to have little experiences of release and lightness. They'll find these experiences truer and more real than going on feeling crummy. Sooner or later, everyone moves in the direction of experiencing what they really are.

When meditation practice first came to America a few decades ago, it was often packaged and sold as a quick fix to immediate happiness and bliss. As people began to practice, they began to understand that this was only partially true, and that things were not so simple. Subtler teachings began to be appreciated; Suzuki Roshi said, "Do not meditate because you think it will make your life better—just do it and eliminate gaining ideas." A few years later, Ken Wilber wrote that, "In the short run, meditation may actually make your life more difficult." People began to understand that meditation is a long-term purification process, not a quick fix.

Meditation is sometimes described as a drill that is working its way into the core of our being. It touches, uncovers and releases subtler and subtler layers, both of truth—our real self and bliss nature—and of our injuries, pain, fear and delusions of separation. Both of these aspects of our selves are inextricably entwined and locked up together in our body, feelings and unconscious mind. As the drill proceeds, subtler and deeper layers of both come to the surface of consciousness.

As we sit with equanimity, patience and courage, we are freed of the defilements and negative energies. When we can just watch and be with them, like passing clouds they gradually dissipate away. The constriction and defensive energy that is tied up with them in our musculature and unconscious mind are released. This liberated energy is now ours and can be used for positive purposes.

The opposite process happens with the positive energies. As the drill penetrates and releases the all-pervading bliss nature, this awareness stays with us as part of our being. It becomes an ally that we can more easily call on, a more immediate and immanent part of our awareness. Although it is what we have always been, we haven't usually been aware of it. The deeper we allow the drill to work, the more we can claim our birthright.

Over a life (or lifetimes), much of the negative energy may 'bottom out' or be 'cleared up,' while the awareness of cosmic-bliss nature increasingly permeates our everyday life. Does the process ever completely stop? Except for the very highest beings, my guess is no. Even those people who bill themselves as 'advanced masters' will continue to uncover new, deeper and subtler levels of separation if they are honest enough to continue practicing and continue the process.

We inevitably realize that this process is not limited to sitting; life and sitting are absolutely inseparable. Life will conspire with a sitting practice to generate just the right circumstances to help uncover that new level of fear and doubt lying below the surface of consciousness. We learn to welcome the difficulties and crises that arise in our lives and embrace them as signs that we are working and growing. The word 'crises' comes from the same Greek root as 'opportunity.' They are our opportunities to grow. The Cistercian Monk Brother David carries it to the extreme: "You should begin to worry when you are not having a crisis in your life."

San Diego meditation teacher Joko Beck describes meditation as like being by a lake with a big junk pile by its side. We can either jump in empty handed or we can carry a piece of the junk with us each time we jump in. One way, after ten or twenty years the pile is still as big as ever, the other way it is lessened and disappearing. In other words, don't use meditation to avoid dealing with your junk pile. Joko also says that a part of meditation is "feeling your psychological discomfort"—being willing to allow your self to deeply feel your fears, so that they can really heal.

The psychologist Jack Engler describes meditation as "grieving and letting go." A broad, well-balanced meditation practice is big enough to include everything—grieving, healing and blissing; it does not push anything out of the way, but is attentive to each sensation and feeling as it comes up. In meditation we recognize that the way to heal our injuries and pain is not to eclipse them by trying to go to some sort of bliss state, but to feel and grieve for our pain as we allow it to work itself out through our bodies, feelings and minds.

On the other hand, Ramana Maharshi once said, "Why look at your trash when you are taking it out." This approach may sometimes work for Indians, but it doesn't usually seem to for Westerners. Perhaps our society is more complex and we are more deeply psychologically injured. It seems that unless we are willing to look at the trash and sit with it to some degree, we'll never really take it out.

Some of the early meditation teachers that came to the West were overly confident of the ability of meditation to lead people to complete liberation and happiness. They advised their students that psychotherapy and counseling was entirely unnecessary, and that meditation was enough. After about thirty years of meditation being widely practiced here, fewer people hold such views.

A more popular view these days is that meditation alone is often inadequate for Westerners. To realize our full potential, many of us also need some sort of psychological healing. It is no accident that a large and growing number of meditation teachers also work as psychotherapists. Meditation and therapy may go hand in hand and be a great aid to each other.

Be very cautious of meditation teachers and approaches that exclusively emphasize bliss states. Rather than just sitting with and experiencing whatever comes up, a bliss-oriented practice can act as a spiritual bromide. Whenever difficulties and anxiety come up, you do your mantra to escape fro investigating and feeling your fears. You never really confront and grow through them.

If you visit a meditation center that is unbalanced in this way it can be really creepy and scary. On the surface, people are all smiles and friendliness—singing 'spiritual' songs, dispensing easy hugs and good wishes, etc. But if you are perceptive, you can often see another story in peoples' eyes, body language and musculature —one of great pain that is largely going unrecognized, unprocessed and unhealed. Such places are applying band-aides to deep injuries and are the breeding grounds of the most dangerous cults.

As I've always been an easy 'smiler' (junior and senior high school yearbook voted 'best smile,' 'dimples,' etc.), such places are especially scary for me. I start to wonder, am I just like these people: hiding real fear, pain and injuries behind spiritual whipped cream? There is a restaurant run by such an ashram that I especially like to eat at, just for this reason (though the food isn't bad, I must admit). When I have lunch there I'm often reminded to be aware that my emotions are real and grounded. For a few days I'm especially careful that a smile is coming from a deep place and is not just a cover-up for unconscious discomfort. I highly recommend trying to find such a mirror for your possible unbalancedness as a sort of reality check.

Also, however, beware of practices that are overly balanced in the more severe direction. If you are always only looking for injury and delusion—this is exactly what you will find. Some approaches don't honor or trust the bliss when it arises, but immediately ascribe it to self-deceit and the ego parading as spiritual experience. If you visit some meditation places that are over-balanced in this more severe direction, many of the people look like their jawbones would crack if they ever tried to smile.

A well-rounded practice has a natural balance between grieving, healing and bliss, between observation and concentration (nest chapter), between opening to and not running from both the difficulties and the bliss, though not necessarily going out of our way looking for either. It lets all of these unfold naturally and in their own time. It allows ourselves space and time to study the injuries which we all have, to grieve and feel the pain that they cause us and in sitting with that pain, to allow it to heal. From this solid foundation a deeply rooted blissful practice will arise.

CONCENTRATION AND OBSERVATION: ZENASSANA

Throughout history, some approaches to meditation have put the emphasis on concentration and others on observation. The concentrative approach puts a greater emphasis on efforts to try to focus the mind and eliminate random and distracting thoughts. In traditional Zen literature, you find many phrases like, "set up your mind like an impenetrable stone wall, keeping out all distractive thoughts." Very generally speaking, within Buddhism, you could call this the traditional Zen approach.

The 'observation' approach is just to sit and observe thoughts, feelings and sensations as they come and go, neither especially indulging them, nor trying to influence, change or eliminate them. Generally, you could call this the Vipassana approach. In the former, the rider gets on the horse and tries to direct it to the water; in the latter, she lets the horse roam the pasture more freely.

In the last few decades, as understanding of meditation has matured in the west, there has been a major shift in emphasis towards the observation approach. To understand this, it is beneficial to look at the history of Buddhism taking root in the West. It has been something like the old tortoise and hare story.

Zen came first and was definitely the hare—the sexy, fast lane. It got all the attention, books and headlines. In the fifties, D.T. Suzuki delivered his ground breaking lectures at Manhattan's New School. They were attended by the hip New York literati, abstract expressionist painters, future beat poets. Alan Watts wrote 'Beat Zen and Square Zen.' Zen was definitely 'in.'

There were a few people in the back row talking about something called Vipassana – but they seemed the nerds of the meditation world: bespectacled, acne-faced boys spouting lists of precepts, paramitas, hindrances, near-hindrances, etc. The sort of things Zen people didn't bother with.

Then in the early eighties, something unexpected swept the western Zen world from one end to the other: roughly, a less well known but equally devastating Zen version of the debacles of TV evangelists scandals. From one Zen center to another, there were similar stories of abuses of power, sexual misconduct, narrow-minded self-righteousness, cliques of inner power elites, and on and on.

As opposed to other religions, serious meditation practice should be hypocrisy proof. It's easy, if you just sit a little, to get a lot of superficially held 'spiritual ideas,' and go spouting off about them. But the long hours of meditation usually required at a Buddhist meditation center are the litmus test. They will be too painful if there are huge discrepancies between your talk and your actual life. The purpose of meditation is letting the barriers and boundaries between yourself, other people and the world dissolve. If you are busy erecting barriers through deceit, conceit and manipulation, these sitting hours will be unbearable torture.

Then how could these scandals have occurred? Here are a few of my theories on this subject. First, as practice was moving to the West, there was a general disruption of rigorousness and duration of training. In Asia, a student would have to have practiced for decades before assuming teaching and leadership positions. Here, the positions had to be filled, but there was a much smaller pool of experienced practitioners to draw on. Duration and depth of practice was often short-circuited to keep places functioning.

Second, we learn over and over that spiritual understanding is a much deeper and subtler process than we first imagine. Someone can have a deep meditation experience and still be far from a real psychological and spiritual maturity. Often these experiences just mark the beginning of the path. The intoxication of having some power or authority can quickly overwhelm whatever one has gained from such an experience.

Finally, and most important: the problems arose from the deficiencies of an overly concentration-emphasized practice itself. This is sometimes known as the 'spiritual bypass.' One can develop great powers of concentration and absorption, have 'tastes of enlightenment,' and still have neglected to examine and heal deep personal injuries. Many older students and teachers seemed to be psychologically stunted and emotionally retarded. Or, another way of saying it, 'enlightenment' is not always so easily integrated into life.

I must note here that this is a very rough generalization. Both Zen and Vipassana are broad movements that include many sub-schools, lineages and wide spectrums of teachings. In many aspects, some Zen styles are closer to some Vipassana approaches than to other Zen schools. The same is true of Vipassana. But still the generalization is not entirely meaningless. As Zen first appeared here, the emphasis was usually more towards the concentrative, and Vipassana more on the observational.

Since this discussion is from the Buddhist perspective, the informed reader may be inquiring, "What about Tibetan Buddhism?" As broad as Zen and Vipassana are, Tibetan Buddhism is even more so; you could call it the 'Hindu Buddhism.' There are so many schools and approaches that you can find almost anything and it's difficult to make any statement; for clarity and simplicity, I leave it out of this discussion.

By now, you will have noted a definite tilt in my prejudices. Allowing space for the more easy going, gradual, Vipassana/observation approach is essential for a healthy practice and life. My apologies to several wonderful Zen teachers I have had, whose teachings were much subtler and all-inclusive than my rough definition of Zen might indicate.

In recent years, after growing through the experiences of the 1980s, a more well-balanced, mature and inclusive approach has developed and is being taught at better informed meditation centers in America. People at Zen places seem more relaxed, people at Vipassana places a little more eager to taste the 'non-dual.' This developing synthesis combines the best and avoids the possible pitfalls of various approaches. I call it:

ZENASSANA.

Let's first review both approaches and consider their strengths and weaknesses. In Vipassana you just sit with what comes up. With patience, equanimity and courage, you practice a precise observation of the interrelated fields of body sensations, thoughts and feelings. This is the "go slow in the shallow end" approach. You don't try to push anything out of the way, but become very familiar with all of these fields. Some approaches sweep the body over and over to minutely experience every sensation, while others carefully note each mental and emotional experience in order to become fully aware of each of them.

The possible shortcoming is that the final, but absolutely most important step, is sometimes neglected or completely forgotten. As the interrelated and usually confused web of body, mind and feelings is sorted out and understood, the observer is gradually distilled out of this once-confused jumble. In this penultimate step, the observer turns back on itself and 'observes the observer.' Finally, 'the observer and the observed become one' or 'the observer dissolves into the pure energy field-awareness.' This experience of non-duality is the real heart of meditation. This is where rapture and the experience of truth arise. The truth being that the observer is not the separate, limited ego, but rather timeless, pure being/awareness. Sad to say, I've sat through Vipassana retreats where the teachings barely mentioned the possibilities of this final, but all-important step.

One could call the Zen approach the way of jumping right into the deep end. The final step, which is sometimes forgotten in Vipassana teachings, is where Zen begins. A theme, or koan, is used to concentrate and focus the mind on pure awareness. This also eliminates extraneous and distracting thoughts and feelings. Although this may give some taste of the deep state of union and truth, it is often built upon a very shabby and unreliable foundation. Zen practicioners often push lifetimes of accumulated baggage out of the way, rather than sorting it out and working through it. This is not to say that this taste is not valuable and worthwhile. It will likely encourage the meditator toward continued practice, eventually integrating insights into all of one’s life.

Zenassana is observation, informed by the possibility of concentration/absorption: going in at the shallow end, but knowing that there is a deep end. It is being aware that observation may lead to concentration and when it does, welcoming it, being embraced in it and letting it fill and bless you. The point is to not push things out of the way in order for this to happen, but to let it grow as a natural ripening. The rider still gives the horse a free rein, but with the awareness that it is a very large pasture and that there is a very delicious trough, which she wouldn't mind if the horse went over to. When concentration and absorption arise in this way, by using up and seeing through our personal stuff, rather than pushing it aside, it will be deeper, and more regularly immanent in our life. One won't have to try so hard for it, but it will be like something that arises from a deep place in the earth, moving through us and filling us up.

When we arrive at this ripened, seasoned and well-rounded practice, rather than us doing meditation, it often seems that meditation is doing us. We surrender to the reality that an intelligence infinitely greater than our limited logical mind is working through us, guiding our practice and opening us in just the appropriate way.

PART THREE
THE HEART OF THE MATTER

I'LL THINK AND I'LL THINK

Right here and right now—what are you? Your idea of 'you' exists as memories of what 'you' did in the past and projections of what 'you' will do in the future, based upon the pain or pleasure associated with the past memories. But if you could enter into a state of just being right here and now—no past, no future—would you be anyone? everyone? no one? Amazingly, meditators discover that as they enter into the present moment, the separate ego vanishes. What replaces the ego? A few of the inadequate words that mystics use to attempt to convey the indescribable are in the right hand circle below.

Experiencing this state depends on learning to focus and/or quiet our usually uncontrollable and random thought processes. People first taking up meditation often have the idea that they are supposed to totally eliminate thoughts. After a few futile attempts they reach the inevitable conclusion; "There is no way I can eliminate or quiet my mind — I must not be cut out to be a meditator." They needn't be so pessimistic. The job of the brain is to think and it usually doesn't stop doing this. Great masters and yogis undoubtedly experience a thoughtless state for prolonged periods, yet before we reach such states there is still room for immense openings of consciousness.

Usually our thoughts are a solid wall—erecting our impenetrable idea of us, the world and their separation. In meditation, rather than being lost in thoughts, we study the nature of thoughts and the thinker; the awareness itself is all important, not the contents of awareness. The thought-wall becomes less solid; little spaces or gaps start to open between the thoughts. In the gap appears truth, reality, the universe, God, unlimited love, whatever you wish to call it. Starting from our limited perception, the gaps and our experience of reality may be tiny. With practice the gaps widen; our experience broadens from a little trickle, to a flow, to a recognition that we are always being flooded in a river of grace.

Our idea of 'I' is usually defined and limited by our thoughts. As we practice meditation, we start to experience an expansion of our self-definition beyond our habitual self-enclosed thought-world. Our thoughts may still be arising; but they are no longer the totality of our self-definition. Rather, they are merely phenomena arising within a much greater experience. They no longer limit or separate us. Although this expansion is limitless and undefinable, mystics have usually not been able to resist giving various labels to it. I've put a few of the more common ones in the expanding circle on the right.

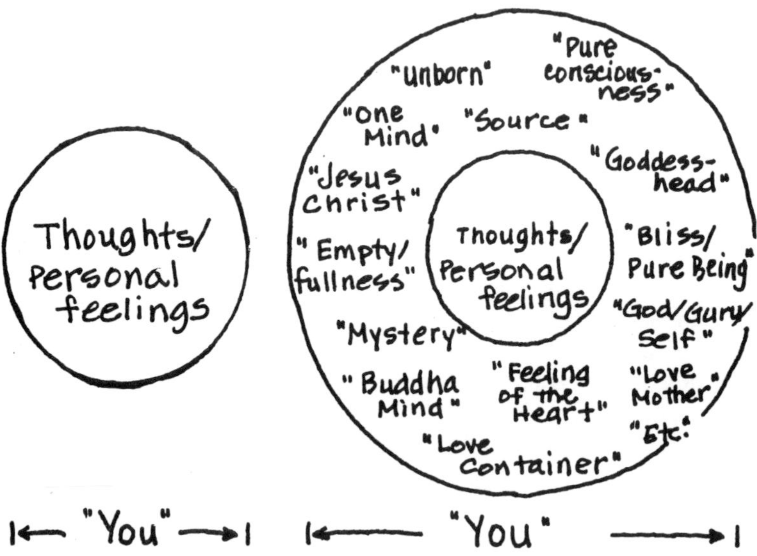

One very simple way to realize that it is our thinking mind that is creating and limiting our idea of 'I' and 'world' is found in Vipassana practice. When meditating, simply label each thought that comes into the mind as 'thought, thought, thought.' Usually each thought convinces us of its reality, and creates the separation of I and world, past and future, here and there. Sitting with 'thought, thought, thought,' is like pricking a pin to each thought balloon. Pop! Instead of grabbing onto the balloon and being carried away, we recognize each thought as just another apparition trying to take us away from here and now. We realize that it is the thoughts that are defining our idea of the world and of our limited ego-self. Behind or before the thoughts we experience a boundaryless being—something immense, timeless, radiant and more real than the limited 'separate self' and 'world' that our thoughts had habitually convinced us of as being real and definitive.

Another way of dealing with thoughts is to contemplate the substantiality of our assumption that they are 'mine.' Questioning whether thoughts are 'my possession' is usually the last thing we wish to do. The western rationalistic world-view was epitomized in the seventeenth century philosopher Descartes' famous sentence "I think, therefore I am." Implied is, "I think ..therefore I am [separate]." We usually don't think about thinking, so we don't question our assumptions: that thinking belongs to us, that it is our thoughts that allow us to believe that we are separate from the rest of creation. A little thinking about thinking will quickly free us from such ridiculous delusions.

We've seen that it is not too great a stretch to contemplate that the breath is not 'ours.' We reach the same conclusion when we consider our body: we know that we can't make the hair grow, the heart beat, the eyes blue, wounds heal. Intellectually, at least, it's not too difficult to see that the body is not ours. As we divest ourselves of these delusionary possessions, what is it that we humans want to hold onto more than anything— the me that's apart, thinking these thoughts, the consciousness to whom they're occurring; these things belong to me. They're not the gift of the universe—they're MINE. The stubborn little person who's inside watching it all happen, trying to figure out how to become happy or get 'enlightened,' to structure the universe to get his wishes fulfilled; the little thinking man/woman is definitely me—separate, apart and autonomous.

Clear reflection will show that thoughts don't belong to me anymore than does the, body or breath. Right now, sit up. Can you make yourself have a mind, thoughts, consciousness? Or a world out there that thoughts reflect a relation to? The perceptions of that world that are dependent on neurons in our brains? A brain for these nerves to fire in? The very space where the thoughts occur? All of these are not ours, but a gift that comes from somewhere beyond us. Thought processes are the last possessions that we divest ourselves of. But when we do, we find that we are actually the radiant unmanifest source out of which all of our thoughts are created.

If we are diligent in our practice, our previously omnipotent thinking mind will gradually loosen its grip. We may not be aware that this is happening, or be able to understand or explain it. All descriptions fail, but the process will inevitably unfold. First the mind gets concentrated, then little moments of silence begin to appear. Then, rather than being lost in the thoughts, we know ourselves to be the very space in which they are occurring; we are the awareness they are occurring to; we are the energy they are made out of. They are just another play of the source that allows all things. By some grace we become proficient at not following the thoughts. We allow them and our awareness to subside in the source.

I must add a disclaimer here. I am not advocating that anyone abandon their thinking mind. We all have to pay the bills and get the kids to school. Our thinking, logical mind has many necessary and wonderful uses. But most of us have gone thinking crazy; the mind is obsessive and running rampant. We are mostly limiting ourselves to living one-sided lives; why not experience both thinking and not-thinking? Why not cut out just 20% of the mental override and put that energy into being in the present moment? In other words, after we have plotted and planned enough, we can learn to go into a different, more quiet mental mode. Somehow this is usually a very foreign idea to most of us. Swami Vivakananda was the first Hindu mystic to come to America. He observed in 1893: “Plans! plans! That is why you western people can never create a religion! If any of you ever did, it was only a few Catholic saints who had no plans. Religion was never, never preached by planners.”

When we start to observe our minds, we realize that we are addictive worryholics. Our random thoughts are largely based on fear—of losing control, not getting what we want, facing a destitute, unknown world alone, dying. Much of our thinking is finally ‘arguing with God.’ Too bad, because the outcome is ultimately beyond our control. At a certain point it is best to abandon the argument.

Dave Letterman asked me, "Can you put me into a 'meditative trance?'" I responded that the belief of meditation is that we are all in a trance already and that meditation will take us out of the trance. People-watching is a fascinating and somewhat frightening experience for meditators. It becomes obvious that almost everyone is walking around lost in the haze of a thought-induced trance world—some in a money trance, others in a sex-trance, a power trance, insecurity trance, victim trance, anger trance, control trance or just a busyness trance.

If one has to be in a trance, the best trance may be to become addicted to being mindfully aware in the present moment. Since there are more and more meditators wandering around these days, it's really not that uncommon to meet someone who is watching their thoughts, rather than being lost in them. Sometimes, in a grocery line or at the laundromat, you can meet someone's eyes and share the smile of just being there – sharing the space, experiencing the moment, being mindful of living.

The vast mass of people, however, still wander around lost in their self-centered thought-dream, far from the present moment. At least the information of the possibility of a more present awareness is widely available today. Previously it was even dangerous to be a mystic. Looking into someone's eyes and wishing to share the timeless and sacred moment can be very threatening to a person determined to maintain the rigidity of their ego boundaries. Lots of mystics have paid with their lives—Socrates, Hallaj, Bruno and, of course, Jesus, are among the most notable examples.

> God, whose joy and love are everywhere
> can't visit you unless you are not there.
> —Angelus Silesius

The "you are not there" the medieval mystic refers to is our usual incessant thinking mind.

> If you sit still you will be grabbed by God.
> —Jiyu Kennett Roshi

Specifically, if you're thinking mind sits still.

> All thoughts are sorrowful...because thoughts take one's attention away from the self, which is undiluted happiness.
> —Ramana Maharshi

This may seem like a totally extreme statement—until our meditation practice ripens enough that we begin to have the experience that pure thoughtless consciousness is bliss and our true nature. Then our meditation becomes an endless letting go into that state. Through our diligent efforts and by grace, this happens with greater depth and continuity.

COMPASSION AND EMPTINESS

Buddhists compare meditation practice to a bird's two wings. One wing is compassion and the other is emptiness. Both wings are necessary for the bird to fly. Roughly, 'emptiness' describes the true nature of ourselves and the world. Compassion describes how our experience of 'emptiness' manifests itself as we live in the world. Really, each wing creates and sustains the other: compassion is emptiness and emptiness is compassion.

With practice we begin to perceive our boundaries dissolving. We experience that at the deepest and truest level, everything is part of us and we are part of everything. Further, we realize that the truth that we discover about ourselves applies to all things—everything partakes in the creation of everything else and is 'empty' of existence as a separate and distinct entity. And as we understand this universal 'emptiness,' compassion becomes inevitable—at a gut and heart level we experience others' suffering as our own.

For over 2,000 years Buddhists have been fond of using the word 'emptiness' to describe reality. In English, this may be bad P.R., as the word has rather frightening connotations—some dark, null, void, non-existence. But actually emptiness is synonymous with fullness. When we discover that we are empty of a discrete, separate existence, then we are full of the source of the universe, unlimited love, God—whatever we wish to call it. Perhaps the Buddhists should expand the word to full-emptiness, potent-emptiness, source-emptiness or *emptiness-head*, equating it to the phrase 'Godhead' that is popular with western mystics.

An old Zen Master once said that if you try to explain emptiness your brain will explode. Emptiness cannot be understood or explained intellectually; when we quiet our minds, it can be understood with our feelings and body. We can't grasp emptiness, but if we sit quietly, it will grasp us. Still, although words are only inadequate pointers, it might be useful to study a few of the words that mystics have used through the millennium in their attempts to convey the meaning of this elusive concept. At the very least such intellectual efforts will predispose us to wish to quiet our minds, and to experience emptiness for ourselves. Here is a survey of some of the phrases that mystics have used and some contemporary concepts that might also help us understand them. All of these words actually mean the same thing, but people try to explain it from various points of view.

Interbeing/Interdependence—All things in form depend on each other for their existence; even more, all are a part of each other. In this century, from the psychology of Carl Jung, the phrase 'synchronicity ' has become popular. This concept points in the direction of what mystics have meant by phrases as 'interbeing' and 'interdependence.' We're all familiar with fortuitous coincidences, the seemingly disparate events that happen at exactly the right time and place to give meaning to each other: the phone call with the information you need arrives just at the most helpful moment or you run out of gas exactly as you are coasting into the gas station. We can't explain it, but can only chalk it up to the mystery. It seems that as we practice a spiritual discipline and give up individual grasping, such 'seeming coincidences' become a pervasive and amazing part of life. We begin to suspect that synchronicity is going on all the time and that we're just becoming more open to perceiving it. A mysterious harmony unites all the people, things, and events of life; everything is linked to everything else, in a complex web of synchronism.

Wholeness—The 'wholistic' or 'whole systems' viewpoint is a modern version of what Buddhists describe as 'interbeing.' The analogy of the human (or any) body is helpful here. If we were inside a body, viewing it at the microscopic level, we might think that the separate blood, muscle, nerve, hormone and other cells were distinct entities, each individually doing their own thing. From a broader perspective we see that the actions of individual cells are not random or independently willful, but are parts of feedback and interaction loops which function for the survival of a whole, which we label 'Jane,' 'Mike,' or 'Bill.'

The whole planet may also be viewed from a limited viewpoint in which geographic, meteorological, biological, demographic and oceanic patterns seem to be random and independent of each other. As science has become more sophisticated, we have increasingly recognized the interconnection of all phenomena; what happens in one area affects all other areas. Seen from this broader vantage, all parts of the earth appear as one interconnected organism, which has been labeled 'Gaia,' after the Greek Goddess of the earth.

When seen from a distant view—i.e. outer space— people experience our planet as one vast beautiful organism; simply put, they fall in love with the planet earth. Astronauts become overwhelmed with the endlessly beautiful interrelations of its light, colors and forms and feel more deeply connected to and part of this wholeness themselves. Soviet Cosmonaut Leonov, the first man to space-walk said, "How bright it is, how incredibly beautiful. So incredibly beautiful I forgot to be afraid." (An easily recognizable symptom of 'falling in love')

However, not everyone can go to outer space. Fortunately the next best place to begin the study of 'whole systems' is at your local lingerie store. Basically, the world is always whole, but our mind and our desire to rationally understand things is always dissecting it. Our deeper wisdom's job is to put things back together. The other day a customer in the garter belt aisle cornered me with a question, "Which is actually sexier for a man—the lace stocking top or the garter belt that holds it up?" (Maybe she was considering saving a few bucks by purchasing stay-up hosiery.) I had to explain the whole systems world view to her. Our minds might separate out things like that, but our truest instincts and wisdom know that such distinctions are only at the very surface of our being. Our society's deepening understanding of this view is the reason that lingerie is its number one growth industry. To complete the whole system, I gave her a deal on lace gloves, cover-up, etc.

Whether astronauts, meditators, or lingerie buffs, when we broaden our perspective to experience phenomena as inseparable parts of a whole, we have a feeling that can best be described as love. It dissolves separation, flowing through and uniting seemingly disparate elements into larger and more real wholes.

Indra's Jeweled Net—This is a phrase that Buddhists use to describe this interconnectedness; all things and events in form are little jeweled mirrors in a huge net that extends infinitely in space and time. The mirrors on each jewel reflect every other jewel—everything reflects and is part of everything else.

We can contemplate how deeply a piece of art may affect us; a Beethoven symphony might change our lives utterly, making us stronger, braver, gentler. The forces acting through and inspiring Beethoven when that symphony was written were not limited to that moment, but were radiating through time and space and affecting people forever. Really, all of our lives are similar. We can't begin to have a concept of the unlimited causes and effects of any of our actions in this infinitely interrelated universe.

Don't just say hello to someone,
A whole universe is meeting
A universe.

As our meditation practice deepens, we have increasingly frequent experiences of the jewel-like quality of this present moment. Things somehow seem lit-up and sacred when we realize that whatever is right in front of us is created by and not separate from ourselves and all of the other things of our life. From a Buddha's point of view, it's all a 'jeweled-net'; over a lifetime of meditation practice, we can move towards that view.

Co-dependent Origination—This concept is often considered to be the centerpiece of the Buddhist world-view philosophy. It essentially teaches us all things of this world arise in a simultaneous karmic birthing. Although we typically see things as being separated by time and space, everything is actually created at once and is co-dependent with everything else.

Books on the correlation of contemporary physics and eastern mysticism have become popular in the last few decades. The views of physics often seem to correspond to what meditators might mean by 'emptiness.' Scientists say that at the Big Bang, approximately 15-18 billion years ago, all matter, energy, form, time and space were latent in one infinitesimal singularity out of which everything then manifested. The mystics, however, beat the scientists to it; and they added that the Big Bang was not just 18 billion years ago, but that it is occurring right here and now—YOU AND I ARE THE BIG BANG. Why put the dissolution of separation back 18 billion years? If it could happen then, why not right here and now? Indeed, as we learn to experience the inter-being, interdependence, oneness, or whatever we wish to call it, the distinctions of this and that, by which we usually live our lives, dissolve and a vast, miraculous and unspeakable energy fills us—the energy of the universe.

As physicists look more deeply at matter, they find that it is 99.9% empty. Again, what physicists find looking into the physical world is what meditators find looking into themselves. Usually our lives appear to be a very solid procession of events, people, places and things. As we start to examine our minds, we discover that this passing parade takes place against a background of fullness, buoyancy and vast space. When we allow ourselves to experience this background space, rather than being endlessly lost in the passing parade, the sense of expansion grows deeper and all pervasive.

Once again, the analogy of the sky and passing clouds is often used to describe the nature of mind. Our mind and essential being is the vast sky, which is always bright and radiant. The endlessly passing clouds are the events and drama of our lives. Usually we are so involved and obsessed with the cloud-drama that we forget that the sky is even there. As our meditation deepens, the clouds lose their power to carry us away from the present moment. They, the passing phenomena of life, are still beautiful, poignant and sometimes painful, but they begin to recede from prominence. Instead, we begin to identify more with the vast, radiant, mind/space sky, which is our true nature.

The next question is obvious: why bother? Why is it worthwhile to devote our time to learning how to divorce our minds from attachment to external forms in order to experience this pure-empty consciousness? Einstein once said that man's greatest question was not whether God exists, but whether "the Universe is a friendly place." It is in the empty/source mind that this question is answered. People use different words to describe the indescribable essence—cosmic love, all-encompassing-intimate-mother embrace, being in our true home at last. It's the friendliest thing that we will ever know and it is what we are made of.

Mystics sometimes describe this as "storehouse consciousness," because it contains the fullness and potential of anything that could ever exist. As the film filament puts a shadow across the projector's pure light and limits it in order to bring it into form, so too is that which we experience in time and space actually a lessening of what we essentially are. Our thought is merely a shadow across our pure all-inclusive mind, bringing it into the world of form.

Oneness—Einstein spent the last forty years of his life pursuing a unified field theory—attempting to find one law that would include the whole physical universe. He was unsuccessful, but contemporary physics continues the quest and has reduced all of nature to two forces.

The delight, fascination and obsession of meditators is very similar. Actually, in our meditation practice, we all become little Einsteins. The world at first appears as an unlimited variety of separation: things, people, places, thoughts, body, feelings, perceptions—all separated into discrete entities by time and space. The job of the meditator, is to experience a oneness that includes everything—at ever deeper and more subtle levels. The broader its embrace of all things, including our very selves, the more we understand our own nature to be benign, blissful and blessed.

Non-Dual—These days 'non-duality' or 'non-dual bliss' have become the most common terms that meditation teachers in the West use to convey the mystical truth which all of these phrases are trying to get at. If I had to choose one word to express the very heart of meditation and dharma, non-dual (or love) would be it.

Simply put, there is nothing that is separate from each one of us; there is no object, everything that exists is the subject and is a part of the one consciousness. This may sound preposterous, but actually it is not so difficult to experience. Zen master Yamada Roshi said "The practice of Zen is forgetting yourself in the act of uniting with something." The Chinese Zen poet Li-Po put it this way:

We sit together
The mountain and I,
Until only the mountain remains.

I first experienced this when I got up to pee late one night at a meditation retreat. Turning on the bathroom light, suddenly the toilet was there, but I wasn't. That toilet was the most beautiful thing I had ever seen, because I wasn't seeing it. It was just shining and radiant by itself; the separate ego had dissolved in the object.

Zen monks have written countless poems about suddenly experiencing non-duality in a branch of cherry blossoms or the cry of a crane over a misty lake. Personally, I've long harbored suspicions that many of them are faking it and first experienced non-duality while peeing. There is something very similar about peeing and meditating—in both cases a flood is released when you allow a tightness in the core of your being to collapse. Since urinals aren't a romantic setting, the monks go on writing about the moon and pine tree branches. To counter this possible omission, I've been writing poems about peeing. Here are a few of them.

Want to be alone,
Best place for

Mike meet Mike—
Go for a pee.

A good pee—
Complete Happiness.

In just this little trickle
Whole Holy Mother's Universe flows.
Quick meditation—
Go for a pee.

You can choose,
One place where you know it.
Why not this?
Only your Guru is peeing.

A stream in a sacred grotto,
A little fountain in a love room.

In a well-known aphorism Zen Master Dogen carries Yamada Roshi's saying (quoted above) one step further:

To study Zen is to know the self.
To know the self is to forget the [little-ego] self.
To forget the self is to be enlightened by the ten-thousand [all] things.

> That the self advances and confirms the ten-thousand things is called delusion.
> That the ten-thousand things advance and confirm the self is enlightenment.

In other words, this sort of radical non-dual experience is nothing you can seek or make happen. Rather, it is the opposite. If you advance towards it, it will elude you. It is grace and it will surprise you when you least expect it. Really, the best you can do is to empty yourself and not seek anything. The deeper your practice of losing the separate-self in formless non-dual meditation , the more likely, when living in the world of objects, that this experience of "forgetting self in the act of uniting with something" may surprise you!

Although this experience, where you completely disappear into an object, takes some spiritual maturity and usually "surprises" you only after lots of practice, it is still wonderful to sit in front of something and meditate on your oneness with it. When I first took up meditation in Berkeley in the sixties, I would often climb up to the hills in the afternoon, seat myself in front of a big oak tree and try to meditate that I was the tree. I don't remember how far I got, but considering Dogen's dictum, the key is to cultivate a very gentle emptiness; then the tree—or deer, or meadow—will come to you and fill you up.

This is a gradual approach. There is an infinite gradient to the degree you can experience non-duality. Over time the 'little you' that's separate becomes a thinner and thinner strand. You know that the source that is giving you life and consciousness—call it the flow of aliveness or the heart that connects—flows through everything. Your heart stops being yours, but feels like God's heart, or the immense, intimate heart that creates everything; the heart in which the separation of inner and outer, of you and things, slowly dissolves.

> Two only among the forty meditational practices are always and under all circumstances beneficial—the of friendliness and the recollection of death.
>
> —Buddhaghasa

This is another way of expressing the concepts of compassion and emptiness. The bottom line of all truly deep meditations is contemplating the meaning of death: investigating if our truest being is something that is unborn, undying and empty of separation. Likewise, feeling a great and widespread affection and outward radiating friendliness is the bottom line expression of compassion.

For me, a solo backpacking trip is like an intense meditation retreat. I invariably have an intense experience of these two aspects of meditation. The first few days I'm often desolate; leaving all my friends and facing the unknown and the high country, alone, I feel lonely and afraid, almost like I'm facing death. After a few days, elation and rapture kick in. There's something about being in high alpine country that is like stepping through a magical door to another world; all the sights my eyes behold are mysterious and beautiful—I'm in heaven everywhere. If I run across anyone, we're immediate best friends. After I've arrived back home, I cherish every personal encounter. In a way, something like dying has turned me into a love-puppy. I've gone from an extreme introvert to an extreme extrovert.

Western psychology led a lot of people astray when it articulated the classic introvert/extrovert split. This dichotomy is certainly valid, but only up to a point. A real and total introvert will also become an extreme extrovert. When we take the time and effort to really be alone, then we realize how much we love and need people. When we experience our emptiness, then we know that other people are really a part of ourselves.

Most of the great enlightened beings whom we have verifiably accurate records and eye-witness accounts of—Ramakrishna, Neem Keroli Baba, Mehar Baba— literally bubbled over with friendliness and humor. They were all comedian sages—sort of hybrids between Charlie Chaplin and Jesus. I suspect that Jesus was also a man of great humor and warm friendliness. Nisargadatta, one of the great Hindu sages of this century, often said that great affection is a sure sign of a realized person: "Your very nature has the infinite capacity to enjoy. It is full of zest and affection. It sheds its radiance on all that comes within its focus of awareness and nothing is excluded."

The more we experience our interbeing with all, the more this affection becomes our natural flavor. We extend ourselves that extra margin to make people feel good about themselves. I met a Buddha at a restaurant recently: he was the smiling waiter. He said, "Let me know if there's anything that you need....And let me know if there's anything that you don't need....And let me know if you don't need anything." The extra friendliness was a greater gift than any of the things I might have needed or not needed.

> I have only one religion—
> Practicing kindness.
>
> —The Dalai Lama

THE FEELING OF THE HEART

Words mean nothing; it's the feeling, feeling, feeling.
—Joe Miller

Joe Miller was an eccentric old codger with big bushy white eyebrows who appeared in San Francisco in the 1960's. He became known as the 'Guru to the Hippies.' For three decades, before he died in 1994, he would lead walking meditations in Golden Gate Park, then sit everyone down on the sides of 'Hippie Hill' and have a meditation session. Here are his last words, "Adjust the feeling part. You can add a little thinking along with it, out at the edges. But the feeling is the main thing, that's what makes the world go 'round."

Throughout this book you will find many different techniques and traditions of meditation described. Hopefully you are now interested enough that I can tell you the truth—none of them really matter much except that they open you up to THE FEELING. Techniques and practices come and go. However, the feeling that you experience through any particular technique will stay with you and deepen and ripen, long after the technique is forgotten. The more you practice, the more the heart-feeling your immanent birthright, a readily accessible ally when you need it, and is there to awaken you when you least expect it.

Learning to open to and experience the heart-feeling is what meditation is all about. Because people write books and give lectures, newcomers get fooled and think that meditation is largely about ideas. This is a big mistake; ideas are preparations and footnotes to the main event. The primary value of words and ideas in meditation is to help extinguish themselves. When the words wear themselves out and you know nothing, the feeling will shine. Then what am I doing writing this book? A good point; please think of this as an anti-book.

The heart-feeling is more expressible through poetry, art and music than through logical discourse. Many of the great meditation masters of Asia were equally appreciated as artists and poets. A student would simply view a painting with a poem attached to it; this was the dharma talk, a valid a way to receive (and give) teachings. In the future, when someone calls on a meditation teacher, the two of them may do a dance together, or sing or walk in the woods.

Although it is indescribable, just for fun let's list some of the inadequate words that mystics have used to attempt to express the heart-feeling.

Light—"I see the light," proclaims the mystic, with uplifted eyes. And the light sees the mystic. As distinctions of seer and seen dissolve, the light intensifies. It is really cool, peaceful and soothing—beyond any visual light or darkness.

Darkness—

But when I lean over the chasm of myself—
it seems
my God is dark
and like a web: a hundred roots
silently drinking.
This is the ferment I grow out of.
More I don't know, because my branches
rest in deep silence, stirred only by the wind.
—Rilke

Mother—Throughout all of nature, the deepest and most widespread bond is the mother's love for the child. When people experience that the universe itself creates, sustains and permeates them with this same love, they frequently use mother images— Mother Mary, various Hindu mother incarnations, Kannon (the Bodhisattva of Compassion) – to describe the all-pervading love-source.

Intimate—

It is closer to you than your very self.
—Nisargadatta.

And everything partakes of this close intimacy with everything else. When the mind is still, we discover that we live in something like a precious and sacred little doll-house. And there is no limit to this feeling of cozy and warm familiarity that connects all the things of our life, mind and heart.

Immanence—

SONG OF IMMANENCE

There's something in the world so near,
The world may be in it, I fear.
And anywhere we ever go,
When we return it's still right here.

There's something in the world so free,
It could become a flower or a tree,
the sky or the sea.
And it has become them all,
and become you
and become me.

There's something in the world so new,
It hardly starts and it is through,
And it is just now being born,
and it is me,
and it is you.

The 'something' is the feeling of the heart. It is always more here than you or I (as the delusional ego-self) are.

Oneness/Unity—

> When the mind eventually sinks in the heart, undisturbed bliss is, overwhelmingly felt. There is then feeling which is not divorced from pure awareness; head and heart become one and the same.
>
> —Ramana Maharshi

Tenderness/Vulnerability/Softness—

> Sitting between heaven and earth....your heart is naked. Your entire being is exposed—to yourself first of all, but to others as well. If you search for awakened heart....there is nothing there except for tenderness. You feel sore and soft.... Even if a tiny mosquito lands on it, you feel so touched. Your experience is raw and tender and so personal.
>
> —Chogyam Trungpa

Strenght/Power/Energy—The heart-feeling is the ultimate softness and its complement as well; it fills us with incredible power and strength. The image of the diamond-like quality of pure consciousness is often used because the true mind/heart is stronger than a diamond.

Real-Self, Grace, Bliss, Love, Awareness: All of these words together cannot begin to encompass the heart-feeling, because it has nothing to do with words or ideas, but begins where they leave off. Even 'feeling' is inadequate, but is the closest word that I know of. In Japanese Zen they often refer to it as 'stream entry.' After a few years of sitting, they will say that someone has finally 'had stream-entry.' The Japanese are usually rather reticent; being a Jew and Westerner, I'm probably more emotionally expressive, so I like 'the feeling of the heart.' Continuing with the Japanese analogy, it starts out feeling like a stream, then like a river; with growing realization, it becomes an ocean. In the end, we realize that there really is no entry, because we are and always have been immersed, but we just didn't know it.

After one has been meditating for a few decades, the heart-feeling becomes so much the unquestioned and indescribable central fuel of practice that it's hard to recall exactly how it was first aroused. At first there are innumerable little sensations that begin to come and go, all of which are part of it and open you to it. Sometimes you might feel like your body is rising or falling, becoming immense or tiny, hollow or filled with light. You might feel a tingling or a warmth, a coolness or a coziness. Sometimes it's a familiarity or deja vu—you're returning to your forgotten home, to the mother's breast or womb. All of these are little ways that the feeling begins to open in us.

It reminds me of the 'Calumny Aria' from Rossini's Barber of Seville:

> .a little breeze, a gentle zephyr
> Which insensibly, subtly,
> Lightly and sweetly,
> Commences to whisper.
> Softly, softly, here and there,
> It goes gliding, it goes rambling....
> In the head and brains
> It stuns and it swells.
> From the mouth re-emerging
> The noise grows to a crescendo,
> Gathers force little by little,
> Runs its course from place to place,
> Seems the thunder of the tempest
> Which from the depths of the forest
> Comes whistling, muttering....
> Finally....It spreads afield, its force redoubled...

Although the subject is opening to the universe, rather than spreading gossip, the heart-feeling is something like this. At first there are a hundred diverse little streams, that might be described this way or that. Gradually they converge into an immense energy/feeling that is usually beyond any descriptive particulars. What begins as little tide pools grow to become an ocean; it fills us up so that there is no room left for you or me as a separate entity. You, I and the world of things feel like little peas in the pod of this enveloping and comforting halo-feeling. As this feeling grows deeper, stronger and all-pervasive, people may want to use words like 'God' to describe it.

Some people, especially those just beginning meditation, might object, "What good is this chapter topic and this 'feeling?' It's not my actual experience or anything I know about or can relate to. How will it help me in my practice? Instead, I feel rather discouraged, because this is quite removed from my actual experience at this time." This is quite understandable. The initial openings are quite capricious and unpredictable—something like the meditator's approximation of the Calvinist concept of Grace. Whether due to childhood experiences, past-life karma, or who knows what, some people begin to feel it right away while it takes other people years.

Actually, the heart-feeling is balanced between effort and grace. It is grace, but it is not entirely capricious and unpredictable. We can experience it when we empty ourselves of our opinions, judgments, expectations, attachments. Usually we are so busy and obsessed with these that there is no space for anything else. Although it is unpredictable at first, eventually it is inevitable; it is what we are.

> The winds of grace are blowing all the time,
> You have only to raise your sail.
>
> —Ramakrishna

*

> You are made of a feeling
> that is always blowing you away.

The best way to get to the heart-feeling is just to feel, feel, feel—whatever we are feeling, with no preference for what it should be or what we want it to be. Simply get down to the root of what we are feeling right here and now. Over and over, soften, let go and honestly feel, feel, feel. We all mostly start with the feelings connected with our little ego-selves—-mine centered around the hopes, attachments and fears of me being Mike, you with your world centered around you being you. This is natural. At the surface, our basic instincts are centered around our fear of loss, the perpetuation of our body, the security of our ego-selfhood and the proliferation of our genes (the sexual-obsession). The job of the meditator is to feel his or her way through these immediate feelings to the deeper and truer feelings of pervading love. If we really let ourselves feel that layer of fear, restlessness and anger with patience and equanimity — then we won't need to let go of them at all; they will fade away of their own accord. There are truer feelings that want to possess us.

Usually the self-centered thoughts and feelings so dominate the mental horizon that they leave room for little else. Compare it to a thumb held right at our eye; it blocks out our vision and won't let us see anything but the thumb. The best way to move through our personal feeling/thought obsessions is simply to step back feel, feel, feel; the thumb moves away from the eye. Actually the thumb of our personal thought/feelings is infinitesimally tiny and the horizon of the heart feeling is immense. Feel, feel, feel, and the thumb will recede farther from the eye. We will know that we are the vast horizon of heart feeling. Sometimes you might try focusing your meditation around some of these questions.

What is the feeling of Space?
What is the feeling of Silence?
What is the feeling of Mind?
What is the feeling of Breath?
What is the feeling of Now?
What is the feeling of Here?

All of these are actually the same; the heart feeling is the substratum in which all phenomena appear. These questions can also be used as a reminder, or a way to center the mind. Rather than asking ourselves, "What is the feeling of space?" simply focus the mind on the feeling of space, the feeling of silence. Or just space, silence. If the practice focuses the mind and limits its wanderings, the opening of heart-feeling is inevitable.

There is another practice that is sometimes helpful to open one to the feeling. You can think back to some past time or place in your life when you felt really contented and fulfilled; remember and recapture the feeling that you had (or that had you) then.

Something like this practice helped the Buddha. For years he had been practicing the most extreme austerities. He was discouraged because they were not getting him anywhere. Then he recalled a time of his youth when he was sitting under an apple tree in a beautiful orchard, feeling a deep and all-embracing peace and contentment. He realized that going deeper into this feeling was the point of practice, and that the extreme austerities had so weakened his body that this had become impossible. He abandoned the austerities and had his first full meal in years (a bowl of rice and milk). This simple meal gave him the strength to continue his meditation, entering deeper into heart feeling.

Sometimes, I like to do this sort of practice using prayer beads. When I am alone, on a long drive or a train journey, I often take them out and use them as an aid in meditation. With each bead, I think of a time that I've felt beauty or love. Amazingly, usually before I'm halfway around the loop of beads, my eyes and heart are opened and I see that the very place in which I'm sitting is filled with that same feeling.

The point is that whatever feeling of happiness we think we are getting from an external object or circumstance — be it from nature, art or some relationship – is, in fact, a glimpse of the innate nature of the mind/heart. A beautiful sight awakens us to what we are. Say you look at an autumn oak against a blue sky, the wind blowing a steady stream of leaves towards you. You are awakened with awe, something out there reminds you to be fully present to feel the heartbeat that is not limited by a body, but is the heartbeat of the nature. Meditation is learning to open to and dissolve into this same kind of heart feeling, without needing to depend on any object or setting to elicit it.

After you've been sitting for a while, especially during retreats, you may get a little 'visionary,' i.e.—see images of Jesus, Krishna, Buddha, Mother Mary, Kali, Hanuman. Some approaches regard this as the final destination of meditation. Other approaches, such as Zen schools, say that although this is certainly a sign that some energy channels are opening, it is still just another level in the world of delusion and not worth getting too carried away over.

There are two important points about 'going visionary.' First, you may enter into a state where the visions are interchangeable. Before your inner eye, Rama becomes Buddha, who then transforms into Shiva, and so forth. This experience is common these days, probably due to our broader cultural exposure, or perhaps because we are old beings who have been incarnating for a long time and practiced devotion in many cultures. Due to present or past life devotions, one form might predominate over others —that is, appear with more frequency or greater visual intensity. Regardless, we begin to understand that these are really all the same being and that they are all the manifestations of our real unlimited self, of the pure energy of here and now.

So these days, when you go visionary, you must be ready to be surprised. When you get into the energized and open state where the archetypal unconscious is flowing through your consciousness, it is kind of like a dream—you never know who or what will show up. I first experienced this at a Zen intensive retreat. I had been raised a good Jewish boy and never had any thoughts or feelings about Jesus. Suddenly, in the middle of one night Jesus came in a sort of dream/vision. You can imagine my surprise. Since then, I'm sort of a Christian, Jewish, Buddhist, Hindu Sufi. Often in my meditations I still feel the blessing and presence of Jesus. Sometimes I think maybe I was a Franciscan in a past life.

Second, and the point that is relevant for this chapter: visions may come and go, but it's the heart feeling in which they arrive that counts. This is the gift and the grace that will stay with you even when the vision passes or transforms. When I had the Jesus vision, it was accompanied by a feeling-cloud that wanted to roll over me and take me out of the body into a sort of love-oblivion. What was that feeling-cloud? Awe, splendor, overwhelming love, infinite tenderness—as always, words fail. Call it anything whatsoever—but I knew that I'd touched the truth of being.

Thoughts and ideas are essentially limited and limiting. They are about boundaries and definitions in time and space. A feeling is a feeling. It is boundaryless, expansive and unlimited. It has no location in time and space; it doesn't know where it is or when it is. It just is. The heart feeling is continuously dissolving our ideas of separation. The deeper we let ourselves become the feeling, the more we know that our true being has nothing to do with time and space.

Meditation practice is always a balance between thinking and feeling. Over years of meditation, the feeling gets stronger and deeper. The thinking mind never entirely goes away, but its power over us diminishes as we learn to dissolve in deepening floods of heart-feeling.

It is, once again, time to inject a note of caution and moderation. I am not advocating that one should totally disband the intellect. To safely tread the spiritual path, a balance of both intellect and feeling is necessary. One definitely needs the intellect to provide a safe framework in which to open to the feelings. People who have totally abandoned the intellect are wandering around glassy-eyed and fanatic in various cults.

Over the last few decades we've seen numerous spiritual groups that espouse universal love and compassion. After a few years headlines often appear concerning drug and gun running, money-laundering, shady political manipulations, death-threats amid vicious and violent in-fighting. The '80's Rajneesh ranch in eastern Oregon is the most notable recent example.

What happens? People who can't see their life in a larger social and historical perspective are easily carried away with delusions of self-importance. They get the idea that what they are doing is radically unique and historically essential. It follows that any means are justified to secure the survival and flourishing of their particular group. Here is a primary criteria with which to recognize a cult. In a true path, the ends never justify the means. The only real means and ends are living a generous and kind life.

I recently came across an old picture book of 'life at the Rajneesh ranch.' It reminded me of other pitfalls in a spiritual path that over-emphasizes feeling without an intellectual foundation. It doesn't look like anyone ever just took a calm walk around there. Everyone seems to be always jumping up and down, running or collapsing in raptures of boundless bliss. I got exhausted just looking at the book. This sort of over-emphasis on ecstatic feeling can easily lead to spiritual hedonism and a lack of social responsibility. Just going 'feeling-crazy,' that is not based on some discipline and balanced with an idea of self-denial and service, is usually spiritual fantasy and self-delusion.

Because Westerners are generally over-balanced towards the intellect, I may have over compensated this chapter towards feeling. Really, both are necessary and reinforce each other.

THE FEELING ISN'T IN YOU: YOU ARE IN THE FEELING—As our perspective transforms, the heart feeling is an ever stronger and more present reminder of this truth—that you are in the feeling and just an infinitesimal part of it. It surrounds you; you are a little fish in the ocean and you are the ocean.

LET GO OF ‘I AM THE BODY’ AND ‘I AM THE THOUGHTS’ IDENTITIES—The heart-feeling is beyond and has nothing to do with body and thoughts. With each breath and moment—as you let go of your usual identification with body and thoughts—the heart-feeling radiance intensifies.

> It's the feeling of 'not you.'
> It's the little bit of lightness that connects.
> It's the heart where there is no distance.
> It's the tiny stitching together of everything.

FORM AND FORMLESS

Form is Formless,
Formless is Form.

—Heart Sutra

These lines form the kernel of the Heart Sutra, the most frequently recited sutra in all of Buddhism.

The breeze at dawn has secrets to tell you....
People are going back and forth across the doorsill
where the two worlds touch.
The door is round and open.

—Rumi

The Sufi poet is referring to the world of form and the world of the formless. The essence of meditation is learning to go deeper into both of these worlds. As our practice matures, we learn that the two go hand in hand; as we go deeper into one world, we naturally go deeper into the other. Finally, we understand that the two are really the same and are always interpenetrating.

Here we find the ultimate, most poignant and delicious paradox of the spiritual path. On the one hand, as we learn to be present and awake, the world of form seems more completely alive and real: we feel like we have never really seen things in their fullness before. And, as our experience of the world of form deepens, so does its paradoxical compliment; we also have a deepening experience of the formless energy field that gives birth to all form. From this perspective, the world of forms seems fragile, ephemeral and like a passing dream—somehow not the ultimate reality at all.

It seems I can't really enjoy this world
unless I'm busy contemplating
whether it really exists or not.

Over a lifetime, as we learn to let go of our limiting little ego identification, both experiences deepen; the aspect of form seems both endlessly more real, and, at the same time, less real. There is no final answer; there is only the mystery and the play of form and formless. We only know that neither can exist without the other. Each creates and is always interpenetrating with the other. And the dance of this play is endlessly delicious.

People with a superficial understanding sometimes have the idea that meditation is about denying this world, blotting out material reality—the world of forms, shapes, colors, sounds—in order to enter some formless, pure energy realm. Artists are especially prone to this misunderstanding. I have a nephew who says that meditation is not for him because his job as an artist is to clearly see and precisely record material reality. Hikers and nature lovers also sometimes fall for this fallacy—that meditation predisposes one to want to leave this beautiful world.

In a way they are half-right, but in this case, being half-right is completely wrong. Truly, part of meditation practice is 'leaving the world of form,' —learning to dissolve in the pure energy ocean that is the substratum, cradle and nursery of all form. But this is only a half of the practice. If someone's meditation is too heavily tilted towards this direction, they will become rather lifeless, withdrawn, bored and boring. In a mature practice, the opening to the formless is balanced with an opening to form.

Sometimes beginning meditation students don't get this; there is a stage where they go off the deep end into the world of the formless, always wanting to close their eyes and disappear into an inner world. Sasaki Roshi would re-balance novice students by asking them, "The world is so beautiful, why would you always want to close your eyes?" The great Hindu Guru Ramakrishna put it this way:

> Dear friends do not enter her sacred temple and meditate before her living presence with eyes closed. Would you return to your native village and sit before your mother without looking at her. Open your eyes every moment to the mystery of Kali.

A friend had just returned from an ashram in India. She was busy repeating a spiritual song that she had learned there, "Oh Mother, take me away, Oh Mother, take me away." As she had tendencies to close herself off from the world, I thought that this was a terrible song for her to sing. I suggested that she should rather be singing, "Oh Mother, bring me right here, Oh Mother, bring me right here." The paradox of the well-balanced spiritual path is that we can sing both songs simultaneously; the deeper we open to the formless, the deeper we open to form, and visa-versa.

Actually, the best way to experience the formless is to love and embrace the world of form. When we are fully present, we know that we are absolutely powerless in the face of the universe's overwhelming beauty. An old Zen master held up a teacup and said, "This is worth one billion yen and can enlighten the whole universe." A tree or just a leaf, a mountain or a stone—anything will do. When we really see something we know that the power to create color, light, form is a miracle beyond us.

Being present in the world of form creates sort of a feedback loop with the formless. We instinctively know that the beauty is not just out there in the object, but is also the very nature of our awareness. Often the Don't Worry Zendo sits in an enclosed courtyard in front of my house in L.A. I close my eyes for a while. I open them. I see the subtle movements an of things —a passing bird, a few grains of pollen filtering down through a beam of light, the waving of the palm fronds. These quiet my mind and propel it to a deeper level. I close my eyes. I open them again. Something new is passing through. Sometimes it seems like there is no end to this delicious dialogue. Then a fellow meditator rings a bell.

I love the nearness of things,
In the stillness where the light touches them,
They tremble for God.

Buddhists sometimes use the words 'suchness' or 'thusness' to describe this numinous quality of the world of form. When we find the sacred altar in the formless heart, then as we go through the day, things in the world of form are also on that sacred altar—somehow holy, numinous and charged with that same blessing that we find in the formless pure energy field. When we can let go of our little selves and really see things, just as they are they are perfect, sacred and interpenetrating with each other, ourselves and the formless.

Trying to explain the mystery of the interpenetration of form and formless is one of the most tempting and futile pastimes of mystics. Simply put, it cannot be explained, but people can't resist trying. Here are a few attempts.

> Each something is a celebration of the nothing that supports it.
>
> —John Cage

> It is not a something, but it makes all somethings....This cannot be known by knowing, but it can be faithed by faithing past and through it.
>
> —Rabbi Nachman

> ...that nothing existed apart from an indivisible and universal consciousness which was experienced in its unmanifest form as being or awareness and in its manifest form as the appearance of the universe.
>
> —David Godman

> To the ignorant and enlightened alike the world is real, however for the ignorant, the world of name and form alone is real, whereas for the enlightened, being, awareness, bliss is the ground and substratum of the world we see.
>
> —Ramana Maharshi

> Love says: 'I am everything.'
> Wisdom says: 'I am nothing.'
> Between the two my life flows.
>
> —Nisargadatta

Mystics often use the analogy of pure space. When we learn to still the mind, we find that the nature of our consciousness is vast, radiant, unbound space; whatever contents enter into this space/mind—the infinite things of the world of form—also take on these radiant qualities. Everything is alive with spirit that permeates all form. If our attention is totally right here, this aliveness in things will return our attention with a sign. It will relate to us and will say, "I'm alive and we are created as part of each other." This always happens in new and unexpected ways, sometimes very simple and sometimes not: a flight of birds in an exquisite dance, hearing a symphony of crickets, grass all waving together in the breeze.

> All things through this space do fly,
> And as they pass they're saying 'Hi.'
>
> —Buffo Sutra Rossini

> If you love it enough, anything will talk to you.
>
> —G. Washington Carver

Another facet of the form/formless dichotomy concerns approaches to meditation. More devotional types are disposed to meditate on some form of divinity—Christ, Buddha, Hanuman, Krishna, Mother Mary, etc. Other people prefer a more direct, formless approach, meditating on pure awareness or sense of being. We will return to this question after taking a short detour in the next chapter.

TWO SPIRITUAL BEACONS

In the past one hundred and fifty years we have seen two great Indian teachers who acted as spiritual turning points and set the stage for our century's discovery of meditation and Eastern spirituality. To understand both the history and contents of this spiritual diffusion it will be worthwhile to consider their lives and teachings.

SRI RAMAKRISHNA

The great Indian mystic Ramakrishna (1836-1886) was a God intoxicated holy man who seemed to spend most of his life in various stages of rapture and divine communion. He lived in a temple on the outskirts of Calcutta and was largely unknown outside of Bengal during his lifetime. In the last years of his life, however, a number of young men became his disciples; it is through them that his influence spread throughout the world. He prepared the way for the West's discovery of Eastern mysticism in four distinct ways.

First, Ramakrishna was instrumental in India's re-affirmation of its own spiritual and cultural heritage, and in the spreading of that heritage to the west. During his life large segments of the Indian educated classes had become disenchanted with traditional Indian spiritual culture and were embracing western materialism and rationality. Ramakrishna helped to change this.

In 1893, the first Parliament of the World's Religions was held in Chicago. The world's attention was focused on the hundreds of delegates that attended this first attempt at a dialogue between all of the world's religions. Ramakrishna's foremost disciple, Swami Vivakananda, was a representative of Hinduism. He was the overwhelming sensation of the Parliament. For three years afterwards he toured North America and Europe, lecturing to sold out and rapturous audiences in numerous cities. This was the first time that an eastern mystic had lived and taught in the west. Vivakananda founded 'Vedanta' centers in a number of cities and his brother disciples came from India to teach at them. The recent western interest in eastern spirituality has all stemmed from these first contacts.

Back in India, word spread that a Hindu was creating a sensation in America. Vivakananda, when he returned to India in 1896, was amazed to discover that he was the hero of the whole country. There was literally a triumphal procession from city to city. Many Indians, needless to say, re-evaluated the wisdom of discarding their own spiritual culture, especially as it was being discovered and valued in the west. Through Vivakananda and his brother disciples, the teachings of Ramakrishna spread throughout India, resulting in a great revival of Hinduism.

Second, the re-emergence of Goddess worship stems from Ramakrishna. He was a great devotee of the Hindu Mother Kali and lived in an exalted state in which he beheld her everywhere. He would say to devotees that, "She is more real to me right now than all the people sitting in this room." A rediscovery of the feminine aspect of divinity is one of the most important spiritual developments of our time. Ramakrishna was the first great modern Goddess devotee.

Third, the ecumenical movement of our times also begins with Ramakrishna. Although primarily divinely intoxicated with Mother Kali, Ramakrishna practiced the meditations of many spiritual paths. With great regularity a guru of some lineage or another would show up and initiate him into the practices of their particular religion. He was the complete nineteenth century religious zelig; his speech, dress, behavior and practices would all conform to his new path. This would continue until he fully experienced its inner truths. In turn he was a Muslim, Christian, Shaivite, Ram Bhakti, Tantric and Advaitist.

Ramakrishna never tired of telling people that all religious paths are wonderful, valid, identical at their core and that we should have tolerance and love for all of them.

> The entire world is being driven insane by this single phrase:
> "My religion alone is true."

The fourth point returns us to the discussion of Form and Formless that we left at the end of the previous chapter. One time, a guru of the formless 'Advaita Vedanta' approach appeared and wanted to initiate Ramakrishna. Ever the love-intoxicated child of Mother Kali, Ramakrishna resisted; he sat by Kali's altar and begged her:

> I long only for my Divine Mother. Her alone do I need. A million salutations to the experience of formlessness. I do not want it. Give calm dispassion to those who seek it, O Mother, but make me mad with love for You. I long desperately for Your Presence, for Your Smile, for Your Touch. O You who are composed of sheer bliss.

Despite his endless protestations, Ramakrishna finally felt that the Mother told him to be initiated into the formless meditation. Within three days he experienced what it had taken his amazed new guru forty years to realize—complete absorption and ego-dissolving in the formless ground of being.

From this time on, Ramakrishna's life and teachings became an exquisite poem describing the subtle dance of form and formless. He both worshipped his personal deity and he abided in the vast expanse of emptiness. Fortunately, in those pre-tape recorder days, a disciple took copious notes of Ramakrishna's teachings: the resulting book, "The Gospel of Ramakrishna" is one of the world's great spiritual classics. Here are a few Ramakrishna quotes on the subject of form and formless.

> The unmanifest is an infinite diamond and the display of manifestation is the variegated radiance of that diamond. There is no gem without its brilliance nor can the gem's brilliance exist without the gem. There is no absolute without the relative and no relative canexist apart from the absolute. God realization is the conscious union of the manifest with the unmanifest; the same reality is experienced as all dimensions of being and also as the dimensionless ground or source of being—the open space of unconditioned awareness.

> Supreme Reality is real and the insubstantial universe as well is real. These mysterious tidal surges, as Absolute and relative, are the ebb and flow of Divine Ecstasy....The enlightened lover swims joyfully in this bidirectional river of God-consciousness—sometimes being swept by the ebb tide into the open ocean of the Absolute, other times sailing upstream with the

> flood tide of the relative. Sometimes the ecstatic lover sounds the deeps and other times plays like a child on the surface.
>
> I used to meditate with my eyes shut, but is the Lord not there if I open my eyes? When I open my eyes, I see that the Lord dwells in all creatures, in man, animals, trees, the sun and the moon, the water and the ground....People who think God is only inside are living in dark mud houses. After the realization that God is within and without, the world itself becomes a glass house.

When people first experience the formless aspect they sometimes become rather unbalanced and world-denying. The subtlest teachers, like Ramakrishna, remind us that the best way to experience the formless source-ocean is through embracing and loving the world of form, rather than through denying it. When we really see and become one with something, in that embrace we, and the world, will both dissolve in the love matrix from which all things take their birth.

SRI RAMANA MAHARSHI.

When I first took up meditation, I came across writings about the life and teachings of Sri Ramana. I devoured them and they became (and still are) my guide. Though Sri Ramana left the body in 1950, really he was my first teacher. Ramana's life is a fascinating story which people always enjoy hearing (and I never tire of recounting).

Sri Ramana Maharshi was born Venkataraman in 1880 in a town in Southern India. As a boy he didn't have any special spiritual leanings and was even something of a ruffian; he much preferred wrestling and athletic games to studying. However, a photographic memory allowed him to receive passing school grades with little effort. The other remarkable thing about Venkataraman was that once he had fallen asleep it was absolutely impossible to awaken him until he awoke himself. After this was observed by his young friends, one of their favorite sports became carrying the sleeping Venkataraman around the town. No one thought too much of this, but it might have been a tip-off that this was not an ordinary person.

The great transformation in Venkataraman's life came when he was sixteen. An uncle passed through the town and told Venkataraman that he was returning from a pilgrimage to Arunachala, a holy mountain which was considered to be an actual incarnation of Shiva, located about 150 miles from Venkataraman's town. On hearing the word Arunachala, all the hair on Venkataraman's body stood on end and he felt an electric current surging up and down his spine. He felt like he was really hearing for the first time. He was amazed that Arunachala was an actual place that one could go to.

Strangely, the energy current never went away, but kept growing for the next six months. (I imagine his hair couldn't have stayed erect for all of that time but must have periodically risen and fallen.) Also, sometime during that six months someone gave him a book, 'The lives of the 63 Tamil Saints,' which he could not put down. He was amazed that people could actually live the kind of spiritual life that was described.

After this six months, the great realization finally came. He was lying on the living room floor and suddenly felt with a great certainty that he was going to die. I will quote from his description of the experience:

> The shock of the fear of death drove my mind inwards and I said to myself mentally, without actually framing the words: "Now death has come; what does it mean? What is it that is dying? This body dies." And I at once dramatized the occurrence of death. I lay with my limbs stretched out stiff as though rigor mortis had set in and imitated a corpse so as to give greater reality to the inquiry. I held my breath and kept my lips tightly closed so that no sound could escape, so that neither the word 'I' nor any other word could be uttered.
>
> "Well then," I said to myself, "this body is dead. It will be carried stiff to the burning ground and there burnt and reduced to ashes. But with the death of this body am I dead? Is the body I? It is silent and inert but I feel the full force of my personality and even the voice of the 'I' within me, apart from it. So I am Spirit transcending the body. The body dies but the Spirit that transcends it cannot be touched by death. That means I am the deathless Spirit." All this was not dull thought; it flashed through me vividly

> as living truth which I perceived directly, almost without thought-process. 'I' was something very real, the only real thing about my present state, and all the conscious activity connected with my body was centered on that 'I'. from that moment onwards the 'I' or Self focused attention on itself by a powerful fascination. Fear of death had vanished once and for all.

The unusual thing was that Venkataraman never returned to ego-consciousness. Most of us study, meditate, try to live a more selfless life, and gradually begin to have little hints of such experiences. Over a lifetime the understanding slowly deepens. With Venkataram it was complete, final and irreversible; i.e. there was no more Venkataraman.

Normal life, needless to say, became impossible. Whereas he had previously never gone to the local temples, now he spent all of his spare time there, standing in front of the images crying. The ruffian vanished; he became docile, passive and lost all interest in outward activity and his studies. This couldn't continue.

Finally, after six weeks, the great break came. Venkataraman was sitting at the kitchen table, supposedly studying a book. Naturally, his eyes were closed and he was lost in the vastness. His disgusted older brother said mockingly, "If your going to live like that, why don't you just go off and become a sadhu." What was said in half-jest struck Venkataraman as obvious and undeniable. Later that day, on the pretext of going to a 'special class on electricity,' he was out of the front door, heading for Arunachala.

Three day later, after traveling by train, walking and begging for food, he arrived at the Arunachala Hill, with the great temple complex at its base. He threw away his clothes, except for a loin cloth (which was all he ever wore from then on), had his head shaved (just at that moment a few drops of rain fell—an auspicious sign), and entered the temple precincts. Having arrived, for 54 years he never left the holy mountain.

For the next few years, he sat in bliss, oblivious of his body and surroundings. He was first discovered sitting in one of the underground vaults of the great temple, literally being eaten up alive by vermin and lice. A few sadhus attached themselves to him and started to take care of him. Gradually, word of this unusual boy spread, and more people came to see him.

In India, it is considered to be a blessing to feed a saint, so people would open his mouth and put food in it. Finally, as crowds continued to grow, the continual stuffing got to be too much for Venkataraman. For the first several years he had not spoken or communicated with anyone. One day when people arrived, they found he had written with a piece of charcoal on the ground in front of him, "Please feed this body only once a day." The young swami could write, and it was in English no less (he had gone to an American Mission High School).

From here, Venkataraman gradually learned to re-integrate his deeply enlightened state with a more normal and communicative state of consciousness. He started talking, so as to be able to answer questions put to him by people who were gathering about him. The austere boy blossomed into a wise and warm-hearted sage whose teachings were filled with innumerable earthy ancedotes and humerous stories. Renamed Sri Ramana Maharshi (great sage) by his devotees, he became one of the most highly revered, respected and influential Hindu Gurus of the twentieth century. As his fame spread and people came from all over India, and eventually the world to see him, a beautiful ashram was built at the foot of Arunachala.

And the story ends even more happily. His mother got news that her young son had become a revered swami at Arunachala. Naturally, with the brother in tow, she moved there and took charge of the kitchen. By the end of her life she was as revered as Sri Ramana. And the brother ran the ashram.

Until he 'left the body' in 1950, Sri Ramana was the model of a real spiritual master. He lived a life of total service and humility. Day or night he was there for people—to answer their questions or just to guide them on the spiritual path by the power of the deep peace that people felt in his presence. There was literally no door on his room. He always refused any preferential treatment for himself, but insisted he was no more or less important than anyone else. If people brought special delicacies for him, they had to be shared by everyone at the ashram.

By the end of his life, Sri Ramana was widely regarded less as a human being than as some sort of incarnation of Shiva/Arunachala, who had taken birth especially to guide mankind. The final evidence of this was a comet, seen by thousands of people and reported in the newspapers of South India, that slowly moved across the sky and disappeared behind Arunachala, at exactly the moment Sri Ramana breathed his last.

Sri Ramana Maharshi's life did seem to have a definite mission; he reintroduced and modernized for our time the ancient Hindu spiritual path of Advaita. This could be translated as self-realization, self-inquiry or non-duality.

ADVAITA/SELF-INQUIRY

Sri Ramana often called the Advaita practice 'self-inquiry.' He taught that the 'I'-thought, the deep sense of being a separate entity, is at the core of everyone's emotional and mental universe. Our whole thought world, our conception of other people, places and circumstances, is spun out of a central concern for I. The first step is just to be aware of this. If we sit still and watch our mind, the momentum and tenacity of this obsession is obvious and undeniable. Like some sort of science fiction monster, we can experience its tentacles reaching everywhere into our flow of thoughts and feelings.

Examining the I-thought is the best way to get a handle on the very root of the thought world. Sri Ramana would enjoin people to meditate on the question 'Who Am I?' or ''What is the nature of this consciousness,' or 'To whom is this thought occurring.' Sometimes Sri Ramana would advise reducing 'Who Am I?' simply to I; sit with the mind focused on I—I—I. Sitting with 'I, I, I' is a tool to immediately and repeatedly discern and reject false ideas of I as they arise. By focusing attention on the small I that is at the center of our thought and feeling world, it becomes possible to let the I and the thought world created from it collapse.

You begin to realize that your idea of 'you' is composed of memories from the past and of projections into the future, based on avoiding those experiences that produced pain and replicating those that produced pleasure. As you learn to disregard the past and future and experience the present moment, miraculously, the idea of a separate 'you' vanishes like a desert mirage—you will never be able to find it. Everything you think you own, know, can do, pertains to the past and future. Further, your body, mind and perceptions are not yours; they are all gifts given to you by something greater. They only exist in co-dependence with everything else in the universe. Being right here and now, things just fall apart.

Here is another way of putting it. Lets say you are some sort of absolute superperson. You have unlimited power to transform yourself and everything in the universe into anything and everything. What is the one thing in which you are absolutely powerless—that neither you nor anyone can ever do?—

—just being/awareness: the ability to be/aware right now. In the present moment this core of being/awareness is the only thing that exists, and it is beyond anyone's power. And only this empty present moment is real, all else is memory and projection.

Inquiry into the emptiness of your separate ego self is also an investigation into the emptiness of all things. You realize that what applies to you applies to everything. All things are empty of an inherent separate existence. You could say that nothing truly exists. But amazingly, this very nothing is full of bliss/love.

The deeper one enters into this truth of existence, the more amazing and wonderful it is. It cannot actually be explained, but people who have had a taste of it get addicted to the attempt. They keep circling around, using different words to try to convey it. Other people might then be inspired to experience it for themselves.

Sri Ramana would tell people to eliminate everything that is eliminatable, that they are not sure of, and see what is left, what they can be certain of. The one thing we can be sure of is that something exists—that there is some sort of being/consciousness that is here. We experience that we are not anything that can be grasped, described or that even exists in time or space. We discover that the real self is illimitable energy; it is pure awareness that has nothing to do with the thought's contents that are centered around the small I.

The above speculations may appear to be merely abstract and intellectual mind games. They are far from it. As we give ourselves to these investigations, we experience, arising from the depths of being, a fullness of love/ blessing that creates everything and in which everything exists. Actually, it is always present but our preoccupation with the little I has kept us ignorant. Our habitual thoughts were always just a tiny little stream. They disappear when we reach the ocean.

NISARGADATTA.

A few years after Ramana died in 1950, a second great Advaita master, Nisargadatta, appeared in Bombay. In a way, Nisargadatta's life was a continuation of Ramana's. Although not a direct successor, his teachings were nearly identical. Many old students of Ramana's gravitated to Bombay to sit with Nisargadatta.

In a way Nisargadatta's life was a great success story and a demonstration of the democracy of the spirit. He was a poor and largely uneducated family man who etched out a meager living from a tiny beedie (the thin Indian cigarette wrapped in a leaf) stand. In middle life, he met a guru, took up meditation and, in between rolling beedies, managed to become deeply enlightened. As he became known, crowds came to fill his tiny apartment in a poor section of Bombay. He was able to give up the beedie business and spend his days answering their spiritual questions. Fortunately, very intelligent people often showed up and asked deep and probing questions. Also, a few people recorded the dialogues and later published them. The best of these books, and one of the great spiritual classics of the twentieth century, is *I Am That*. It is the most articulate exposition of dharma that I have ever found. You'll find several quotes from it throughout this book. If you are inspired to go out and get a copy of *I Am That*, then this book will have served you well.

It is interesting to compare the personalities of Ramana and Nisargadatta. In Ramana's presence, people felt great peace, warmth and grace. His answers to questions were usually patient and compassionate. People perceived an infinite gentleness in his appearance. I've known many people (myself included) who like to meditate looking at his picture. The depth, wisdom and love that radiate from his eyes is miraculous and indescribable. People said that when he smiled the whole world would smile.

Reading *I Am That*, a slightly different kind of personality emerges. I wouldn't exactly call Nisargadatta a spiritual thug, but more of a classic Zen master type personality: up-front, outspoken, blunt, altogether humorous and not too worried about hurting anyone's feelings.

His responses to questions were unfailingly brilliant and immediate. No matter how deep and difficult the question, almost before it was completed, the answer was there, perfectly articulated and illustrated, coming from the place of deepest enlightenment and pulling the rug out from under the questioner's particular limited perspective.

Of these two great Advaita teachers, Sri Ramana would more frequently emphasize awareness whereas Nisargadatta gave a little more emphasis to the sense of being. Let's consider both.

Sri Ramana says to let go of the thought, feeling or perception and be the pure experiencer—this is the doorway to realize that you are not a being limited by body, time and space—but that these all exist within the pure unlimited consciousness which is what you always are. Nisargadatta also enjoins turning inwards to pure awareness. He calls it 'witness consciousness' and frequently advised students to become the pure witness, observing but untouched by all events. However, in Nisargadatta's version of self-inquiry, there is slightly more emphasis on feeling a sense of being. His leitmotif is 'I am.' Sitting, working, traveling, whatever you are doing all day, just keep a sense of I- am; feel that there is being here, but let all particulars, definitions and limitations go.

> The only fact that you are sure of is that you are. The 'I am' is certain. The 'I am this' is not. Struggle to find out what you are in reality. To know what you are, you must first investigate and know what you are not. Discover all that you are not—body, feelings, thoughts, time, space, this or that—nothing, concrete or abstract, which you perceive can be you...The clearer you understand that on the level of mind you can be described in negative terms only, the quicker will you come to the end of your search and realize that you are the limitless being.
>
> —Nisargadatta

These are not distinct or different ways at all, but use a slightly varying emphasis to get at the undefinable and indescribable reality which is beyond all ideas and words. From whichever way you conceive it, as practice deepens you understand that the essence of meditation is to experience that being and consciousness are identical. The consciousness to whom each thought is occurring is pure being—vast radiant space that includes everything. And vice versa—the very nature of being/space is alive and conscious. Here we arrive at the classic Hindu description of reality—Sat Chit Ananda—being, consciousness, bliss.

BEING=CONSCIOUSNESS——›BLISS

Alternatively, we might use the words space and mind. Usually, we think of these two as separate. There is space, the expanse within which we exist. And there is mind, the little bit of enclosed and separate consciousness to whom our thoughts, feelings, memories and sensations are occurring. Meditation is experiencing these two as identical; mind is not 'yours,' but is the vast space. As we experience this identity, we disappear into it. We know that we are always this being which is conscious and alive with a bliss that creates and contains everything.

In English these days, bliss may have some sort of superficial, pollyannaish connotations. When asked to describe the nature of the experience of the Supreme, Nisargadatta replied, "Immense peace and boundless love." These may be more suitable alternatives. Anyway it is indescribable.

NON-ATTAINMENT

Advaita teachers usually use the word 'self' for the absolute. This stresses the truth of non-attainment: spiritual wisdom is realizing what you actually are and have always been, rather than attaining anything new or outside of yourself.

> No one is ever away from his self and therefore everyone is in fact self-realized; only—and this is the great mystery—people do not know this and want to realize the self. Realization consists only in getting rid of the false idea that one is not realized. It is not anything new to be acquired....once the false notion 'I am the body' or 'I am not realized' has been removed, supreme

> consciousness or the Self alone remains and in people's present state of knowledge they call this 'realization.' But the truth is that realization is eternal and already exists, here and now.
>
> —Sri Ramama Maharshi

The use of 'self' also helps eliminate excessive theorizing and rampant metaphysical rumination. When asked about God, creation, the nature of the universe or reality, Sri Ramana would almost invariably reply that just knowing who you are is all you need to do and, really, all you can do. There's no need to think about anything else; when you know who you are, then everything else will be answered.

Subtle meditation teachings usually begin with this 'big view': affirming that we are already enlightened, that enlightenment is the very nature of our consciousness and being. The next step is to realize that we do not need to seek anything, but just to realize this true nature; i.e. the very mind that is seeking some sort of enlightenment, peace or bliss is actually made out of what it is seeking.

BUDDHIST TEACHINGS

Looking at Buddhist teachings, we find many that are identical to Advaita. The great Zen masters often taught meditation using koans (questions) that essentially embody the same kind of self-inquiry taught by Ramana. Here are a few of these koans.

> "What was your original face before your parents were born?"
> "Who is the master?"
> "Who is it that is dragging this corpse around?"
> "Who is it that comes and goes through the six sense doors?"

The preferred practice of some schools of Korean and Japanese Zen is simply using the koan, "What is this?" All of these approaches can be used as either a question or as an affirmation: 'Who am I?' 'I am' or just 'I;' 'What is this?' or just 'this, this, this.' We can call it being, consciousness or "this:" it is the ever present ground of being that is an infinitely more real "you" than whatever your ideas of your separate "you" are.

Please try sitting with just 'this, this, this.' With only 'this, this, this' in your mind, there is no preference or choice or rejection. All distinctions dissolve; 'this' includes everything going on around or within you as well as the pure space/being/consciousness within which and to whom it is all occurring. A mind focused on 'this' has a key that will open it to subtler, more radiant and spacious energy.

Non-attainment is also central to many Buddhist teachings.

Practice is enlightenment.
Enlightenment is practice.

This is the most famous epitaph of Dogen Zenji (1200-1253), the founder of Japanese Soto Zen. The heart of Dogen's teaching is "the oneness of practice and enlightenment." In this practice, one sits with the attitude that meditation is not trying to attain anything, but is rather the very expression of enlightenment. The very act of sitting affirms that we are already enlightened. It is also the experience and enjoyment of this realization.

The great exponent of the Soto Zen path in this century was Shunryu Suzuki Roshi, who founded the San Francisco Zen Center in 1958 and was one of the greatest inspirations in establishing Zen practice in this country. Non-attainment is a recurrent theme in Suzuki Roshi's masterpiece *Zen Mind, Beginner's Mind:*

> When you try to attain enlightenment, you have a big burden on your mind...Your mind starts to wander about somewhere else, when you do not try to attain anything, you have your own body and mind right here.
>
> When you are idealistic, you have some gaining idea within yourself; by the time you attain your ideal or goal, your gaining idea will create another ideal. So as long as your practice is based on a gaining idea, and you practice zazen in an idealistic way, you will have no time actually to attain your ideal.

In other words, our very mind, right here and now, is complete, peaceful and at one with the universe. We only need to really experience it, rather than let it be directed outwards, as it chronically is.

How sad that people ignore the near
and search for truth afar.
Like the child of a wealthy home
wandering among the poor.
Like a fish in the midst of water
crying out in thirst.

These opening lines of the "Song of Zazen," by Hakuin (1685-1768), the father of modern Japanese Rinzai Zen, are chanted in most Rinzai temples after evening meditation. They hold the same intent and message: our very nature is affluence and plenty. The ocean is our being, but we habitually do not look at what is right here nor do we look at the looker himself, and so we do not experience what we actually are.

Another classic Zen story:

Student, "What is the Buddha way?"
Master, "Ordinary mind is the way. The mind thinking this and that right now is it."
Student, "How do I contact it?"
Master, "The more you try to approach it, the further you get from it. The more you chase it, the further it runs."

When we first take up meditation, we often grasp after some idea of enlightenment as an external thing. At this point, we have to drop the idea of 'enlightenment' itself. When we have an idea about enlightenment, we are making it into an object that is separate from ourselves, a barrier between ourselves and the actual experience of life. With time we learn that there is no thinking about enlightenment; there is only being it, moment by moment.

Another famous Zen saying: "If you are an inch away, you are 10,000 miles away." If you have any ideas of separation, of attaining rather than being, you are universes away. A novice inquires about the 'gateless gate.' The master explains that if you think there is a gate, it will always elude you. If you know that you are already through the gateless gate, then you are it.

> If you can't find the truth right where you are, where else do you think you will find it.
>
> —the Buddha

The truth is always and only what is right in front of us. Right here and now we are complete and whole. Through discipline and practice, we experience this once, then twice, then again and again. We begin to understand that spiritual life is not about having any ideas: on the contrary, it is repeatedly letting go of all ideas and remembering to experience this precious right now moment.

In recent years, Dzogchen has become the most popular branch of Tibetan Buddhism in the west. Dzogchen teachers emphasize non-effort and undoing, rather than doing. I recently attended a 'meditation retreat' with Tsoknyi Rimpoche, a respected Tibetan teacher. Rimpoche would always be ringing a bell and imploring us, "OK, non-meditation time, just open your eyes, relax and smile." It is, unfortunately, easy to get into some overly concentrated, constricted and up-tight state in meditation. The subtle meditation teachings, as Dzogchen, constantly remind us that there is nothing to seek or wait for; if we just open our eyes, heaven is right here.

When I was in Katmandu recently I met a Dzogchen monk. I told him that I had attended a retreat with Tsoknyi Rimpoche. He exclaimed, "Retreat! Retreat from what?"

Here are a few verses from a Dzogchen sutra:

> Seeing that everything is self-perfected
> from the very beginning,
> the disease of striving for any achievement is surrendered,

and just remaining in the natural state as it is
the presence of non-dual contemplation
continuously spontaneously arises.

*

Monk, "The thousand expedient means all lead back to the source. I wonder what that source is really about."
Master Yunmen, "Where there is a question, there is an answer."

Monk, "Though this is constantly my most pressing concern, I cannot find any way in. Please, Master show me a way in!"
Master Yunmen, "Just in your present concern there is a way."

Yumnen(864-949) was the last of the great Tang dynasty Chinese Zen masters. I love to read the record of his dialogues. He makes the above points over and over: our very thinking mind is not ours; it is the universe's and it is unlimited energy and intimacy. The mind, when it turns around and studies itself, realizes that the very thoughts of this and that are made up of the stuff of the universe. Unfortunately, our preoccupation with the this and that keeps us from knowing our true nature. The answer to all questions is in the very consciousness that is asking or that has a concern. Only turn inwards and discover the nature of that consciousness. In the dialogues he has with his students, Yumnen immediately turns every questioner back to the very mind that is asking the question.

> Someone asked Master Yunmen, "What is most urgent for me?"
> The Master said, "The very you who is afraid that he doesn't know."
>
> Someone asked, "What is 'being silent while speaking'?"
> The master said, "A clear opportunity just slipped through your fingers."
>
> A monk inquired, "How about when one makes a hole in the wall in order to steal the neighbor's light?"

Master Yunmen, "There it is."

A questioner inquired, "How about after reaching the light?"
The master replied, "Forget the light; give me first the reaching."

As your practice ripens, you will have experiences of blissful and all pervading light. But the very source of that light is the reacher. The light intensifies as separation dissolves; the consciousness to whom it is all occurring is made of and disappears into the indivisible light. At this point,

YOUR HEART IS THE BRIGHTEST
PLACE IN THE UNIVERSE.

But it is no longer your heart, it is the heart.

*

In his recent book, 'Ambivalent Zen,' Larry Shainberg asks his Zen teacher, Dokyu Roshi, to explain the meaning of this old Sufi tale:

One day, a student of the great Master Nasrudin passes by his house and finds him on his knees, rummaging in the grass.
"What are you doing, sir?"
"I'm looking for my key."
"But, sir, didn't you lose it in your house?"
"Yes," says Nasrudin, "but there's more light out here."

Can you guess at the Roshi's explanation. This chapter should have primed you. Don't look below; hazard a guess before I give it away—okay, now you can look:

"Easy," says the Zen Roshi. "Looking is the key."

INQUIRY II BEING A NOBOBY AND BEING A SOMEBODY

ALL DEFINITION IS LIMITATION

Do I even exist or am I
just a bunch of crazy ideas?
Thought thinking it's someone,
HAH!
Big joke.
This idea of Michael
is the stupidest idea
I ever had.
How did it take over?

Our thinking mind is always busy defining us. Once we start to experience our true being, we know that it is beyond any idea or description or limitation. Meditation is about sitting with a firm affirmation of renunciation: I have not, I want not, I know not. I am not definable. I am not male or female. I am not Oriental, Jew, Black or White. I am not even a person. I have no job. I have no age. I am not poor or rich. We all have anger, tightness, pride, regrets built up around ideas of who we think we are. As we learn to let go of all definition, we experience what we really are—unlimited energy and love.

NO NAME

Meditation schools and sects are often fond of re-naming people. By the time one has been around the spiritual block a few times that person is likely to have picked up a few spiritual names. I have a number myself: a Sufi name, a Hindu name, and several Buddhist ones as well; having all these additional names is a good reminder to help pry me loose from the solid certainty and attachment to the idea "I am Michael Attie." Please go out and add a few names to your portfolio. Then you'll be more easily reminded that the real you has nothing to do with any of them.

You get the idea. What we think we are is fine—as far as surface appearance goes. But names can remind us that we are also something deeper and limitless. At the Don't Worry Zendo, a lot of us have taken new dharma names. My name is now Mike's Appearance. There is also Seems Phil, Activity that Answers to the James Name, Marsha's All Love Disguise, Ronnie's Best Moment, She'son Hanuman, etc. Please make up your own name that says, I'm this separate appearance and I'm also________.

Besides our names, in English we've evolved extremely separate-self oriented personal greetings. Stepping outside of our culture, we see that such greetings are not at all essential but show a definite bias based on deeply-entrenched dualistic thought patterns. Throughout India, for example, people greet each other with a name of God: "Hari OM," "Radhe Shyam," "Jai Ma," "Ki Jai" and many others, depending on the locality. Or they often greet one another with a simple "Namaste"—which means, "I honor the divinity within you": in effect, "You are much more than what you seem." Since we are stuck in this "How are you?" mode, maybe we could at least ask, "How are not-you today?" or "How not-are you?" or "How is more than you today?" This would be a little reminder in our daily greetings that we are not just this individual self.

NO BODY

The same thing that goes for the name goes for the body; the mystics say that belief in the idea that 'I-am-the-body' is the greatest mistake one can possibly ever make. Our true self is far greater than the bodies that come and go. To the novitiate this statement may seem absurd and preposterous. To the veteran meditator, it is obvious. It is not that we are not our bodies—of course we are. But with some meditational opening we experience that we are also much more than our bodies.

It is not too difficult to explain this concept intellectually. Here is Nisargadatta again:

> All exists in the mind, even the body is an integration in the mind of a vast number of sensory perceptions, each perception also a mental state...Don't bring the idea of a body into the picture. There is only a stream of sensations, perceptions, memories and ideations. The body is an abstraction, created by our tendency to seek unity in diversity.

No amount of intellectual persuasion, however, will convince anyone that they are not their body; but at least it might prepare them to let themselves experience it through meditation. Please try it for yourself: simply meditate on the theme, 'I am not this body.' You will see that as you give reality to the idea that you are your body, then the world of other bodies and things comes into existence. It is not so difficult to step back and experience yourself in the state of primal immanence, before there is any manifestation. You can allow yourself to be filled with the fullness that creates all bodies, minds and space—before they are created. It is always right here, you just have to quiet the mind a little to experience it.

> You are so accustomed to think of yourselves as bodies having consciousness that you just cannot imagine consciousness as having bodies....Bodily existence is but a state of mind, a movement in consciousness; the ocean of consciousness is infinite and eternal...You are not in the body, the body is in you.
>
> —Nisargadatta

NO DOER

Let's not stop with name and body; the sense of doer-ship must go as well. We can eliminate the sense of doer-ship by contemplating our interdependence with everything and by practicing non-attachment to results. Whatever we think we are doing, we can only do it because everything in the universe has conspired to allow us to 'do it.' That which has given us the means to act is ultimately responsible for the results; we do our best and then let go.

The way to enlightenment is to do your best and then step back.
—Lao-Tsu

THE NOBODY STORE

My little corner of L.A., tucked between Beverly Hills and West Hollywood, should be re-named and called 'Manicure' – there is a nail-parlor on almost every corner. It is usually sitting between a beauty parlor and a fashionable clothing boutique. Basically, the stores in my neighborhood have one purpose— selling people things by confirming their assumption that they are a somebody. In the middle of the neighborhood sits a mega-mall, the Beverly Center. Huge billboards proclaim the arch-somebodyist statement and Beverly Center motto—'Don't Blend In.' The truth is that, no matter what we may try to do about it, we are blended in. Experiencing this is not so terrible, actually it is the best thing that one can do in life.

I would like to see just one store devoted to the truth—that we are all nobodies. What would the store sell? Eyeglasses with inner mirror inserts— reminding us to look back at the looker. Cellular phones that call you with dharma messages. Portable mindfulness bells—when the bell randomly strikes we're reminded to breathe and simply be right where we are. Clocks with no hands or that always keep the wrong time; to remind us that time is in our minds and not in reality. And on the macabre side, all sorts of Day of the Dead stuff. Jewel encrusted little casket knick-knacks to remind us that the unmanifest self is unborn and undying; press a button and a voice box sings out,

Play it dead,
Your sitting in a casket.
Just be here,
The world is your gift basket.
—from the Buffo Sutra Rossini

The nobody store would also sell Hanuman dolls; pull a string and Hanuman laughs. Hanuman is the Hindu Deity that symbolizes the cosmic joke. Humor is basically pulling the rug out from under pretentious people. Of course, since we all think we are somebodies, we are all pretentious – and Hanuman is always laughing. The store would sell mirrors where your image suddenly disappears in a blaze of bright light. We mostly live our lives in a house of mirrors. We see our reflections through the people and circumstances of our lives. We build our whole lives on an idea of ourselves that we cannot directly see. When we finally look at the awareness of the looker, we are amazed; we are not what we thought we were at all. The true nature of our consciousness has nothing to do with the little separate self, the 'mine' that has been reflected in the mirrors which we have taken so seriously. When the looker looks into the anti-mirror (or the true-mirror), the light shines and a little automated voice attached to the mirror will sing,

And with no mine,
The mind,
It gets lost in the shine.
In the shine everything,
Everything is fine.
—from Non-Dual Drinking Songs
(sung to the tune of Drinking Song
from La Traviata)

I'm not sure what else this store would sell, but with meditation becoming popular the public may be waiting for it. If this book sells enough copies to raise the capital, I'll open it myself and call it the 'Nobody Store.' I'll put the famous Emily Dickinson poem on an easel in the window:

I'm a nobody. Who are you?
Are you nobody too?
Then there's a pair of us.
Don't tell—they'd banish us, you know.

How dreary to be somebody,
How public—like a frog—
To tell your name the livelong June
To an admiring bog.

I don't think that ego-confirmation is inherent to capitalism. Maybe I'll make more money by telling the truth, that we are nobodies. In a hundred years there may be nobody stores on every corner, with just an occasional nail-parlor here and there. And the nail parlors will all specialize in Buddha, OM and yin-yang designs.

One could say that meditation is merely a question of hedging our bet a little. During all of our waking hours, our thinking mind is usually centered around the assumption that we are a somebody. Basically, we've bet all of our money on this proposition. But what if we are wrong? What if we are betting all of our money on a figment of our imagination? Meditation is devoting a little money to a side bet; say devoting a few minutes a day to investigate the possibility that we've bet on the wrong horse. It is like taking out an insurance policy, just in case the truth is that we are a nobody—or an everybody.

> Understanding no-self as spaciousness, rather than annihilation, is crucial.
>
> —Johanna Macy

A clarification might be in order here. Sometimes people get kind of a gloomy feeling around the concept of no-self: that it is sort of a scary non-being or an extinction of consciousness. Vivakananda had such fears when he first went to Ramakrishna as a young man; he told Ramakrishna that he would rather just skirt the edges of samadhi (complete annihilation of separate-self in deep meditation.) Ramakrishna scolded him for indulging in such superficial understanding: "You foolish boy, how can one lose consciousness by merging with Pure Consciousness."

> The truth is that individuality is not lost, but is expanded to infinity or infinite relationality...One who truly renounces actually merges in the world and expands his love to embrace the whole world.
>
> —The Buddha

People will only loosen around their separate-self identity when they find something better, more real or which makes them happier. In meditation, by some grace, we first have little intimations of the vast spaciousness of our true nature. Only then, when we know that it is nothing to be afraid of, do we gain the courage and self-confidence to allow ourselves to become enfolded in deeper levels of no separate-self. I promise you – you will not lose anything in the process – except for some very heavy baggage that you've been lugging around for far too long.

BEING A SOMEBODY

> Form is emptiness, emptiness is form.
> That's not too difficult to understand.
> Form is form, emptiness is emptiness.
> This may be more difficult to understand.
> —Suzuki Roshi

We honor the truth that form is emptiness, that we are a nobody. But we must also honor the truth that form is form, that we are a somebody. In other words, we don't want to get carried away with excessive self-effacement or some sort of twisted self-abasement. There is an old saying that the Buddha was the biggest egoist. This is just saying, at the level of form, that he had an accurate assessment of his self-worth and personal power. The truth is that to get rid of the ego we first need a healthy and self-confident ego. Before we can experience the deepest truth, that we are a nobody, we need to know that we are also a solid and strong somebody.

Some meditators get carried away with the idea that they should be egoless. They may experience agonizing guilt over their ego's every appearance and become easily outraged and angry with themselves. Or they may become overly cautious and tip-toe through their lives like they are walking on eggs and become rather paralyzed and afraid to do anything.

A friend of mine has taken up an almost daily recitation of a sutra that is a long elaboration of all the ways that one can be deceived and trapped by the subtle ego. Really, I'm not sure if it will do him much good. It may be helpful to read it once in a while, but one can't really make the ego go away by contemplating its tenacity and ubiquitiousness. This might just cause one to become morbid and feel rather helpless and hopeless.

The best way to diminish our separate-self delusion is to give ourselves something better. As we begin to experience non-duality, less efficient and counter-productive ways of thinking and living just fade away. We outgrow fear-centered habits and manipulative games of the past. We realize that blatantly assertive and self-aggrandizing behavior is ultimately self- defeating, and only keeps us from experiencing the source of our real happiness.

People sometimes have the idea that the end goal of meditation is that the sense of a separate-self is totally and abruptly wiped out. This may happen in a few rare cases; maybe a Nisargadatta or a Ramana comes along every century or two. I quote them to inspire us and to show the possibility of complete liberation; but not to impose any set-goals or spiritual guilt-trips.

Beyond these rare exceptions, I doubt if anyone is totally egoless. We all have an ego; it won't really do us any good to fight it or try to deny it. We cannot get rid of the separate-self delusion by worrying and fretting over it. If we devote some energy to meditation practices, the flood of non-self will eventually come and drown the ego. Until then, we may as well enjoy the separate ego self, there's really not much we can do about it anyway. And when the flood comes, we can enjoy non-self even more.

With mature practice we discover how broad and immense we really are, how much room there is in us for all sorts of seemingly contradictory parts of ourselves. We let go of our ideas of who or what we think we should be and just gladly accept what we are. I've been a meditation addict for over forty years and have cleared enough space and had enough intimations that I can write this book. Here and there (and hopefully a little more deeply and regularly as I age) I have experiences of no-Mike (or big-Mike). At the same time, I know very well that there is still a big 'I am Mike' identification left in my psychological make-up. To be honest, the idea of totally divesting myself of the idea that there is a Mike getting rid of Mike, that there is someone meditating deeper, writing a book or founding the 'Don't Worry Zendo,'. is almost inconceivable. That's OK. I'm not overwhelmed with ego-angst. If I keep practicing, it will all evolve in its own time. Its not anything I can control or need to be too concerned or worried about. Who knows, I'll be happy if the Mike-obsession is 30% (or, if I'm feeling optimistic, 40%) cleared out by the end of this life. Even that 30% gives me enough spaciousness to experience immense and wonderful heart treasures. So please, don't worry about getting rid of the separate-self delusion. If you practice diligently realization of no-self will evolve along with your sense of self. Both a somebody and a nobody will exist within you; you may as well enjoy them both. It is enough to know that no-self is the deepest and truest reality. If you keep practicing as much as your life permits, this realization will inevitably evolve and ripen.

THE DEFENSIVE SHIELD

When we touch a really intimate, unarmored and vulnerable place in meditation—a raw and naked embrace with the source of the universe — we realize the contrast it creates with our day-to-day life. We become sensitized enough to be able to feel the tightening and fear that usually runs through our bodies as we interact with people and situations. We all go through our lives with a defensive shield that is up and on the alert; we say to the world, "Come in, but not too far." Meditation teaches us to be more perceptive of our subtle defensiveness.

Watching the defensive shield through our day-to- day lives may actually be more valuable than meditation. It is just when our sense of 'I' comes up strongly that we can realize that we don't have to react—with self-justification, with anger, with insecurity; we don't have to always be right. It is okay to be wrong, it's okay to let someone take advantage of us. We don't have to get in the last word. If some one cuts in front of us, sometimes we can just let them. If someone puts us down, we don't have to defend ourselves. There's really no one to defend.

Here is a famous old Zen story:

> Tokusan one day descended to the dining hall, bowls in hand. Seppo asked him, "Where are you going with your bowls in hand, Old Teacher? The bell has not rung, and the drum has not sounded." Tokusan turned and went back to his room.

Tokusan was the old abbot of the temple. The schedule may have been off and the dinner bell late, upsetting the rhythm of the monastery. Although he had seniority and could have complained, asserted or countered, he had no need to, but just quietly returned to his room. Tokusan had no defensive shield; he had no need to be right.

One day out for a walk, I passed by the Self Realization Fellowship temple when the afternoon meditation was beginning; I went in and joined the meditation. Afterwards, in the courtyard some fellow and I looked at each other and spontaneously embraced. He said, "You look like you just came out of meditation." I coyly replied, "Is there any coming and going in meditation?" And he, authentically, replied: "I don't know, I don't have many answers these days."

I felt like I had met the real thing and that I was just a meditating wise-ass. Really meditation will give you personal empowerment, but the ego oftem expropriates it; Ah, I'm somebody who knows something and has answers. Meditating is learning to be a nobody over and over and over. You don't need to have the answers.

Day after day
I throw myself out there
and hope it will peel me away.
Look for scenes to convince me
of the foolishness of this notion,
'I exist.'

'Peeling-away' is a good description of meditation, 'turning inside out—totally most alive and totally most not you.' But this is still the beginner's game. The most valuable and fun challenge is to see all of the situations that arise in your life as opportunities to feel and defuse your subtle defenses and peel away a little more.

With time, being a nobody will be your greatest challenge and pleasure. You will go anywhere and seek out any situation that will remind you that you are a nobody. In my neighborhood there is a very hip and fashionable cafe—the tables filled with soap opera starlets, producers, agents, models, etc. I love to go there because I feel like a real misfit— a total nobody. To heighten the effect, I have a special jacket I wear when I go there. It has broad fuzzy lapels and a thick wide belt. I call it the nerd jacket. When I wear it sometimes the waitresses won't even wait on me. If I don't feel rejected enough, I may try to strike up a few conversations with some of the young starlets. To make an understatement, I haven't gotten any dates. But this is excellent! I am perfecting the art of being a nobody. This may be more valuable than meditation, and a faster way to enlightenment.

A few years ago there was a protest for Tibetan Independence in Santa Monica. Before attending I had to park my car and carry my picket signs ('Boycott Chinese Goods' and 'Dalai Lama Can Save China') around town with me on errands to the bank and post office. Usually I'm pretty inconspicuous in my daily life, but I quickly realized that this isn't Berkeley in the sixties and demonstrations are not that popular anymore. Everywhere I went people were giving me wide berths and strange looks. Fortunately, I took this as an invaluable opportunity. Usually our ego-defensiveness is so deeply ingrained that we are barely aware of it and so we don't question who we are. When uncomfortable situations arise, though, we are propelled to investigate our usually unconscious social masks. Embarrassment, humiliation, rejection, condemnation—these are all godsends to the seasoned meditator.

I used to wonder why various religious sects required robes, long beards, and other conspicuous counter-culture items. Perhaps they understood the advantages of social discomfort. Now I am looking forward to the next demonstration.

> The great way is easy
> For those who have no preferences.
> —Third Zen Patriarch

These are among the most famous lines in Buddhism. When one takes up meditation seriously, these lines highlight the solid wall that one runs into over and over. Basically, we realize that we are feverish with attachments and aversions; they form the basis of our usual self-centered mental processes—our somebodyness. As we let go of our craving mind, we find that sitting is amazingly easy. There is no need for exhausting ourselves with great outputs of will-power and endurance. We are not striving and we are not pushing away. A radiant and easy going fullness becomes immanent.

The great Thai master Aachan Cha came to America in the 80s and led a few retreats. While students were sitting, he would go from one to another with an impish smile on his face. Laughing, he would repeat over and over:

> "Suffering today?
> Big somebody, big suffering,
> Little somebody, little suffering,
> Nobody, no suffering."

If one really lives as a nobody, the way will be so easy that there will be almost no need to meditate. However, because almost no one lives this way, meditation can help us become aware of the depths of our attachments and, when we loosen our grip, of the happiness inherent in our true nobody-nature.

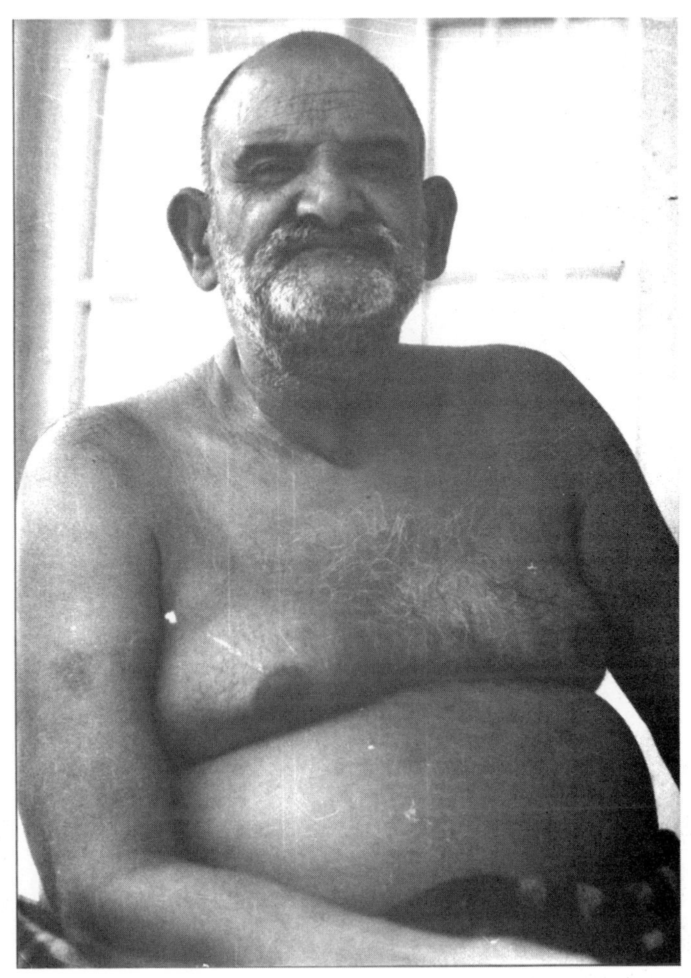

Neem Karoli Baba

Shunryu Suzuki Roshi

Swami Vivakananda

Sri Nisargadatta Maharaj

Sri Ramakrishna

Joshu Sasaki Roshi

Sri Ramana Maharshi

PART FOUR
DHARMA IN OUR EVERYDAY LIVES

MICROCOSM/ MACROCOSM

Extremely small is extremely large.
—Third Zen Patriarch

The truths which are first discovered in the microcosm of sitting meditation are also valid and relevant in the macrocosm of one's life. Meditation is often referred to as 'practice' because it is practice for living fully and wisely when we are off the cushion. The skills, virtues and wisdom which one obtains through sitting become the best allies for living one's life impeccably.

We could call meditation the test tube of life. In a scientific experiment, to get at the core truth of a situation, we simplify things by eliminating as many variables as possible. Similarly, in meditation, by not stimulating or activating the body and mind, we get at the deepest truths. Then, we can take our insights with us when we step into the world and use them as our guides.

Lets consider a few areas in which the lessons learned in the microcosm of sitting overflow into the macrocosm of life.

IMPERMANENCE

Understanding and accepting the impermanence of all phenomena is one of the basic teachings of Buddhism and all other schools of meditation. Basically, everything in form is constantly transforming and evolving—i.e. nothing stays the same. We first discover this in our sitting practice. The more subtle our understanding of the interrelated phenomena of body sensations, feelings, thoughts and perceptions, the more we realize that they are all part of an endless flow—nothing lasts. Everything breaks up and transforms into something else.

The most obvious case is pain in the legs. We panic and think it's terminal. We are sure that it's just going to get worse and worse and more unbearable until the bell rings. Amazingly, it doesn't. After a while it may lighten, shift and change into something else.

We also learn that pleasant sensations are subject to the same law of impermanence. With our deepening practice, an endless variety of blissful feelings will arise. "Oh, I'm in heaven forever" we say. But we're not. The bliss comes, stays a while and passes on, just as anger comes—and goes. Fear, planning, lust, sorrow, aches, inspirations and on and on—each has its moment on the mind-stage and then passes. Really, all of one's life (and more) comes and goes—but nothing lasts.

Our experience of impermanence belies our solid and permanent concept of self. If all the things we thought were 'me' turn out to be evanescent, then we are faced with the question, if our identity isn't to be found in these fleeting sensations, then where does it reside? We will never find a fixed spot where the real "me" exists. Ultimately, all that is left is pure awareness or being. An appreciation of impermanence makes our life seem something like a dream. The past disappears, but where did it go? Did it really exist? Contemplating the impermanence of everything, we let go a little easier. When my friend Lou was dying of cancer, his last words to me were, " Everything seemed so important. When you get wise, nothing seems too important—you let it all pass."

People often experience some confusion or perceive a contradiction around the subject of impermanence. Is the ultimate some unknowable, unspeakable something, some background against which and within which everything occurs or is there completely nothing/no thing—just endless transformation? Reading the pronouncements of the great mystics, sometimes it sounds one way, sometimes the other, and sometimes both ways. It's an endless game the mystics play with themselves. After eliminating everything but transformation, yet, yet, they still can't resist sneaking in a name for whatever is left. Although the word used is the most indefinable and incomprehensible that they can find—i.e. the unborn, emptiness, formless, pure space, unlimited love,etc.— still the way they use it often implies a subsisting something.

To tell you the truth, I can't understand this matter myself. Do these names imply a something or a nothing—or a some nothing? Really, it's not worth devoting too much time worrying about. This is just getting hung up in futile attempts to grasp the ungraspable. When these sorts of questions come up, it is actually a good reminder to stop thinking. Words and ideas are a poor means with which to understand reality. The answer will be found in feeling beyond any ideas.

The more that we broaden our view and embrace the truth of impermanence, the more we will sit and live with equanimity and patience. The Buddha said that these are two of the most characteristic qualities of the seasoned meditator.

EXPANSION/CONTRACTION

Zen Master Yasutani Roshi said that a meditation retreat is like a civil war; every part of us comes to the surface and does battle with every other part. As we become more perceptive, we simply experience subtler aspects of this civil war. We stop fighting the battles, and, instead, start to notice how the battles are born, long before any armies take the field.

We are basically composed of tendencies of expansion or contraction; expansion is the heart and love, contraction is the mind and fear. Over a lifetime of practice, the power of expansion becomes greater – however our proclivity to contract will always be there. But we get used to it, accept it and have a deeper faith that it is ultimately not real.

The Chinese call this the yin-yang of the Tao. Our personal lives, our society and the world all evolve like a dialectic or pendulum. Everything has the seeds of its opposite within it; when it gets too far to one extreme, the seeds germinate and give birth to its opposite.

The skillful meditator learns to use this dialectic in their sitting. Each contraction can be a wake up call, reminding us that we can cultivate its opposite. Restlessness reminds us of our true mind that does not need to go anywhere. Boredom reminds us to experience the peaceful mind that needs nothing. A bout of sleepiness can wake us right up.

In a way, feeling this expansion and contraction within ourselves unites us with the universe. It is not just our rhythm, but is the rhythm of everything around us. As our sitting becomes subtler, we find the breath of the universe in everything: the ebb and flow of the ocean, the rise and fall of the wind, the cycles of the sun and moon.

At a sacred spot I visit every few years high in the Sierra Nevadas, I've found a perfect symbol for the dialectic. It lies in Evolution Basin, which is surrounded by Mt. Spencer, Mt. Fiske, Mt. Huxley, Mt. Haeckel—all named after the nineteenth century social darwinist philosophers. These men were proponents of the most materialistic, uncompassionate, mechanical and rational philosophy ever conceived of by man. Yet, exactly in the middle of this basin, surrounded by these thirteen-thousand foot peaks, there is a sacred spot that is a powerful symbol, altar and expression of the black goddess of mystery — the exact antitheses of social darwinism.

Streams come down off of these peaks and go underground; they then reemerge in a perfect giant nipple, about one hundred yards in diameter. The whole mandala is made of glistening and shining black cobblestones, with an island of large black rocks and a few tufts of grass in the middle. I do a day long vigil, slowly circumambulating around the mandala, stopping every few degrees for meditation, prayers and to worship the Goddess. I'm always amazed to have found this natural altar to the mystery of love and infinite possibilities right in the middle of the peaks named after the philosophers of the diametric opposite. I take in the whole scene as a powerful reminder of the dialectal nature of all phenomena.

'AN INTENSE POWER OF CONCENTRATION.'

Attention deficit disorder is a chronic disease of our times. For whatever reasons—electronic over-stimulation, a shortage of funds for education, bad diet, environmental pollutants—the tragic fact is that people are losing their ability to concentrate. Meditation is a powerful counter measure to this scary trend.

Some people have the mistaken idea that meditation is just about relaxing—laying back on the lounge and going soft and woozy. Nothing could be further from the truth. The exact opposite is the case—meditation requires and develops skills of intense concentration.
The concentrated meditative mind is sometimes compared with the molecular structure of metal. All the atoms are lined up so that the charges are aligned in the same direction. Through the intense effort and endurance required to disregard all distracting thoughts, the focused mind attains a similar order and harmony.

Achieving this sort of one-pointedness results in great intensity and power. It was said that when Baso, the great Tang Dynasty Chinese Zen Master, shouted "Kwatz", people would go deaf as far as three miles away. In the East, meditation practice was always considered inseparable from the traditional arts of the culture. Poets, potters, martial artists, painters, sculptures—all were meditators and applied the intensity and concentration learned through meditation to their particular arts.

INTEREST AND AFFECTION

> And above all, infinite affection, love, dark and quiet, radiating in all directions, embracing all, making all interesting and beautiful, significant and auspicious.
>
> —Nisargadatta

Years ago, I did some retreats with Master Kusan, a great Korean Zen Master. He said, "The gift of meditation is that once you have some real experience of it you will never be bored again." This is completely true. There is nothing more challenging and fascinating than learning to experience the very nature of consciousness. Psychologist Fritz Perls said, "Boredom is just a lack of attention." As your skills of attention grow, you find that everything within consciousness is both fascinating and worthy of interest and affection.

Perhaps more important than never being bored again, you will never be boring again either. This is the art of—'Zen and the Art of___________.' As almost everyone is interested in lingerie, in my life this was especially easy. Once I inherited Playmates of Hollywood and people heard that I was a meditation bug, it didn't take long before requests for interviews on 'Zen and the Art of Lingerie' were coming from all directions. Before I knew it, I was 'The Lingerie Monk.' Of course the connection between intimate apparel and intimacy with the universe was an easy fit–but whatever your circumstances, if you look deeply enough you will find some metaphysical significance. Everyone is doing it these days. My cousin Maurice gives workshops on the 'Inner Lawyer.' Why not the inner truck driver (the endless road), the inner garbage collector (Sasaki Roshi said, "I am a garbage can"), the inner financial counselor (the real bank account),the inner nurse, and even, the inner window washer.

If you are attentive, you'll see symbols for the ultimate everywhere. Your conversation will be deep, interesting and stimulating. Of course, a lot of this has been done already: Zen and the art of Tennis,

Zen and the art of motorcycles, Zen and screen writing, gambling Zen. But I don't let this limit me. Don't let it limit you. If you meet a hunter you can say, "I am also a hunter, I hunt the most difficult thing—the thoughts of my own mind." Or just quote Zen and the Art of Archery; "The goal is not the target—it's yourself." If you meet someone in the mining business: "I mine the true gold of the heart." Maybe you'll be an insufferable smart-aleck—but at least you'll be remembered for having strong opinions.

And if you meet a golfer, you can say that you are also trying for a hole in one—'a cosmic hole in one.'

Right where you are
there's a hole in the universe.
Make yourself small enough
and you'll fall into it.
Smaller still,
and you become the hole.
Smaller still and there's no hole,
no you,
just the universe.

LOVINGKINDNESS

Lovingkindness, or *metta* in Pali, is a basic practice in many traditions of meditation. Metta meditations typically begin with a period of affirming the all-pervading love which is the nature of our minds and reality. The next step is practicing some sort of self-acceptance, self-forgiveness and self-generosity. If we are deeply injured and suffering, we cannot really wish love and fulfillment to others. First we must learn to love ourselves, or more properly, to experience that the universe always loves us. When we are full, then we have enough to overflow and give to other people and our surroundings. Lovingkindness is expressly not based on self-sacrifice or the denigration of our own happiness for the sake of others. First we put ourselves in the circle of this love and then we visualize the circle expanding to hold all the people and places of our lives.

Here is a typical lovingkindness meditation. It can be slowly read to yourself or practiced with friends for ten minutes to a half hour or longer.

> Sit comfortably, relax, close or half-close your eyes. With each breath let go of a layer of rigidity, tightening, defense. With each breath let yourself open to a flow of gentleness and softening. Deep in your heart and belly a flower is unfolding, petal by petal. With each breath, let go and let the pure love at the core radiate more intimately through you.
>
> The mother's love is unconditional; she embraces her baby with soft tenderness, generosity, acceptance, forgiveness, intimate attention and caring. As you soften and let go, you feel that the universe loves you in the same way.
>
> You may repeat the phrases the Buddha used when he taught metta meditations:
>
> May I be filled with loving-kindness.
> May I be well.
> May I be peaceful and at ease.
> May I be happy.

After you have placed yourself in this feeling of lovingkindness, you can begin to visualize other people and places in this same way. Place them in this heart of lovingkindness which has unfolded within you.

Begin by visualizing family members in this heart of loving-kindness. Then include friends and loved-ones who are dear and near to you. Say the phrases for them.

May _________ be filled with lovingkindness.
May _________ be well.
May _________ be peaceful and at ease.
May _________ be happy.

Let this heart keep expanding. Include benefactors: people who have helped you in this life. Include teachers and people who have inspired you. Place people towards whom you have neutral feelings in this heart, for example, the strangers you encounter during the day. Then, and this is a very powerful part of the practice, include a person or people who have caused you difficulties or whom you're angry with.

Think of the people whom you work with and say the phrases for them. Think back in your life to the circles of people with whom you lived and wish them all well. Be with animals in this loving heart. Bring people who are physically ill or mentally distressed into this circle. Be with ones who have passed away; hold their hands and embrace them. Open this expanding heart to your neighbors and then to your whole neighborhood. Let it continue growing to include your city, state, and country. Feel the whole world bathed in the peace and radiance which is at your core.

As your meditation deepens, you may develop your own phrases and ways of expressing the blessing that will naturally flow from you towards the world.

Metta need not be done just in the setting of formal sitting, but can be practiced anywhere and at any time. Rainy days lend themselves to metta, as does camping. I especially like metta on long trips—curled up and cozy in the back seat of a car, or on planes, trains or buses. An especially long trip might lend itself to the 'Whole Life Love Review.' (See 'Daily Love Review' below.)

It's time to insert a note of moderation. Obviously, we are not always drowning in the oceans of love I'm perhaps over enthusiastically describing here. We all start where we are, often injured and contracted. The question of intent is important to metta. By repeating the phrases and doing the best we can with visualizations and well-wishing, we slowly reshape our minds in a more altruistic and open direction. A more complete experience of lovingkindness will inevitably follow.

Also, becoming a 'metta-bug' doesn't blind one to peoples' shortcomings and faults. You won't become a naive and superficially cheerful pollyanna. If anything, you'll become more perceptive of the rampant 'greed, hatred and ignorance' that often rule the human psyche, BUT you'll also be an ultimate optimist. Defilements come and go, but love is what we are made of. Sooner or perhaps much (i.e.—lifetimes) later, everyone does realize this inherent nature.

Having this awareness of the inherent goodness of human nature, we don't sign people off as hopeless quite as quickly; we relate to them with a little more patience. Having touched the pure spaciousness of our being, we see Buddhas everywhere, although they may be unrealized Buddhas. The more we interrelate with people from this consciousness, the more we can be a mirror for them to see their potential and allow them the space to grow into it.

'Love,' of course, is a confusing and often misused word in any language. What passes for 'love' may largely be a disguise for our insecurities and our need to be accepted. We suit our social intercourse to get approval; we give ‘love’ in order get it. A dose of skepticism and caution is undoubtedly a necessary balance when contemplating 'love.'

When we experience real lovingkindness or metta, however, it is unmistakable. Metta is not dependent on anything; it arises within, and then overflows. When the sun is shining it has no strategy for pleasing anyone, because it doesn't need anyone. When we experience that the universe loves us, we can give love more freely and with less strings attached.

In lovingkindness practice, prayer and meditation merge. These two words are used to describe a variety of often overlapping experiences and practices. Generally speaking, prayer implies petitioning or communing with an all-pervading power that we conceive of as being outside of ourselves. Meditation can start in a similar way, but the assumption is often that we and this power are one. Hallaj, a great mediaeval Sufi, was burned for proclaiming, "I am God." He also meant, "Everyone is God." This is where the meditators take their ultimate stand.

Prayer can be self-centered: praying or chanting for material objects, health, prosperity, etc., or it can be more altruistic: praying for love, health, fulfillment and understanding for ourselves, loved-ones and the world. In the latter, prayer is similar to metta meditation.

Some meditation approaches emphasize immediately and directly experiencing the non-dual: going directly to the root of consciousness by allowing our boundries and ideas of separation to dissolve. From this point of view metta practices involve unnecessary lingering in the idea of ourselves and others as separate entities. A pure non-dualist might claim that as thoughts and memories of people and places arise they naturally subside in the source consciousness and a spontaneous metta inevitably arises without our needing to deliberately cultivate it.

This all sounds good in theory and is partially true. In actuality, however, if you go to a meditation center where the practice emphasizes the non-dual, you sometimes feel a stiffness and dryness in the people. You might feel they could use the wetness of a little more deliberate metta in their practice. Actually, consistent metta practice will generate so great an opening of source-energy that it will become like a roaring furnace devouring all form. Likewise, practicing the non-dual must eventually result in feelings of lovingkindness towards all manifestations in the world of form. Each approach really helps the other; either way, you can't go wrong.

METTA/ leads you to NON-DUAL
LOVINGKINDNESS ....experience .... MEDITATION

NON-DUAL leads you to METTA/
MEDITATION ....experience .... LOVINGKINDNESS

In other words, it's best to practice everything. Sometimes it is wonderful to practice pure awareness, and other times it is wonderful to do more deliberate metta. Although each will eventually lead to the other, you might occasionally feel a need to balance your practice more towards one way or the other; your intuition will guide you.

As meditation practice matures, it increasingly becomes a choiceless awareness that is permeated by metta. If someone comes up in your mind, don't try to push them away, but embrace them in lovingkindness. When you are fully with someone in this way, your communion will be complete and without any residue; a deeper letting go and a more intimate dissolving will naturally follow. Sitting then becomes an unfoldment of pure non-dual consciousness and compassion/ lovingkindness. Actually there is no you or other, there is just love; sometimes this is perceived as the pure source/substratum and sometimes it is seen as the manifestation of things.

More deliberate Lovingkindness meditations can take many forms. Here are two Tibetan Buddhist practices. The first is called 'taking and sending.' Think of someone near and dear. With each in-breath take from them some of their suffering, contraction and confusion. With each out-breath send them peace, understanding, love and generosity. (You can also use this practice with someone more difficult or estranged.)

The second practice is the 'Universal Relationship Contemplation.' This involves a belief in or an acceptance of the possibility of reincarnation. Contemplate the endless eons of our past lives; going back far enough, we may all be related. Everyone you meet, in some past life, may have been a parent, child or sibling. Repeated contemplation of this possibility results in seeing everyone as a large related family and feeling an open-hearted kindness towards all the people in your life.

My personal favorite lovingkindness practice is the 'Daily Love Review' – or, DLR. I often do this at night when I go to bed. Lying down, I review the course of the day from the morning on and recall every person I encountered, whether briefly and in passing—a clerk, a bus driver — or in a more involved way. I hold each person in the heart and wish them lovingkindness. Often, I don't make it through the day, but fall off to a peaceful slumber by the time I reach the afternoon. If you practice the DLR, besides having good sleep, you'll also have deep and inspiring dreams.

A question that is always paramount with any meditation practice is, how do you integrate it so that it's part of your daily life? Here is another great advantage of the DLR. As the practice becomes habitual and regular in the evening, it will begin to permeate your life and stay with you during the day. With each encounter, you'll remember that you'll be seeing that person in the evening's DLR, and so you'll be more present and open right there while relating to them.

Here I must insert a disclaimer and a note of caution; if you do these practices regularly, you are likely to find lovingkindness taking over your life. At this point you will begin your ascent upwards through the:

LEVELS OF LOVINGKINDNESS

Some may call this a descent downwards into lovingkindness obsession. I don't know, you'll have to decide for yourselves. Personally, I don't think you'll have any regrets.

First, you will reach the level of the LOVE PEST:

At fifty, I finally realized
what I want in life,
just to be free to love people.
If they think I'm a love pest—
too bad.

After attaining lovepesthood, if you persevere in metta practices, you will further attain the level of the LOVE ADDICT. When you reach this stage it may limit your social circle; you will only want to associate with other love addicts. It will be physically painful to be with people who aren't kind and open- hearted in their day-to-day social interactions. Marching forward with your fellow addicts, you will constantly remind each other of the meaning of your life: relating to the world with the soft, all-inclusive heart will become your treasure, your pleasure and your daily challenge.

Before you know it, you will have become a LOVE CRUSADER. You play the game in infinite guises, but really only love is given and taken. You maintain your normal, day-to-day 'front': "fill it up on pump number six," "have you heard the weather report?" But the veneer is growing thin; the things that have to be done are just your excuses to be with people and acknowledge the mystery and sacredness of the moment together. When you are empty— in the world with no itinerary or agenda, not needing anything from anyone—then you can provide that space of complete attention and contact. Routinely superficial and self-centered social intercourse becomes unbearably dry and boring. When you incessantly repeat your mantra,

> Today is the best day of my life.
> This hour is the only hour
> I can really be with someone,

you will advance even further to the level of the LOVE ANARCHIST.

You can wear the mask for a while, but you become obsessed with pulling it off. The love anarchist is looking for any excuse to disrobe in public. Straight conversation and social intercourse is just an excuse to say "I love you." As a love anarchist, you will do anything to wake people up from their usual somnambulistic and unconscious existence. Unconventional and shocking behavior is often required; the best way to awaken people is to break the rules and surprise them with the unexpected.

The love anarchists credo is: "The universe creates us, loves us equally and has mysteriously put us in this same spot together." You feel it incumbent upon yourself to inform people that being right here together is the occasion and just cause of a celebration. If someone opens the door a quarter of the way, you will try to open it half-way.

If, by some miracle of God's grace you are not arrested in the love anarchist phase, you might advance even farther and become a LOVE ARTIST. You've been turned loose with your metta brushes and want to fill in the world. It is your canvas. You've touched the delicious palace where your heart is dissolving into the one heart; you want to touch everyone from the source that is radiating from this heart.

By this time you've likely gone completely LOVE CRAZY. You don't care if people think you are deluded and living in some dream world; what you feel in the heart is truer than anyone's cynicism and negativity. Once you've gone love crazy there's no looking back, you sing the song of the smiling idiot:

> I may be a fool,
> but at least I'm a happy one.

You follow the advice of the Hindu Guru Ramakrishna:

> The conventional world of honor, leadership, scholarship, refined comforts, giving publicly in charity and exercising the eight occult powers—cast all this away and just cry. Be mad with love for God! Let people know that you have simply gone crazy and cannot handle mundane responsibility any longer. Then no one will come to you for advice or suffocate you with adulation. Throw aside ceremonial religion, duty as well.

But wait, you can go still farther—to the place where there is no you and other, just love. You are now completely LOVE INTOXICATED and LOVE POSSESSED. Once the dam has broken, there's no calling back the flood waters; they've got to flow out through you and the world. At this point there is no you, just Hanuman, Neem Karoli Baba, Buddha, Krishna, Christ. If I even tried to say what you would do, it would be wrong; if there were any rules, ideas or expectations, they would all be broken.

When all is said and done, what is the point of meditation and the point of life? Meditation teacher Jack Kornfield is fond of asking, "When you are on your death bed, what questions will you ask—Did I live well enough? Did I love well enough? How deeply did I learn to let go." Meditation practice is a useless waste of time if it does not help you learn to love.

TAKE IT EASY, SLOW DOWN!

In meditation, we discover that it is our thoughts which create the idea of passing time. When we are able to sit in the ever-present moment—no past or future, not waiting for anything nor wanting to go anywhere—that is exactly when the boundaries of our self-definition collapse and we experience that we are always in an ocean of grace. An appreciation of the wonder of the moment will inevitably overflow into our lives. This is an example of the microcosm/macrocosm principle: our meditation practice teaches us lessons that apply to our life as a whole.

In both sitting practice as well as our life, it is the difficulties that force us to experience deeper resources of energy. In our sitting practice, this is exemplified in the pain we may experience in our knees and legs, especially during long retreats. It may be unfortunate, but it is nevertheless true that a greater or lesser degree of self-imposed physical pain is common to many spiritual paths; besides cross-legged meditation, witness Christians kneeling in prayer, American Indian sweat lodges (and more extreme sundances) and shamanic dance-till-you-drop trance states.

In a beginning primer on meditation, perhaps I should not allude to such unseemly realities. I don't think this will deter people; they will find them out sooner or later anyway. Half the kids I meet today are going in for body piercing, which is, as far as I understand it, a similar effort at courting some physical pain (hopefully for a compensating gain). Meditation may be a gentler approach. People today are desperate enough for spirituality in their lives that most are willing to put up with some discomfort. Countless meditators have experienced repeatedly that courting a little physical pain is one of the best ways to deepen meditation practice. The fact is that people come back and sit again and again – as their experience deepens they find the discomfort minuscule compared to the rewards.

If you are experiencing some leg-pain and are anxiously waiting for the bell that signals the end of sitting, your physical and psychological distress will only increase. The discomfort level may get to a point where one has to let go, stop waiting for the bell, and just be in the moment. This is the doorway to immanent grace. This is indescribable—a sort of lightening or half-leaving the body, being flooded with light or whatever. And, miraculously, when the bell finally does ring, you'd rather it hadn't. The pain has receded in a flood of 'spirit.'

Usually when pain comes we tend to panic and to run from it. The best thing to do, however, is to open our eyes, calmly look at what's right in front of us and experience what we are actually feeling. This brings us back to the present from some interior panic. If we calmly sit with the pain, we find that our suffering comes more from our reaction to it—our fear that it will get worse and go on interminably—than from the actual sensations. The deepest source of our panic is actually our fear of the letting-go that is finally the only way we can deal with the pain. Stepping into the unknown is actually a much greater cause of concern than the actual pain.

> You will find in pain a joy which pleasure cannot yield, for the simple reason that acceptance of pain takes you much deeper than pleasure does
>
> —Nisargadatta

Meditation could be described as just practicing non-resistance—to any and everything in our bodies, lives and world. Whenever difficulty arises, this is our opportunity to practice non-resistance at a deeper level. Paradoxically, it is the difficulty that can lead us straight to its opposite.

Similarly, in our lives, difficulties can often make us aware of our unconscious scattered minds. Being in the circumstances of feeling rushed can be our best reminder to wake up to its opposite—slowing down and appreciating where we are. Feeling anxious and harried in the supermarket line won't get us to the cashier any sooner. If we stop, relax and look around, we will see that what is right in front of us—the dance of people, merchandise, lights, colors, and rows of checkout counters—is an endlessly fascinating and beautiful scene, actually much more interesting than our thoughts of where we think we should be rushing off to. A favorite motto I try to remember in a line is, "Waiting is the opportunity to stop waiting." Feeling the anxiety of impatience can be an instant reminder to use this mantra and just be here.

Some meditation-minded people claim that the Los Angeles' freeways may eventually bring about the greatest mass-enlightenment in human history. Why fight it?—you're not going to get there any faster anyway. A few years ago I received a speeding ticket on my way to a meditation retreat. I keep a copy of the ticket above my desk—it's a good reminder of the absurdity of having thought that wherever I was going could possibly be any better than enjoying a beautiful Sunday morning drive down Sunset Blvd.

Times when things go wrong can be our opportunity for deep inquiry. Recently, driving the Interstate to Northern California, I returned to my car after stopping for dinner, turned the key and discovered a dead engine. At first the superficial aspects of my program fell apart—the selected route, contemplated arrival time, tomorrow's program. This led to a deeper collapse and a sort of mini-enlightenment: the rapid questioning of the idea that I was actually going anywhere or that time or 'I' really exist. Fortunately there was a motel nearby where I spent a blissful evening contemplating such absurdities.

> All the way to heaven is heaven.
>
> —St. Catherine of Siena.

An old rabbi once said that in each life there is one great opportunity for awakening, but we don't know when it will come, so we have to be ready for it all the time. Of course that one moment is always right here; when we're not rushing anywhere, we find that we are more than in heaven—we *are* heaven. Another rabbi said; "You could wait your whole life to see a sight like this; you know—it's what's right in front of you."

After all is said and done, Nature may be our best teacher for learning to slow down and appreciate the moment. The tide comes in, autumn winds take the leaves from oak groves, ice breaks up on a winter stream—things get done thoroughly, but in their own time—an elegant, exquisite and always perfect dance.

> Whatever you think you are waiting for is a mistake. What your deepest self really wants is always right here and now.
>
> —Nisargadatta

This may seem like a radical statement, but with some meditation experience we recognize that it is the deepest truth. We are all busy doing things and trying to find our happiness. That is okay, but the deepest peace and happiness is already ours; it is in the very nature of our awareness.

> Where do you think you are always rushing to? Maybe it is just to the cemetery.
>
> —Thich Nhat Hanh

ANGER

In dealing with anger, we are best advised to follow the general rule for dealing with all difficulties—don't repress or deny them, but study and honor them; when used wisely they are our best teachers. They can wake us up, help us to understand our attachments and energize our practice.

We start with a major premise: in relating to people and circumstances the 'enlightened' person reacts with compassion, rather than anger. This may begin only as an intellectual concept or an ideal, but it can become a reality as our meditation practice deepens. Once we start to experience our true self, we know that we and everyone are made of love. We know this is true because the more we are able to let go of our identity as a separate self, the deeper we disappear in the embrace of this all-pervading love. It is what we are all made of.

As this happens gratitude and compassion replace pride and anger. We are increasingly filled with gratitude that we've had the exposure to the teachings of the dharma and the time and opportunity to practice and realize them. We increasingly have compassion towards people who have not had this exposure and are still lost in greed, anger and delusion. We feel sorrow at the suffering that their ignorance causes in the world and a desire to be of service is awakened within us – to serve in any way that will possibly alleviate the suffering.

Of course, in our world of rampant greed, social injustice, environmental catastrophe, ethnic cleansing, wars and torture, the objects of our anger are often well deserving of it. Sometimes anger may be unavoidable. It can, however, exist within us in a larger, compassionate framework of understanding that people often act from their ignorance. This awareness need not lessen our efforts to alleviate suffering and the destruction of our planet.

In any situation, the 'enlightened' person acts from the motivation, 'How can I best help?' This does not mean that we become sops or wimps. Sometimes the situation may require that we show our 'claws.' This 'enlightened' anger is not congealed or solidified, one doesn't obsess or hold on to it, rather it just passes away like waves from a pebble thrown into a pond. This apparent anger is sometimes the appropriate way to help.

As our meditation deepens, we don't as readily project our anger outwards as turn inwards and use it as an opportunity to learn about ourselves. Inevitably, in the process, we begin to suspect that we may not really be mad at the particular situation and/or persons we are confronted with. We are already angry. The current situation just gives us an excuse to express the rage already in us which we haven't yet processed. Our anger may stem from early childhood family situations, a mother who was stressed in pregnancy, past life injuries—who knows? This is popularly known as 'having one's buttons pressed.'

The universe always generates just the right situation that we need in order to grow and free ourselves. Our anger is the perfect opportunity to understand and process our unhealed injuries and unfinished karma; it is the perfect indicator of our attachments and aversions. We are angry because we don't get something that we want. We are attached to certain outcomes of a situation and we want people to behave in a certain way. When someone frustrates our 'program,'we become afraid and angry. The arising of anger is our opportunity to investigate our attachments and soften their sharp edges.

Anger assumes a certain intellectual arrogance and self-righteousness—that we know what is good, just and required both for ourselves and others. A good dose of self-doubt will diffuse the sharpness of our anger. A great Rabbi once said that the best mantra is "I may be wrong." We assume that we know the whole picture when maybe we only see a little part of it. We can hazard educated guesses but usually don't know for certain the best outcome for events. What we are most worked up about wanting to happen might produce our worst disaster.

A Chinese folktale tells of the farmer whose horse ran away. The neighbor sympathized; the farmer just replied, "Who knows." A few days later the horse returned, followed by a wild horse. The neighbor congratulated him on his good fortune; the farmer would only reply, "Who knows." The farmer's son was thrown and broke his leg trying to break the wild horse; the neighbor mourned the farmers poor luck. The farmer just replied, "Who knows." The barbarians invaded, the government drafted all the village's sons, except the one with the broken leg. The neighbor praised the farmer's new reversal of fortune; the farmer merely said, "Who knows," and on and on. Similar stories abound in almost all cultures. We think we know what we want and need, but we don't; what the universe produces is our perfect lesson. Fear and lack of faith are always underlying our anger.

As with all other difficulties, the energy that comes up with anger may stay with us and strengthen our sitting, long after the circumstances that we think have caused it have passed away. At meditation retreat centers it sometimes seems that things are structured expressly to arouse people's anger. A good example is at Rinzai Zen monasteries where a tough and mean looking monk is often given the monitoring duties. In the early years of my practice some of the most intense and deepening meditation sessions have come in just this situation. I could swear that a certain monk was particularly picking on me; whether I was walking or sitting, he was constantly correcting my posture, yelling at me, correcting my eating, etc. After many fantasies of slugging him if he didn't leave me alone, I, of course, had no choice but to just sit, bear with it and forget it. The energy aroused stayed with me and became a fuel for deepening practice.

I was angry because I was sitting with some idea of 'attainment,' of 'getting enlightened,' which I felt the monk was frustrating. We get angry because we don't get something that we think we want. With some luck or maturity, our anger will begin to raise the bigger questions of what it is we want and who it is that wants it. With more maturity of practice we realize that enlightenment is not something to be attained, but is what we always are when we let go of our grasping. When I was believing the stories that my anger was telling me, there was no way that I could have seen this. That monk may have been much wiser than I realized.

Similar examples from other meditation situations are numerous. Guerdjieff taught at a center outside of Paris in the 1920's. There was one particularly uncouth resident—inconsiderate, self-centered, loud and dirty—who was detested by everyone. When Guerdjieff returned from a trip to find that this gentleman had left the center, Guerdjieff pursued him to Paris and begged him to return. When he refused, Guerdjieff offered to pay him to return. Guerdfieff later told some students, "I need him like yeast for bread. Without him here you would never learn about anger, irritability, patience and compassion."

> Even if someone is our sworn enemy,
> who uses lies and slander
> to persecute and torment us,
> we recognize that person
> as a Boddhisatva of wisdom and mercy
> who uses skillful means
> to help liberate us.
>
> —from 'Song of Enlightenment'
> 7th century CE. Chinese Zen Scripture

Eventually, we may learn to value and even love our difficulties—anger among them. When a difficult situation arises, if we can practice non-judgment and forgiveness, it becomes our precious opportunity for liberation. Recently, I found myself up late one night, angry with someone. This led me to inquire: who am I to hold myself as above, different or better than anyone else? I can't claim credit for anything I think I have or know, but must be grateful to fortunate circumstances of birth, friends, teachings, life-situations, etc. Investigating my anger led to a deeper loosening of the 'I' assumptions that had originally allowed the anger to arise. Instead of allowing the emotion to take hold of me and take me on its roller-coaster ride of suffering, I turned it around, and used it as a springboard into my own self. Thus, compassion was born for myself – and for the person with whom I had been angry.

The Hollywood Blvd. branch of the 'Don't Worry Zendo' is a loft we share with a neighbor. Sometimes it seems she could be a little more considerate with her stereo's noise level on our weekly meditation nights. We've reminded her a few times, but sometimes she's forgetful. This is above the din of Hollywood Blvd. and the noises from her room are actually no louder than the traffic, boom-boxes and other sounds drifting up from the street. Still, it's easy to get worked-up and spend the evening stewing: "She doesn't give a shit… she's so inconsiderate… we go out of our way to do things for her… she's just doing it to bug us," and on and on.

Here is our great opportunity. The anger immediately brings up our idea of us as distinct and separate— wanting something, making judgments and thinking we're better than someone else. When things are brought up so strongly we're given a precious opportunity to let go of it all. As we soften and let her music merge with the symphony of Hollywood Blvd., we begin to include the neighbor, whether (probably) just negligent or somehow willful in our meditation. And then she and all of our judgments merge into the big all-embracing heart.

To work up a real anger requires a very solid idea of the world—self righteous and impregnable judgments of good and bad and right and wrong. We know too little and the world is too great a mystery. Well be healthier, wiser and happier if we're a little less certain of things.

BRINGING MEDITATION INTO EVERYDAY LIFE: YOU ARE THE BOSS

My father had a motto, which was his first and last piece of advice to me when he handed over the keys to Playmates of Hollywood: "Customer, customer, customer."

Over the years, at employee meetings, I elaborated his advice into a standard speech. The older employees heard it so many times that they knew it by heart, but I forced them to listen again and again anyway. Here is some of the 'Playmates manifesto.'

> At some businesses, you feel a joie d' vivre, a lightness, a special energy and enthusiasm permeating everyone . At a restaurant, it seems that the waitresses and busboys are almost choreographed, moving in time to each other. At a market, the boxboy is a juggling artist or performing a magic act as the merchandise disappears into the bag. Sometimes a bus driver is leading a tour as he announces the streets and stops. These are the places you want to eat and shop at, or the special bus you want to ride on.
>
> Gauging the employees spirit, I can almost always tell when a business is going to go broke several months or even a half a year before it does. And we can also know what establishments will succeed. Since my fathers days, Playmates has flourished due to a few rules.
>
> Thank Customers—Let them know that they have done us a favor and not the reverse. I hate it when I go into a store and thank a clerk and they just accept the "thank you" without returning a bigger "and I thank you."
>
> Smile—Of course, if someone is having personal problems and is miserable, a fake and forced smile may be worse than no smile. But I let everyone know when they are hired that if glumness becomes chronic they won't last long at Playmates.
>
> Make Contact—Have some interaction other than just the unconscious and rote exchange of goods for money. This can be

anything: a brief moment of eye contact, a joke, an appreciation—some way of saying, I'm really here, you're really here. Of course, if a customer is dedicatedly in their own world, don't bug them, just let them do their own thing.

Drop Everything—Don't make the customer wait, even for a second. The customer is more important than anything else a clerk may be doing, be it stock work, ordering, straightening or especially personal business.

Break Rules—Do everything humanely possible to make the customer happy. Extend or break all rules concerning exchanges, try-ons, fittings, etc. Of course, many people are opportunistic and, if given a chance, will misuse the store. This is especially true of a lingerie store, where one must be especially careful not to allow exchanges on used merchandise. Fortunately, for many years our manager was the infamous 'Cranny Annie.' People believed she had a built-in electron microscope with which she could detect even a molecule of soilage on any questionable merchandise being returned as 'unworn.'

Extend Yourself—Do that something extra and unexpected. If you hear a customer say she's hungry, send out for some food. Change the music to suit the customer, take a trip to the factory for that emergency order.

Basically, at Playmates, people buy clothes for clubs, fun and partying, so the atmosphere has to be light and fun. We celebrate all birthdays with cake and drinks and share them with customers. When someone comes into the store they never know if they might be coming into a party.

All the rules can be summed up in one rule—

Love The Customer—Playmates is not a store, it is a 'Temple to Hanuman and the Love Goddess' disguised as a lingerie store. I tell my employees that I really mean this. I'm more concerned with being kind and helpful, with making the customer feel good about themselves, than with whether someone buys anything or not.

Of course, it's just this concern that will create business. People want to trade where they feel good. By repeatedly being open-hearted and loving to customers an atmosphere is created; people feel that vibe and want to return again and again.

To clinch my employee-orientation/love harangue, I then play a selection from a tape by Ramdas, in which he tells one of his favorite stories. Here is a part of it.

> When I came back from India, I was going out to teach at Esalin. I started out on the New York Thruway....I'm singing to Krishna...when I notice in my rear view mirror, a blue flashing light....a state trooper gets out of the car and I opened the window and he said, "May I see your license and registration." Now I was in such a state that when I looked at him, I saw that it was Krishna who had come to give me darshan, because how would Krishna come in 1970? Why not as a state trooper? Christ came as a carpenter, I don't understand why he couldn't come as a state trooper. And so Krishna comes up and says, "May I see your license." He can have anything, he can have my life. All he wants is my license and registration. So I give him my license and registration, and it's like throwing flowers at the feet of God and I'm looking at him with absolute love. So he goes back to the car and he calls home. Then he comes back, he walks around the car and he says "Well, what's in that box on the seat." I say, "They're mints, would you like one? [laughter] They were mints."
>
> He says, "Well the problem is you were driving too slow on the freeway and you'll have to drive off the freeway if your going to drive this slowly." I said, "Yes, absolutely." And I'm just looking at him with such love. Now if you put yourself in the role of a state trooper, how often do you suppose they are looked at with unconditional love, especially when they're in their uniform. So after he had finished all the deliberations, he didn't want to leave. But he had run out of state trooperness. So he stood there for a minute and then he said, "Great car you've got here." That allowed me to get out and we could kick and spit and hit the fenders and say, "Don't make them now like they used to," and tell old car stories and talk about straight eights and slant sixes. And then we ran out of that. And I could feel, he still didn't want to

> leave. I mean why would you want to leave if you were being unconditionally loved. Where are you going to go? You already got what you want. What are you going to do? That takes care of your power needs , all of it. So finally he runs out, he knows either he's got to come clean, that he's Krishna. So he says, "Be gone with you," which isn't state trooper talk. But what the hell, he can have a little sloppiness in his lines, that's all right. And as I get into my car and am about to drive away, I look into my rear view mirror and he's standing by his cruiser and he's waving at me.

Of course, my employees haven't just returned from two years meditating in India. It may be a bit much to ask them to see every customer as Jesus or Krishna. But after they've been listening to the Ramdas tape for a few years, I hope a little begins to rub off.

YOU ARE THE BOSS

> Usually, without being aware of it, we try to change something other than ourselves, try to order things outside us. But it is impossible to organize things if you are not in order....YOU ARE THE BOSS. When the boss is sleeping, everyone is sleeping. When the boss does something right, everyone will do everything right and at the right time...When we have our body and mind in order—everything will exist in the right place, in the right way....That is the secret of Buddhism.
>
> —Suzuki Roshi

Playmates is not only the 'world's largest lingerie store,' but has the most risqué clientele as well; it's undoubtedly the world's foremost supplier to exotic dancers, erotic masseuses and x-rated models. Some men have offered me large fortunes to hire them, others claimed they would go immediately insane if they worked there. This may be true; I largely gave up hiring men because usually I would have to fire them within a few days as they unraveled in a sea of lechery. I realized I could only hire gay men or extremely well-mated men, preferably those whose wives were also employees and could keep an eye on them.

People often wondered how I, being single, navigated these treacherous waters. First, I must clear up the common misconception that a lot of meditation somehow results in an easily sublimated sexual libido. The exact opposite is usually the case. Meditators are right up there with politicians, fundamentalist preachers and navy pilots as among the horniest, and most sexually obsessed of people. Perhaps if one lives in a cave, or has been meditating for forty or fifty years, the sexual energy gets sublimated to higher centers. Usually though, as one learns to open to expanded energy, it travels in the most familiar circuits, and in our obsessed culture that often means SEX.

As it's been over twenty years since I moved to LA, it's now difficult to remember exactly how close I actually got to a complete nervous breakdown. But I remember getting up mornings and thinking, here I am, the world's horniest man, going off to the horny store again. I didn't fight it for too long. Let's say I embarked on a program of 'product testing' and 'special owner's discounts' with a string of willing customers.

A short detour, and then we will return to this story of moral depredation. At this same time, when I wasn't devoting myself to 'customer servicing,' I embarked on a project of converting Playmates into a 'Temple to the Goddess.' I commissioned a well known artist, Steven Arnold, to convert the back wall of the store into an altar to the 'Lingerie Goddess.' The altar was unveiled and consecrated with a large and elaborate ritual, modeled after a 3,000 year old Mycenaean ceremony. Priests and priestesses of the Goddess chanted her hymns; incense, bells, gongs and conches supplicated her. Afterwards the packed store celebrated with a late night boa-dance.

The altar became a focus of the store. Fresh flowers are supplied, an employee 'priestess' keeps it clean and dusted, customers or employees light incense and say a silent prayer. The Lingerie Goddess represents the divine attribute of beauty. Other altars have been added over the years. Hanuman represents the divine attributes of playfulness and humor, and the Illuminating Angel represents love. I'm also anticipating that an altar to the dark Goddess of mystery will manifest one day in an empty space reserved especially for her. All of these altars focus energy and reinforce each other; an energy field is created; people feel good when they're in the store, even if they're just obliviously shopping.

I soon learned, however, that creating such an altar cannot be taken lightly or frivolously. Once empowered it has a life of its own; it may affect you in a way deeper than you intended or in surprising directions you never contemplated. It becomes a symbol and lightning rod of your higher aspirations and will accelerate the working out of your karma and your spiritual evolution.

About this time something completely unsettling and unexpected began to happen; money—large amounts of money—started to occasionally disappear from the company safe. Enough money that it seemed that all of my work would become something like Sisyphus endlessly pushing the stone up the hill—a lot of effort for an empty bank account.

The overriding question and mystery of my life was trying to figure out how this was occurring—my brain was feverishly contemplating the possibilities. I changed the keys, locks, and combinations, administered lie-detector tests, installed new security systems—still the money would occasionally disappear. I got no help from the police department; the strangely unsympathetic Detective Smith seemed convinced that I was faking it for tax write-offs.

Finally, with a new and improved security system installed, one night the alarms went off. The security company called me at home and I rushed to the store. Detective Smith, other police and I entered the store together. The mystery was solved. The store's light fixtures were comprised of three rows of spherical halos, with bulbs in the middle, running down the length of the store. In the rear of the store, the light halo right in front of the Goddess had been converted into a sparkling spotlight that perpetually shone on her. This one halo had been unhinged, revealing a hole opening up into the attic.

It was obvious that thieves had come in through that hole, lowered themselves into the store with a rope and, when they tripped the electronic motion detectors, made a quick exit the way they came. The amazingly obdurate Detective Smith claimed that the unhinged halo was a coincidental accident, and that they got in some other unknown way. Reinvestigating the roof the next day, I found a removable air duct through which the thieves could have gotten into the attic; this just confirmed the obvious.

None of this really mattered though. The point was that of the thirty-six halo lights, the thieves entry portal was through the one that was the Lingerie Goddess's spotlight—the Lingerie Goddess had sent the burglars herself! More than that, it was very obvious to me – that she herself was sent burglar. My mind realized that the most recent burglary had followed a very recent case of 'product testing.' Thinking back to past thefts, I realized that they had all immediately followed similar 'owner's special discounts.' The Lingerie Goddess was sending me a message and giving me a very strong teaching on appropriate and inappropriate use of sexuality in my life.

Needless to say, that ended my extracurricular customer liaisons; I reformed my life. But, the story continues; the Lingerie Goddess wasn't done with me. Additional difficult lessons taught me that I shouldn't have any prurient exchanges with customers at all. If I even helped someone find the 'right item,' or gave my opinions at the dressing rooms, some catastrophe would inevitably ensue.

A few memorable episodes—

A beautiful young woman was starting her first stripping job. No one seemed to be around to help her find a few costumes (or so I told myself). Ten minutes after I finished helping her there was yelling from the bargain basement. My trusted maintenance man was interrupted while engaging in indiscretions with a customer; it seems he had his own exchange policy going. I personally favored giving him a stern warning and another chance, but the other irate employees insisted that he go (I think that was the last straw of a growing list of grievances). It took me several months to find a good replacement, during which time I had to do everything myself.

Another time, an extremely pretty young woman told me she was going in for breast enlargement the next week (Playmates is sometimes known as the 'silicon capitol of the world'). I couldn't resist showing her that such enhancements were absolutely unnecessary; with good costumes properly worn (and removed) she was absolutely irresistible and could pretty much empty anyone's pockets of all the tips she wanted. Within five minutes all hell broke loose. Some long simmering feuds between three employees erupted into open warfare: spitting, kicking, scratching, wrestling on the floor, hair pulling, hurling racks and baskets of merchandise at each other, yelling insults and curses across the store—real roller-derby, TV women's wrestling-style mayhem. As a result, several people quit or were fired; it took more than several months to rebuild a stable staff. Again, during this time I pretty much became a slave to the place, working long hours filling in for the departed employees. (An L.A. Weekly reporter happened to be shopping that evening and joined other customers in gaping-mouthed disbelief at the spectacle they witnessed. She later reported, "If you're bored some evening, just go up to Playmates and catch the employee cat fights.")

After this, I was almost afraid to talk to or even look at customers. And I absolutely never went within thirty feet of the dressing rooms. But still I fell again. Ted Aguilar, publisher of the "California Glamour Girls" lingerie calendars, came in with a van of models for costuming. He insisted I pose with them. I ran to my office and barricaded the door. He sent one emissary after another, "Come out, he wants a picture of you and the girls." Finally I relented and told myself, "What harm could it do?" Within thirty seconds of taking the snapshots, the merchandise security alarm went off. I ran to the front door to be confronted by four mean looking gang members who threatened to 'blow me away' for even suggesting that they might be stashing any unpurchased items under their jackets. I agreed that it must be a faulty alarm system.

By this time, as studying, teaching and writing about meditation were taking over my life, and as my activities were severely restricted anyway, I sold Playmates. But I'm not completely removed, because I sold it to my son, who allows me an occasional visit.

And I can say that I am totally and absolutely grateful to the Lingerie Goddess for everything she has done for me. In a way, she let me have my flings when I needed to; I lived through a lot of sexual karma and hopefully 'used it up.' Then, she let me know in very strong terms what was no longer appropriate at my stage of growth.

I would also say that the Lingerie Goddess saved me from early senility. It's a proven fact that this is the number one occupational hazard of lingerie store owners. Fred Menninger, the founder of Fredericks, and my father Eli, who was losing his bearings at the end, are the two most well known examples. If She hadn't interceded, perhaps I would never have had the fortitude to retire. With my brain slowly receding into a confused though contented mental fog, I would still be manning the dressing rooms today. This is now my son Jake's problem; with this warning, hopefully he will pull out before it's too late. *

I tell this story for one reason. It is the strongest and most extreme case in my life of the secret of Buddhism—"YOU ARE THE BOSS." When things go wrong and you have difficulties, don't be so quick to look outside of yourself. Usually the outside world is a reflection of the inner world and events are trying to tell you something about yourself. It's best to first fix yourself before judging and finding faults with others. Amazingly, most of the time when you do this, the outer conditions will indeed transform.

> If your heart is pure, then all things in your world are pure.
>
> —Ryokan

---

*In 2003 Jake sold Playmates. Though now out of the family, it is still flourishing at the corner of Hollywood Blvd. and Wilcox Ave.

GENEROSITY/GRATITUDE

If you understand the true nature of the universe, you will not let a day or an hour pass without practicing generosity.

—The Buddha

Whatever joy there is in this world, all comes from desiring others to be happy. Whatever suffering there is in the world, all comes from desiring myself to be happy.

—Shantideva

Student during retreat: "I am discouraged, what should I do?"
Soen Roshi: "Encourage others."

Give yourself to another human being; drop your ego and take care of someone, or you'll have a lot of pain in your life.

—JoyaMa

Generosity is not merely the overt act of giving somebody something material; it can also be the giving of care, of protection of kindness and of love. Looking at people and communicating that they can be loved, and that they can love in return is giving them a tremendous gift. It is also a gift to ourselves. We see that we are one with the fabric of life.

—Sharon Salzberg

The more intently you work for the well being of others, the more oblivious of yourself you become. In this way, as your heart gradually gets purified by work, you will come to feel the truth that your own self is pervading all beings and all things.

—Swami Vivakananda

Even though you do not realize the oneness of this 'Big I' with everything, when you give something you feel good, because at

> that time you feel at one with what you are giving. That is why it feels better to give than to take.
>
> —Suzuki Roshi

> One must learn sooner or later that one cannot get salvation if one does not try to seek the salvation of one's brothers and sisters.
>
> —Swami Vivakananda

> The deepest happiness you can have comes from that capacity to help relieve the sufferings of others.
>
> —Thich Nhat Hanh

> No true spiritual life is possible without a generous heart.
>
> —The Buddha

> Take always the position of the giver. Give everything and look for nothing in return. Give love, give help, give service, give any little thing you can but keep out barter. Make no conditions and none will be imposed. Let us give out of our own bounty, just as God gives to us.
>
> —Swami Vivakananda

> Self-cherishing is the source of all pain,
> Other-cherishing is the source of all happiness. In life, death and countless lives, my only prayer is to cultivate generosity.
>
> —The Dalai Lama

Hooray! I've collected so many quotes that I don't need to write a chapter. What else can I say? It's as simple as this—as our meditation deepens, practicing generosity will be as natural and inevitable as breathing. And the converse as well, our meditation will never really deepen very much unless we practice generosity. But one more quote, just to give us something to reflect upon.

> In Asia, the classical sequence of teachings and practice is generosity then morality and then meditation and insight. But here in the U.S. the sequence seems to be meditation first, then morality

and after sometimes, as a kind of appendix, there is some teaching about generosity. What's going on here?

—A visiting Thai meditation master

As our practice matures, we increasingly understand that meditation and interpersonal relations cannot be isolated from each other; they go hand in hand and are each a reflection, a test and an encouragement to the other.

The sole purpose of meditation is learning to let our illusory boundaries dissolve: on the universal level, with the primal energy source and on the level of form, with nature, cityscapes and people. We begin to sense that the dissolving of our boundaries is always immanent and that all-pervading grace is always waiting to flood us. We also sense that there are limits to how deeply we can open to this flow; they are set by the degree to which we've purified our lives by living with honesty, helpfulness, generosity and non- attachment.

Some approaches put great emphasis on precepts—rules to guide our lives—i.e. honesty, non-stealing, avoiding harmful gossip and addictions, etc. They believe that when we are living a self-less, honest and generous life our meditation will naturally be filled with an effortless grace. These approaches see sitting as a waste of time unless our lives are in impeccable ethical order; at first they may not emphasize much sitting at all. The opposite approach, which the Thai Master observed is dominant here, is that intense sitting will naturally lead to living by precepts, as we learn to experience that we are not separate from other people. Often however, as we've observed in earlier chapters, this takes longer than one might expect. A balanced approach is best.

The use of psychedelic drugs is an extreme illustration of this question. If used in the right setting and with good guidance, they can certainly give people a glimpse of the possibility of mystical union. There is no doubt that the voluminous quantities of LSD coursing through the western brain in the sixties played a major part in that decade's precipitous growth of interest in Eastern mysticism. Once one has had that taste though, one must begin the lifelong work of ordering one's life and bringing it into accord with that experience. Unfortunately, psychedelics often short circuit this work. With continual and chronic use, they usually produce a subtle (or not so subtle) spiritual ego trip;

people live in a psychedelic delusion of 'enlightenment' and often use it as an excuse for living self-centered, selfish and self-righteous lives.

The point is that all the meditation (or drugs) in the world are a waste of time unless we deal with each situation that arises throughout the day with scrupulous honesty, openness, generosity and kindness. Every situation is an opportunity to put meditation into practice. Unless we use these opportunities, meditation will never really be deep and profound.

Our human psyche holds an endless tension between the mind and the heart. The mind lives in constant fear of the heart. It is always trying to limit our exposure to suffering in the world, for fear that the heart will react with over-extravagant compassion. It's afraid that the heart will give away all of the money or invite all of the homeless in for a meal.

The mind probably can relax its tight grip a bit; with the exception of the few St. Francis's scattered over the millennium, we usually keep enough mind around to assure that we are provided for with what we really need. But our definition of 'what we really need' might also loosen a bit. As our meditation deepens we realize that happiness comes less from material things than from being able to help other people. The more we feel the heart's fullness, the more we'll naturally want to be more generous with our time and possessions.

In Hinduism, the elephant God Ganesh is a symbol and reminder of generosity. He is huge, out going, free-flowing and without self-doubts or second-thoughts. He represents an inner over-abundance, so full that it overflows into great generosity. All over India—in shops, tea stalls, temples and little roadside shrines—one encounters images of big pot-bellied Ganesh. It is wonderful to be in a country where this reminder is everywhere: to be generous, kind-hearted and—if there is any doubt at all—to not hesitate to give something away.

Life is sort of like a karmic bank account. Through some inexplicable good fortune, when compared to most other times and places, anyone living in our time and country is born with a relatively full account. The broad sweep of history generally consists of an endless succession of oppression, poverty, disease, instability, anarchy, wars and invasions. As we realize what a relatively unique and stable situation we live in, this life truly seems like a precious opportunity. We may not know why this was given to us or what we've done to deserve it, but we must feel a deep gratitude.

And we may want to take out a karmic insurance policy. I try to remain balanced and not too get hysterical, but in my life I feel a sort of meditation Protestant work ethic. Some unknown good fortune has brought me to this amazingly fortunate birth. I consider the infinite possibilities of less fortunate rebirths and I want to be sure to not deplete my credit line. So how do I add to this bank account? Diligent practice. Not living too extravagantly, but making some effort at self-control and restraint over rampant and excessive desires. Making use of my time efficiently and wisely. And practicing generosity. The universe has been so generous, I must pay it back. Generosity is the best way to express gratitude and bring it in to action.

> Gratitude is the hallmark of a realized person. Not gratitude towards something, but the spirit of gratitude directed towards everything.
>
> —Robert Aitken

As our meditation deepens, we are grateful. We may not always be certain to whom or what we are grateful, but we are just grateful. We are grateful for the exposure to the dharma that we have had in this life. We are grateful that we live in a time and place where there is the leisure, opportunity and freedom to practice and realize the truth of the dharma. While writing this book, sometimes I've contemplated that in many times of history, just one chapter would have gotten me banished or executed. In Europe especially, until a few hundred years ago, I'd have a quick ticket to an auto-da-fe.

Throughout the eastern religions, bowing is a widely spread expression of gratitude. Westerners, at first, usually find this practice anywhere from a little uncomfortable to totally repugnant. As their understanding deepens, however, they often become bowing-addicts themselves.

When I first went to Sasaki Roshi in the early sixties, he had just arrived from Japan and was living in a tiny tract house in a Japanese suburb of L.A. Basically, there was never anyone else there; I could show up at any time, take tea with him, sit and have an interview. After a few visits, one day someone else was there. She appeared to be more experienced in the ways of proper Zen etiquette than I; peeking out of the corner of my eye, it seemed that she had gone bow-crazy. Before and after sitting, coming and going to interviews, she couldn't sit or stand up straight, but was bowing all over the place. Being a good Jewish college sophomore, I wasn't ready for this; it struck me as particularly creepy and arcane. I felt like I was suddenly in the middle of a secret Japanese cell in a W.W. II spy movie. I didn't come back for a few years, during which time I sat and studied on my own and got used to the concept of bowing.

Bowing and prostrations pervade the rituals and practices of most eastern religions. One bows to the altar and teacher on entering a Hindu temple. In Buddhism, before and after sitting, reciting sutras, bathing and going to the teacher, one bows once or a number of times. In Tibetan Buddhism, doing 108,000 prostrations is a part of the foundation practices which are required before receiving advanced teachings. In ancient China, and in Tibet even today, bowing pilgrimages are common. A pilgrim may take months or a year to walk across the country to a temple, sacred spot, or master, bowing every few steps of the way. They're also doing it in Thailand, Burma and Ceylon. (This is starting to sound like a Cole Porter song.) For millennia, Asia has been seized by a bowing frenzy. What does all this bowing mean?

To a Westerner bowing symbolizes servitude and obedience: that you are relinquishing your autonomy to someone and something outside of yourself. In the East, you are really bowing to yourself and to the Buddha nature that is inherent in all beings. Bowing is identical to meditation; with each bow you throw away your idea of an ego self as a willful separate existence and honor the all-pervading source.

A few years ago I sat some sesshins at the Zen Center of San Diego. Once a day there they have a bowing period. To the rhythm of a bell everyone bows repeatedly together. Before the bowing practice someone suggests a theme for the day's bowing. It might be to bow to let go of one's expectations from the sesshin, to bow to illusions and impermanence, to bow to our difficulties.

But especially, I think, one bows to express gratitude. As one's practice deepens, expressions of gratitude are often the first and last thoughts one may have. The mind is empty of everything except, "thank you, thank you, thank you." One begins to feel that just expressing it with words is inadequate, one wants to express it with the whole body. This feeling of gratitude can become so powerful and deep that really nothing can express it; bowing is often the best solution that one can find.

But what if you have a bad back or hip, are just lazy or can't get over an inborn bowing-phobia? This is no problem; there is a good alternative for expressing gratitude—you can go altar-crazy. Set up altars all around your residence, in every nook, cranny and corner. Place flowers, incense bowls, candles, icons and pictures, holy water and special stones all over the place. Throughout the day you'll be reminded to be grateful; each time you pass an altar you'll light a stick of incense; this will be like having a little bow—to gratitude, to appreciating the moment, to surrender, to remembering that life is a gift. Our arrogant ego is insidiously tenacious; ubiquitous altars are an excellent aid to loosening its grip over us.

There is only one possible drawback to the altarmania alternative—you may begin to run up a high incense bill. Especially if you get addicted to a high class Japanese incense habit. Their best grade is the olfactory equivalent of a fine Seiko watch or a Lexus roadster—designed for use on the roshi's birthday or at intimate tea ceremonies with the master. Once you get started on the high class stuff, and unfortunately it's easy to get hooked on this grade, you'll want to use it all the time. And it's not cheap: it's a habit that you can't easily break but it can quickly break you. As one who is suffering withdrawal as I write, I must warn you that as your incense bill goes ballistic, you may have to cut down on other habits—i.e. eating, clothes, etc. Bowing is definitely a cheaper gratitude-alternative.

And another altar-warning. Once you get started with altars on shelves and bureaus, they may get out of control and spread; you will start to see altars everywhere. Walking in nature, you will be in the Garden of God. Wherever you go you'll see sacred arrangements: little groves of saplings perfectly framing an old grandfather tree, oak branches arching over rock gardens like the fans of a divine attendant.

Everything will seem to be placed in just the right way by a magical and conscious hand. Taking a walk in the city, you'll find the same run-away altars. You will be in a Whitmanesque world where merchants and workers are all sacred priests, each presiding over their shop and workplace altars. And the altarmania won't have saved you from bowing anyway, because by now you'll be like one of those elder Tibetan Lamas who, when you first see them, appear to be hunchbacks. All of the bows have merged into one long bow. And you'll have no regrets, because like theirs, your eyes will sparkle. Your life will have become a perpetual bow of gratitude to everything.

SLEEPING, DREAMING

When people first take up meditation, they often go through stages of chronic sleepiness. This is not surprising. When the mind quiets down its instinctive first reaction is to fall asleep. It is finally getting a break and it wants to take it fully! With some experience of meditation people learn that much more than sleep can be found in a quiet mind — it is a portal to experience the radiant energy that we are all made of.

Mystics often use the example of sleep to illustrate all sorts of points about the nature of meditation. Deep meditation is often described as being awake and being asleep at the same time. What would that be like? In both sleeping and meditation, we forget all of our problems. But meditation has an obvious advantage; through it we can consciously enjoy the world of no problems or conflicts. The one indisputable characteristic of deep sleep is that everyone loves it. When we awaken we want to go back to it, but all we keep is a sort of fading subliminal peaceful afterglow. Our only regret is that we can't be aware of sleep while it happens. This is an indication that everyone wants to be a meditator, even if they don't know it.

Besides sleep serving as an intimation of the nature of deep meditation, meditators also learn to value and use the state between sleeping and waking. When understood and skillfully used, sleepiness can serve as an important doorway to deepening meditation. Meditators eventually learn to welcome a little sleepiness during meditation; they even cultivate it by sleeping less. During retreats, it sometimes seems like you can't really get into a good meditation unless you are a little sleepy. A nod or two can be like the clanging of an alarm clock, you are awakened completely but might leave your logical mind behind.

> We have a glimpse of the real self everyday. Between sleep and waking there is a momentary twilight. The waking consciousness begins with the 'I' thought. Just before the up-surge of the I-thought, there is a split second of undifferentiated, pure consciousness. First unconsciousness, then the light of pure consciousness, then the I-thought, with which the world-

> consciousness floods in, this is the order. The middle state is self-awareness. We can sense it if we are sufficiently alert and watchful.
>
> —Sri Ramana Maharshi

There is a little energy vortex right at the point between sleeping and waking: i.e.—you wake up with a little start. Let's say you were meditating on the wall of a deep well—a little nod would give you a real jolt and wake you right up. As our attention becomes more subtle, this border of sleep and waking is experienced similarly. The skilled meditator learns to ride this energy cyclone and uses it in three ways.

First. The raw energy stays with you; it permeates and diffuses through your body and consciousness and lightens and strengthens your meditation. Call it a free shot of caffeine, adrenaline, neuro-transmitters or whatever, but that raw energy is a spark from the motor of the universe; each jolt opens the door a little wider to awakened experience.

Second. The jolt helps recollect and gather the mind. You had the little nod because your mind was not totally right here. In some subtle way it was wandering around. The nod and jolt brings you back and reminds you—here, here, there is only here.

The Rinzai Zen school especially are the sleep deprivation specialists. During sesshins, meditators sleep very little, and at intense sesshins, not at all. The sleepiness becomes a very powerful tool to enter deep states of absorption. Here the infamous stick comes into play. Talk about the big jolt from the little nod—when a big mean looking monk carries a stick around and tries to catch you nodding, you'll know what I mean. It may sound a bit gruesome, but the truth is it works. Please find a good Rinzai temple and try it.*

---

* The stick is used differently in various Zen traditions. In the gentler Soto temples it is voluntary. If you are feeling a slackening energy, tired or sleepy, you may request it. A few slaps on the shoulders can act as an amazingly invigorating tonic. At some temples you bend way over and are hit on the back, on both sides of the spine, rather than on the shoulders. This can be like an excellent massage. Maybe the acupressure points are struck there. A good stick monitor, who knows what he is doing, can take your back aches, besides sleepiness and exhaustion, from you with a few well placed slaps. You'll want to hug and thank the monitor; quite a different feeling than what you might have

Third. The little bout of sleepiness is a potent aide to help wipe out the logical/rational mind. In that sleepy nod the mind often has a few flashes of dreamlike gibberish. A wisdom arises that knows that the surreal static is not so different from our usual waking mind which, from the enlightened point of view, also consists of nonsensical ravings. With each bout of sleepiness this wisdom takes over and the mind lets go of all thoughts—both the seemingly rational waking thoughts and the surreal/half-sleeping ones. With each letting go the vortex expands and grows more powerful, helping the mind to further dissolve itself and to let go of thinking.

> In a tired condition you are free of 'certain certainties' and can enter easily into the mythic dreamlike dimension where zazen is most effective.
>
> —Robert Aitken

At the intense Rinzai sesshins, the logical mind pretty much gets demolished. As long as sitters are in a meditative, non-rational state, they can stay awake and alert, but if they start to think too much they immediately fall asleep. This is best illustrated during the Roshi's daily lecture. As soon as anyone starts to think about what the Roshi is saying, they immediately doze off. No stick is used during the lectures, so basically everyone immediately falls asleep. I have sat in a Japanese Zen monastery with the Roshi lecturing to a roomfull of sixty nodding monks.

In Japan this rather absurd and surreal aspect of Zen training is understood and accepted. People expect that the lecture is the time to get in a little nap. In American Zen the sesshins are usually not as severe and people haven't been exposed to this particular Japanese quirk. When I returned from Japan and did sesshins here, taking a nap during lectures was still an ingrained habit. People would poke me and think I was extremely rude. Later, I would sometimes try to explain that taking a nap

---

towards the sometimes scary Rinzai monk. The difference between the Soto and Rinzai stick use generally reflects the Rinzai sect's approach of greater emphasis on sleep deprivation and on sudden breakthroughs, rather than gradual maturation.

was the greatest compliment you could pay to the Roshi and that staying awake was actually rude. I don't know if anyone ever really appreciated this particular piece of Zen illogic.

One of the classics of medieval western mysticism is the 'Cloud of Unknowing.' A great title, which aptly describes the true meditative state, although it could as well be called the 'Cloud of Unknown Love.' Sleep and meditation are both something like a cloud of a great unknown world that moves in on you and into which you disappear. Your rational mind never really knows what it is, but it is much greater than you and it sort of swallows you up.

The emphasis on the Zen approach in the above discussion may add an ominous edge to it. Leave it to the Japanese kamikaze mentality to push things to the extreme. To balance it, here is a Sufi poem.

Don't go to sleep one night.
What you most want will come to you then.
Warmed by a sun inside, you'll see wonders.
Tonight, don't put your head down….
The day is for work.
The night for love. Don't let someone
bewitch you. Some people sleep at night.
But not lovers. They sit in the dark
and talk to God, who told David,
Those who sleep all night every night
and claim to be connected to us, they lie.
Lovers can't sleep when they feel the privacy
of the beloved all around them....
—Rumi

Really, it all comes to the same thing—if you're always rather lazy and attached to excessive sleep, you may not get too far in meditation. When some discipline, determination, longing for union and/or pain of separation keeps you up, this is when the heart- flower may open. This can all be summed up in the words of Perry Como, maybe a '50's secret Sufi. Remember the refrain from his old song:

Love blooms at night,
In daylight it dies.

DREAMING

Exploring the sacredness and mystery of dreams can be an important part of the path to awakened awareness. Through dreams we recognize that the source of wisdom and enlightenment is within our own being. Dreams are messengers from a place of peace and wisdom, and they are trying to teach us how to untangle ourselves from the confusions of our lives so that we might live in these states.

Besides teaching us that everything that we need is already within us, dream study also teaches us that there is an intelligence far greater than the rational/logical mind. Call it what you want—universal intelligence, the unconscious, cosmic consciousness—but it is through our dreams that we can contact this intelligence and source of creativity within us. Our mere rational mind is amazed and confounded by the interconnection of dream symbols with our inner growth and all the events of our life. Because of this, dream-work is an excellent preparation to help us let go of the rampant thinking mind during meditation. The deeper one has explored one's dreamlife, the more readily one understands that the logical/rational mind is only the tip of an iceberg of consciousness.

> [The enlightened person] knows the waking state to be a dream.
> —Ramana Maharshi

Mystics sometimes describe a state of being 'dreamy.' This state is often experienced during intense meditation retreats, but it can happen at other times as well. Being dreamy is something like a prolonged deja-vu which can sometimes last for hours or days on end. The waking state and dream state become a little mixed up and the waking state starts to seem like it is all a dream; everything seems familiar, like it has happened before. At this point, one often has intimations that dreaming and waking are not that dissimilar and that there may be something more real than either of them.

When seen from the perspective of the enlightened state, dreaming and waking are actually identical: our usual consciousness is just another dream and it is not much different than the dreams we have at night. In both states, the clinging to a sense of "I" generally dominates. Enlightenment is described as waking up from the dream of our separate existence.

A number of years ago I spent a few days at a Trappist Monastery. The schedule was: up at 3:00 AM for a service, then back to our cells for a little nap, then back to the chapel for mass or prayers, back to the cell for a nap, up for more vigil, another nap, etc. Something like this, up and down, up and down from the middle of the night through the early morning, until breakfast.

I really liked that routine and sometimes I like to recreate a similar morning schedule. I get up very early, have a cup of tea and sit for a good period, then take a nap, then sit a period, take a nap, etc. etc. Please try this sort of a morning sometimes. Even if you don't do all the ups and downs, one nap after a few good periods of morning meditation can be the most pleasant beginning of a day. I can promise you one thing, you'll have deep, interesting and meaningful dreams during these naps. If you are persistent at meditation and slowly purify yourself, these post-meditation dreams will turn increasingly inspiring and blissful.

It's time to inject a note of caution here. As with every subject in this book, as well as every subject on the mystical path, I recommend a balanced and middle way. One can't rush the meditation's maturation, it will ripen in its own time. In the case of this chapter's subject, please don't go sleepless until your intuition tells you that you are ready for it. And when you get sleepy meditating, don't always try to push through it. It is wonderful to sit up straight and sit your way through the sleepiness. But it is also wonderful to just lie down sometimes, and take a nice nap. I do it often.

Someone asked a Zen Master: "What is Sesshin?"
Zen Master: "A bright ball of nothing."
Sitting, sleeping, dreaming, waking,
What is real?
Sometimes they get all mixed-up.

That's when you'll experience yourself as
"A bright ball of nothing,"
with no circumference and no center,
extending everywhere
and including everything.

PART FIVE
MANY WAYS, NO WAY

DEATH I

> Without being mindful of death, whatever Dharma practices you take up will be merely superficial.
>
> —Milarepa

Basically, meditation is practicing dying on a cushion. As we learn to experience that we are empty of a separate self, we discover that we don't go to some a lonely, fearful, void place. Rather, we dissolve in unfathomable and limitless source-radiance. We consider that this boundless radiance is our true home: what we always are and what we will be when we finally do leave the body.

To some degree, meditation can be just a 'feel good' game. It may help us to relax, live this life more creatively, courageously and generously—all wonderful and worthwhile results. But the contemplation of death drives meditation to the most ultimate questions of our being: 'Who Dies?' 'What am I?' 'Can I really die or am I some formless, all pervading essence—unborn and undying?'

One doesn't need to wait for death or for a serious disease of the body in order to contemplate these questions; over the centuries, mystics have woven the contemplation of death into meditation in numerous ways. Meditating in cemeteries or among corpses in charnel grounds has long been popular in order to intensify the question of 'Who dies?' Sitting in places in places where there were wild animals has also been popular.

In Los Angeles, I hold meditation meetings in a room above Hollywood Blvd. This is getting to be a scary neighborhood at night; the serious meditators are separated from the dilettantes. Admittedly, on most evenings, the meditation hall is largely empty; but those who do come have the opportunity to pursue a deep inquiry into the meaning of life and death. I also do late night walking meditations on L.A. side streets, also a no-no for the more timid population. I've survived so far, but as cars pass slowly by, the inquiry of 'who dies?' is often deepened and intensified. Don't get the wrong idea. One doesn't want to tempt fate too far; except for those truly and deeply enlightened, I wouldn't recommend backpacking in Afghanistan. There is a middle ground here. Do what you are ready for.

The Buddha said, "Death is my guru" and I must admit meditators often become obsessed with death. This may at first seem a bit morbid to the more cheerful general population. But this fascination does not result in any terminal depression.

In my case it often manifests in an interest in anything old. I can spend days looking through history books, old magazines, wandering museums and watching old movies. I am fascinated by the fact that everything flowers so briefly and is gone—the people, the places, cultures, whole worlds. Sometimes I get addicted to a painful and delicious nostalgia that reminds me how quickly my world and I are also passing. However, this pain is actually beneficial because it leaves me with no choice but to seek the ultimate anecdote for all pain—really being here in the present moment.

Some Deities in the eastern world are especially associated with death, and their inclusion in our practice can lead to profound results. Death is the central theme when one meditates on these deities, yet this contemplation leads the devotee to bliss and peace, rather than to some morbid despair. In Hinduism, Kali and Shiva come to mind. Kali is depicted as a ferocious Goddess, holding a sword, wearing a garland of bloody skulls and dancing over prostrate dead bodies. She destroys in order to create. Ramakrishna, the greatest modern devotee of Kali, spent his days in divine rapture, singing and dancing his love for Kali, and through her, for everything. Shiva is called 'the destroyer'; a huge, hooded serpent is his necklace and canopy. In Shiva's other familiar form, he is depicted as the cosmic dancer, joyously dancing through all creation.

Tibetan rosaries are usually made out of bodhi seeds (from the variety of tree which the Buddha sat under when he was enlightened), intermixed with skulls carved out of bone. I like to wear mine because, besides reminding me to be mindful of death, it often starts good conversations. In the East, people are used to it, but in the West, they are often shocked and ask me why I'm wearing a necklace with skulls in it. I can reply in all sorts of ways: "To remind me that death can come at any moment, so I'd better be fully alive right now," "To let fear, self-grasping and attachment die," "Because it's always just now, can now die?" I have some fun, break through the usual superficial conversations to really touch someone's heart and maybe exchange a few words of dharma.

Even if you don't resort to such props, as a natural progression your meditation will eventually turn to the question of death. Basically, in the course of a lifetime of meditating, one starts to feel great happiness, at first sporadically, and then more regularly and deeply. However, we might tend to think that this happiness is "ours," or the result of particular circumstances. Yet, this 'great happiness' that we feel is strictly a gift; it comes from some place much greater and beyond the 'little you.' There is no way that it is "ours" or due to any circumstances. Rather, it is the opposite. The more you let yourself be peeled away, the deeper this happiness—call it bliss—permeates your life.

As we live our lives and are feeling so good—sitting, walking, working, relating—the questions inevitably begin to arise, grow more insistent and become an obsession: "If I was dead, would I still feel this good?" "Is this radiance dependent on my having a body and material brain for me to experience it? Or is it greater, timeless and outside of the body and brain? Are the body and brain just part of a little wave that appears within this radiance?" As incredible as it may seem, coming from a materialistic mind-set as most of us do, when our practice matures and ripens, the scale tips towards the latter conclusion.

Things like reincarnation seem less far-fetched and even likely. One begins to feel that this present life is just one little step in a much greater and all-inclusive process of evolving love. It seems that everything that happens to us is part of this process and when death of the body comes, we have a growing faith that this too will be a part of the journey. Death no longer holds the terror that it used to. Our identity has shifted to the wholeness of all things which are conspiring to abet this evolving love.

The 'near-death' experience may be the great new religion of this century. Medical science has made it increasingly common for people to be resuscitated after being clinically dead for five to ten minutes. We are being inundated by a veritable flood of books, videos, articles and movies on the subject. It's almost gotten to the point that people feel they haven't really lived unless they've had a near-death experience.

The 'near-deathies' almost universally report similar experiences—being absorbed in extremely intense, blissful, all-pervading light; finally feeling at home; meeting dear ones—either still in a body or not—with great love; meeting guardian angels, love-mothers, gurus, guides, saviors; experiencing intuitive and non-verbal understanding of people; seeing the world that they've departed from with great love; understanding that this love is the true meaning of life. Most report they would have been very happy to have stayed 'dead,' but were drawn back into the body by unfinished business or responsibilities on this material plane.

The life-threatening illness falls somewhere between the near-death experience and ordinary life. You could say that this is an intense, though forced, meditation on death. Strangely, if illness canbe approached as a meditation—whether the illness results in the cure or demise of the body—many people feel that they learn so much from having the disease that they become grateful for it. It may sound macabre, but you sometimes hear statements like, "I wouldn't have traded my cancer for anything in the world." People with life-threatening diseases often go through various stages: denial, panic, pleading. Finally a stage of acceptance, letting go and opening to the spirit arises.

Being a care provider for people who are dying is also an intense meditation. As people open at the doorway, they often take those around them to the edge. Ramdas, who has done a lot of work caring for terminally-ill people, said, “It's such incredible grace for me, that in the morning when I know I'm going to be with such a [terminally-ill] person, I get absolutely thrilled in my body and being, because I know I'm going to have the opportunity to be in the presence of truth.” Out of context, this may sound a little self-serving, but actually Ramdas has dedicated his life to selfless and compassionate service.

In critical illness and the near-death experience we recognize very strong and intense experiences of what one usually learns to experience more gradually in meditation. Just as dying is a crash course in meditation, the obverse is also true; meditation is a gradual course in dying. In other words, we don't need to die in order to have the near-death experience. Meditation is practicing it over and over. As planning, craving and attachments arise in sitting, we learn to let them go and just be; these are all small deaths. This 'letting go' then begins to permeate our lives.

We also recognize that, in fact, we are dying and being reborn all the time. Life is endless transformation. Not only are we "new" all the time – new breath, new motion, new sights, new moment – but we see that precisely because of this new-ness, that there really is no "us" that continues on as a discrete, separate entity. As we live with this understanding, we become more porous and life becomes a string of precious moments—though they are happening to no one in particular.

You could say that the trick is in learning to die before the death of the body. If you can do this, I guarantee that life becomes permeated with great fun, spaciousness, freedom and tender-hearted love. But this ego-death does not happen so easily. We are all deeply programmed to perpetuate our delusions of separation; our incessant craving and planning mind is usually in complete control. People generally don't want to think about the big death or the many small deaths.

> Why, when I look
> at all the faces in the room,
> is there no face that says,
> 'Someday I will die'?
>
> —Soen Nakagawa Roshi

It usually takes a systematic and dedicated meditation practice or some rude shock to the system—often the experience of the real possibility of dying—to get us beyond our habitual separation-thinking mind. This is one of creation's greatest jokes, paradoxes and mysteries, because the greatest happiness is found when we are free of our limited ego identification. Then, all the trials, transitions and uncertainties of life can become opportunities to practice little 'letting go' deaths and to experience the part of us which is undying.

Someone once held a teacup up to Aachan Cha and asked him, "Isn't it painful to know that this cup will eventually break?" Aachan Cha took the cup and replied, "To me the cup is already broken." This is another step; not just to contemplate that we can die with each moment and with each breath, but to contemplate that we are already dead. Living as 'already dead' didn't lead Aachan Cha to any morbid state, but to a great freedom that inspired almost everyone who met him. He was rarely seen without a big, bright, mischievous and sparkling smile on his face.

If we live as if 'already dead,' then we are the eternal dance of everything coming and going; we are the oak tree in the garden and we are the busy street. If we are dead, then everything else will be very alive. Usually our ego-self is very alive, so everything else is dead. Zen master Suzuki Roshi taught that this is the deepest meaning of the commandment, "Thou shalt not kill." We are usually lost in our ego's mental fog, so the world is not really alive for us. In effect, we have erected a thought-wall that is killing the world all the time.

Unflinching courage is a sure sign of a deeply enlightened person. Physical death is no longer real for them and they have no fear of it. Bankai was thought of as just another eccentric monk hanging around the neighborhood in sixteenth century Japan. During the funeral procession of a feudal lord, an immense lightning storm broke out. Everyone ran for safety, except Bankai, who sat on top of the casket to 'guard it.' After this people began to appreciate his spiritual stature, a temple was built for him and he went on to become the most highly revered Zen Master of that time.

Bankai called his style of teaching 'unborn zen.' One sits with the certitude that our true being is both unborn and undying. Besides dying and being dead, you contemplate that your true being has always been dead. This may sound like a twisted Halloween special, but––it works. Please try it for yourself. With each breath and thought-moment, let your awareness be filled with nothing but death, death, death. You will be left with something that is not born and can never die. It is indestructible consciousness right here and now and it is the source of everything.

There is the strange idea of a separate 'me,' sitting in the middle of our thought world. But it has no power to make itself be born, or die, or to just to be right now. It is actually always powerless, but somehow our whole life becomes centered around it. When we let our illusions die, we experience our true nature and realize that we really are the formless power that creates all things—vast, peaceful, radiant and limitless being/consciousness.

DEATH II

Belief in reincarnation is a commonly shared world-view throughout the East, in Sufi schools of the Middle East, and in the Jewish Kaballah. The Egyptians elucidated it in their 'Book of the Dead," it was commonly held among early Gnostic Christians until outlawed by the Council of Nicaea in 325, and it was an underground heretical current among medieval Christian mystics.

No culture, however, has made as deep and profound study of death, dying, intermediate states and reincarnation as the Tibetans. And no culture has integrated this understanding into their way of life as thoroughly. It will be worthwhile to take a digression and consider the unique qualities of Tibetan culture that, in part, are based on this belief system,

My theory is that Tibet's unique significance for the whole planet stems from its geographical situation. There is something especially sacred about the location of the highest water source in a watershed. When I go backpacking I often climb to the highest spring or glacier and do a vigil for a day. I inevitably find that this is a sacred spot that flows with a special blessing . I become addicted to the taste of the pure, sweet water, but even more so to the delicious blessing that my heart is receiving.

Tibet functions in this same way for the whole planet Earth. It sits atop the tallest and youngest mountains in the world, the Himalayas, and the major rivers of the Asian land mass—the Yellow, Yang-tse, Indus, Ganges, Mekong—all flow down from its high peaks. It may be no coincidence that Tibet became the only country in the known history of the planet to have completely and unilaterally disarmed. Instead of devoting their excess wealth to armies and conquest, as has been the accepted norm throughout recorded history, they devoted it to monasteries and enlightenment. When the Chinese invaded in 1950, there were 6,000 monasteries in the country of six million people—one monastery for every one thousand people. And the monasteries were generally not "two monk" establishments. The three largest, on the outskirts of Lhasa, each had populations approaching 10,000. This is unprecedented in world history. Spiritual unfoldment and enlightenment was the industry and raison d'etre of the whole country. Before the Chinese invaded, Tibet functioned as the world's unique 'enlightenment factory.'

Tibet seemed to be a country that was half on this earthly plane and half on some astral plane. The culture was a unique interpenetration of the material and spiritual. I know of no other country that developed a system of state and local oracles who acted as mediums for protector deities. High lamas —through prayers, meditations and visualizations— helped people die skillfully, guiding them through the intermediate states of death, bringing them to the most beneficial rebirths.

The system of 'recognized reincarnations' is also unique to Tibetan culture. When a high lama dies, he often promises his students that he will return in a new body. He gives indications of the region in which he will reincarnate. After his passing, oracles are consulted and divination methods used to obtain assistance in finding the reincarnation. When a candidate child is found, he or she is rigorously tested before being accepted as the reincarnation: from a collection of similar items, the candidate must be able to choose the one object used in his or her past life, recognize past associates, etc.

This may all seem far-fetched, but the truth is that it works. For generations, leadership of the lineages, monasteries and nunneries has been in capable hands through this process. If you meet some of these little 'recognized reincarnation' children, you can't help but be impressed that something more than the thorough training of randomly chosen children is going on here. I was amazed at five-year-old Kalu Rimpoche's ability to sit still for hours, seemingly in some sort of absorbed state (though perhaps playing and giggling a little), while, around him, long and complex ceremonies and meditations were being conducted. My greatest impression, however, on meeting a few of these little kids, is their seeming lack of self-centeredness and self-importance. Given the fact that they are the center of an almost constant hubbub of activity and attention, this seemed almost impossible—any normal kid would have become spoiled rotten.

For me, however, the greatest evidence of the likely validity of the profound beliefs of Tibetan religion can be found by just associating with Tibetan people. Although often living in conditions of great poverty and oppression, whether in Indian refugee camps or in occupied Tibet,

Tibetans are remarkable for their warm-hearted, good-humored, kind and resilient qualities. One cannot be other than impressed, and certain that these people carry some great truth in their hearts.

All of the above is just a long introduction to a brief outline of the Tibetan views of death. The Tibetans believe that immediately after dying one enters the 'first bardo:' a state of complete annihilation in radiant self-effulgent bliss. If you have done a great deal of spiritual work—i.e. attained Buddhahood, this is your true self, there is no returning to the delusion of separation. Some people may have attained this stage, but have taken vows to return in a body to help others—they are the 'recognized reincarnations' or 'bodhisattvas.'

Most 'dead people,' however, only taste this state for an interval and then descend to more mundane dualistic levels. Someone who has done a lot of spiritual work may abide in the first bardo for a longer time. Those still deeply lost in separation and delusion will pass through so quickly that they are barely aware of what is happening. Unfinished karma, the unburned seeds of ignorance and craving, will manifest as a consciousness of separation. Various stages approximating western ideas of after-death states may then manifest: reviewing life and judging one's actions as beneficial or harmful and then enjoying or suffering the fruits of one's actions in mid-level bardo states. These heavens, hells and purgatories are stages we pass through; they are not final, as in the western conception.

As our ideas of separation manifest themselves on grosser levels we are drawn to take another body in which to continue our evolution. The conditions of this next life are determined by the decisions and actions of past lives. Thus, the true heavens and hells are right here.

A few notes of caution, and an appreciation of an ever-present paradox, are appropriate here. If ideas of karma and reincarnation become central to one's thinking, it is possible to lose one's sense of compassion; one might easily fall into the trap of dismissing peoples' suffering with a cursory 'it's their karma.' Tibetans are also aware of this paradox; to balance it they are usually compassion obsessives. If you ever go to teachings by a Tibetan Lama, you'll quickly notice that almost every other word spoken is "compassion, compassion."

The world is much more complex and mysterious than any of our ideas about it can begin to encompass. We may believe that peoples' lives are a reflection of their past actions, i.e. karma. Yet, we have to temper this idea with an appreciation of the limits of our knowledge. Who knows what is really 'good' or 'bad karma?' What appears to us as suffering, even the greatest and deepest suffering, may also be great blessing; it is through difficulties that we grow and evolve. The idea here is not to be too final, certain or definitive in our judgments of anyone or anything.

Personally, I apply ideas of karma to myself more than to other people. When difficulties arise in my life, rather than being angry at the world or someone, I try to accept the situation as karma and to see the arising phenomena as the perfect lesson and the inevitable results of my past actions. As for other people, who am I to judge anyone?

> I'm such a sinner, I just try to take care of myself and leave the judgment of other people up to God.
>
> —Gandhi

> I have gone all over India on foot and have seen with my own eyes the misery, ignorance and squalor of our own people. Let no one talk of karma. If it was their karma to suffer, it is our karma to relieve the suffering.
>
> —Swami Vivakananda

How important and helpful to meditation practice is having a belief in reincarnation? It is quite central to Tibetan beliefs. Many Hindu meditation teachings also emphasize the importance of reincarnation. Most Zen teachers, however, accept reincarnation as probable, but don't place a central importance on it. Some great teachers have avoided all talk of reincarnation. From the point of view of absolute truth, any idea of a separate entity that reincarnates is descending to the realm of relative and dualistic delusion. Some teachers prefer to keep their point of view fixed at that uncompromised, non-dualistic level.

If not guarded against, people can turn into 'reincarnation obsessives,' spending their time and money going from past-life regressors to psychic readers. Rather than liberating themselves, they just become more deeply attached to the idea of themselves as a continuing separate entity. Ramana Maharshi replied to a question about reincarnation: "You don't know who you are in the present life, why worry about past lives? Just find out what you really are in the present life and all your questions about other lives will be answered."

Sometimes, however, to understand and liberate ourselves from a deep wound or recurrent psychological tendency, it may be helpful to know that these recurrent patterns may be due to events in a past life. If we are practicing a spiritual discipline, this understanding might come through dreams, in meditation or through meeting a psychic person at just the right time. We need not become a 'regression-junkie;' if it is necessary for our growth the understanding will seek us out, we don't need to seek it out.

Although it is not essential, an understanding and acceptance of karma and reincarnation is helpful to meditation practice. Having faith that our lives are the manifestation of some ultimate harmony and perfection may make it easier to let go of the rambunctious and intractable rational mind. At first, this faith may be provisional, but as it helps us experience our true self, we fully embrace this perspective.

As our practice deepens, we accept the likelihood that we're on earth to learn certain lessons and do certain work. and we'll stay for as long as this takes and leave when we've done what we came here for. I don't want to be simplistic. Of course, the workings of destiny are mysterious and often full of surprises; death often comes knocking long before we think we are finished and ready. And although this life is beautiful and we do all we can to prolong it, if the knocking persists, we must surrender, and have faith that there is an intelligence greater than ours — one that knows the proper timing of things better than we thought we did. Amazingly, in this surrender, we find the greatest joy and peace; we come to understand that our true being is inside of a vast mystery, beyond the comings and goings of this little body.

There is an old tradition of Zen masters and poets writing a death poem when they are about to leave the body. Here are a few of my favorites.

A bright and pleasant
autumn day to make
death's journey.
—Fukyo

As one approaches death's doorway consciously, the opening heart radiates 'bright and pleasant'

This year I want
to see the lotus
on the other side.
—Jokuro

This must be
my birthday
there in paradise.
—Joseki

Most of the great enlightened beings have not been big 'birthday people;' they usually don't make a big deal out of celebrating the birth of this body. Ramana Maharshi went even farther: "Rather than celebrate, we should mourn taking birth in this body of illusion, the real day to celebrate is when there is a birth of realization of the true self."

A death poem by a western poet:

Death is just
infinity closing in.
—Jorge Luis Borges

Infinity is closing in right now. Just "be still and quiet."

Basho, one of the greatest haiku poets, at first reprimanded his students when they requested a death poem: "You fools, every poem I've written in the last thirty years [since his enlightenment] has been a death poem." He then relented and wrote:

> On a journey, ill:
> my dream goes wandering
> over withered fields.
>
> —Basho

Is our life a dream-journey? If so, let it be a beautiful dream, filled with love. Sadness is inevitable too; everything that we love passes. When we awaken, and know that we are not only the dream but the fields as well, we can watch both our love and our sadness pass, with a full, though sometimes broken, heart. And gentle humor too. Many monks and haiku masters used this opportunity to get in a last joke.

> Had I not known
> that I was dead
> already
> I would have mourned
> my loss of life.
>
> —Dokan

> Today, then, is the day
> the melting snowman
> is a real man.
>
> —Fusen

This is not to say that westerners don't also try to get in a last laugh. If you wander through Hollywood's Hillside Cemetery, you'll come across the gravestone of song and dance comedian and old Friar's Club kibitzer Eddie Cantor:

> Deep in Mother Earth I nestle,
> Freed at last from Georgie Jessel.

To some people—especially my mother—it may seem that I have contradicted myself all over these death chapters. Contemplating the ultimate topic of death raises the dialogue to a place where paradox and seeming contradictions are inherent in any discussion. We all have many parts of our being, and they co-exist at different levels of our consciousness. One day, Ramakrishna was told that his much beloved cousin had died. He had no immediate reaction; he seemed indifferent. But he spent the next day crying his heart out, soaking up towels in endless tears. The first day he was on a spiritual plane where there is 'no coming, no going, no birth, no death.' The next day his consciousness was on a relative plane and he grievously missed his nephew.

Once, someone came running up to Neem Keroli Baba with the news that Hari, one of the old Ashram workers, had "fallen off a ladder and died." Baba just laughed like a little boy, repeating over and over, "Hari is dead, Hari is dead." It turns out that the information was premature and Hari wasn't even too seriously injured. Did Baba, who often displayed some sort of omniscient psychic knowledge, know that Hari wasn't dead? Was he callous, closed-hearted and just didn't care about Hari? Or was he at a level of consciousness where birth and death are not real, and refused to display the usual and expected sentimentality over these issues?

Ramana Maharshi developed a tumor in his arm. After undergoing several operations at the instigation of devotees, the tumor recurred. With tears in their eyes, devotees implored him not to leave them, but to cure the body with powers they believed he had and could use. Ramana answered, "You say that I am dying but I am not going away. Where could I go? I am here."

We can have growing intimations of the completely enlightened views of death described above. Mostly, however, we are all too human. When death comes, it is a great mystery; grieving is very real and must be honored and indulged until we heal.

Some of the most notable meditations on death in western culture are in the great operas; really they are among our deepest and most moving requiems, the western equivalent of the Zen death poems. It has always been axiomatic that opera is depressing because 'everybody dies.' At the climactic moments the despair and pain pushes the characters over the edge; they then often let go and experience a spiritual love that transcends death. Gilda, dying in Rigoletto's arms, sings to him:

> There in heaven, near my mother,
> Forever, I shall pray for you.

In Lucia de Lamermoor, Edgar, about to plunge a knife into his belly, sings:

> Oh Beloved, if separated we were on earth
> God will unite us in heaven.

Aida and Radames, entombed in the death crypt sing:

> Heaven is opening for us,
> All pain ceases.
> Our wandering souls fly to
> The glow of eternal day—
> The ecstasy of immortal love.

In La Traviata, Violetta departs her body singing:

> All my pains are gone.
> I feel reborn,
> A new strength is reviving me!
> Ah! I'm coming back to life!
> Oh, Joy—

In most of these operas, until the final moments quoted above, the approach of death is quite gruesome and cataclysmic. This need not be true in our lives. By incorporating an awareness of death into spiritual practice over a lifetime, we can make a friend of death. We will have prepared a groundwork of understanding our pure consciousness and it won't take the immediacy of impending death to shock us into realizing our true nature. We will find such joy and fullness in our life that, paradoxically but true, we won't look at the body's death as a final catastrophe. Embracing life fully and without fear, we will do the same for death.

LET YOURSELF GO: OUT OF CONTROL

People who take up meditation often study Tibetan or Sanskrit in order to read the various scriptures in their original languages. This is helpful, but certainly not necessary. Irving Berlin has already put all the essential teachings into English.

Come get together,
Let the dance hall feel your leather,
Step as lightly as a feather,
Let yourself go.

Come, hit the timber,
Loosen up and start to limber,
Can't you hear that hot marimba,
Let yourself go.

Let yourself go, relax,
Let yourself go, relax,
You've got yourself tied up in a knot,
The night is cold, but the music's hot.

So come, cuddle closer,
Don't you dare to answer 'no sir,'
Butcher, banker, clerk and grocer,
Let yourself go.

Someone asked Master Aachan Cha if he could put all the teachings of meditation into a few words. Aachan Cha replied, "Two words say everything—LET-GO." Meditation is just practicing and learning to be proficient at letting- go. Usually as each thought arises, it carries us away from here and now to the world of us and others, hopes and fears, past and future. Meditation is simply letting-go of each thought before it carries us away. Letting-go becomes habit forming; the more one practices, the better one gets at it And it becomes easier because we learn that when the mind and body are completely filled with letting-go, this very moment is a radiant and boundless treasure.

People reading books on meditation may encounter long discussions of concepts such as the seven factors of enlightenment, the eightfold path, the ten perfections, the five hindrances, the five training precepts. They may feel discouraged and are sometimes overwhelmed by the cerebral overload that they think is assaulting their brain.

Here is the good news. Of course, studying is helpful; it lays an intellectual foundation that can only help us; it accustoms the mind to run in beneficial pathways; it offers us techniques to help us approach the various difficulties of the spiritual path. However, it is also only a side dish to the main entree; the real meditation begins when one lets- go and forgets everything.

> The best way towards perfect composure is to forget everything.
> —Suzuki Roshi

> Monk to a dying master, "Remember all the teachings master."
> Master: "I've forgotten them all and anyway there is nothing to remember"

If you've let go and forgotten everything, then who are you? Or, what are you? No one? Anyone? Everyone? Can you think of a greater challenge than answering this question ? You will become fascinated by the challenge as you realize that when you forget everything, there is something that will never forget you. Call it what you wish: God, the Love Mother of the Universe, Guru.

A Zen koan asks, "What is your original face before your parents were born?" When you've forgotten everything, then you will see this original face. You will become like a new born baby—everything new and fascinating and not separate from you.

Meditation is often described as experiencing being 'out of control.' The usual workings of our rational mind are largely devoted to one thing—maintaining control. Our thinking mind is frantically trying to maintain a buffer of safety and comfort between us and the outside world. We erect a fortress around our lives and try to control conditions to keep ourselves safe within this fortress: safe from unpredictability of nature, from threatening social situations, from political and economic uncertainty.

This is all natural and inevitable. BUT, at a certain point it is unproductive. After we've planned and plotted enough, it is best to finally let-go. Meditation is acknowledging the truth—that, ultimately, things are out of control. We've been given birth, we're given life, we'll be given death. We do our best with what we have while we have it. But no matter how tight a grip we may try to keep, the bottom-line is that things are out of our control.

When we release our tight grip, we actually find our liberation. In our attempt to maintain control, we erected a dam to hold back the unknown. When we finally give up and let the dam burst, we discover that we had actually erected a wall against our intimate connection with all things, as well as against our fears.

Hollywood disaster movies, popular because they remind us of the out of control nature of our lives, may eventually lead to mass enlightenments. We do what we can, but we never know: that volcano, that twister, the earthquake, the high-rise fire or terrorist bombing may be coming up next. I saw a volcano movie a few years ago. The whole theater cheered when the mountain finally blew its top. It felt like the release of a contagious mass-enlightenment. People cheered because they subliminally recognized that things are 'out of control.'

Of course, the 'reality videos' are even a step beyond the disaster movies. I have one called 'Caught on Camera': every sort of crash and accident, fires, floods, rescue attempts, etc. I proposed to the Don't Worry Zendo that we watch these scenes between sitting periods. They may be a great aid to meditation: the modern approach to assimilate the out of control nature of reality.

Another Irving Berlin song says it all:

How it felt when I fell
I just can't recall.
But her arms held me firm
And they broke the fall,
And I said to myself

As I hopelessly kept spinning all around:
"I got lost,
But look what I found."

A Zen master described meditation as "taking a leap off the edge of a cliff into the unknown." BUT, as the song says, when we take the leap, the arms of grace will catch us. What we find, or rather what finds us, is much greater than whatever it was that we let go of.

Another way that people often describe meditation is 'being open.' If we are attentive , with each breath we can release a layer of tightness: in our bellies, musculature, nervous system. Ramakrishna was out there at the extreme fringe; he had gone so far in opening and relinquishing control that:

> His shirt is unbuttoned, because he cannot tie knots, button clothes, bolt doors, close boxes, tuck the mosquito net under the mattress, or even bind his own cloth firmly about his waist. So released is the Paramahamsa that he can confine or manipulate nothing.

There is no limit to how far you can go in letting go of control. You may end up like Ramakrishna, with no tightness or constraining power left in any way. Of course, you might not want to go that far out unless you were sure you had attendants around to tie your shoe laces and tuck in your bed for you—which fortunately Ramakrishna usually had.

> Nothing of value can happen to a mind which knows exactly what it wants.
>
> —Nisargadatta

This may seem rather extreme, but I love this quote. Of course, sometimes we do know what we want; or, we have things that have to get done and we just do them. But the trick is to have another mode of consciousness that we can shift into—more non-directed, open and non-controlling. In this frame of mind the things of our life will vibrate with a deeper and more intimate aliveness.

One day while they were out walking, Soen Roshi asked his student Eido, "How do you define beauty?" Eido demurred an answer, so Soen answered himself, "If an event is unrepeatable, that is beauty."

Control-addicts are ultimately trying to preserve or recreate the past conditions that brought them happiness. They are usually destined for a life of disappointment. Things often don't unfold as we expect them to. If we are off on a planning-cloud, we miss the absolutely unique, unrepeatable and beautiful treasure that is right in front of us, moment after moment.

FANATICISM

Basically all humans want to be happy and we all seek this happiness in some sort of union, love and connection with something greater than ourselves. Unfortunately, people usually choose something limiting with which to find their primary connection and self-identity—a particular political party, nationality, ethnic or religious group. They then create barriers that separate themselves from 'outsiders.' This is too bad, because we all already have a complete and intimate connection with the greatest thing, the source of the universe.

As I wrote in an earlier chapter, it is helpful to have a sangha —a setting of group support in which to practice meditation. But one must also be very cautious in choosing a group. First, be sure that it does not have an 'us vs. them' mentality towards outsiders; if it does it is not a sangha but a cult. If you contemplate practicing with any group see if they are open, generous and friendly towards everyone—members and non-members alike—without any ulterior motives of wanting anything in return. Also check that the group does not try to control or limit your life in anyway. And be sure that you don't feel there are any dark secrets in the back room or subtly unmentionable topics.

Look for a place where spirituality is not abstract and self-centered, but where people are engaged in society and dedicated to helping in some way. The resurgence in spirituality since the sixties has, unfortunately, often become rather twisted with consumerism and all sorts of selfish indulgence. Under the 'new-age' banner I see articles on 'prosperity consciousness;' "I deserve to be rich" and "I deserve abundance" have become mantras of spiritual materialism. The corollary is never mentioned, "If I am richer, then some one else is poorer." I would personally prefer the mantra "there is enough for everyone."

Also, given our situation today, people are in a spiritual vacuum if they are not living lightly, conscientiously and respectfully on our planet. Our psyche and soul cannot be healthy if our practice does not include caring for our seriously ill planet. Real practice is realizing our interbeing with nature and all creatures.

Also, find a group where the people have not gone overboard with proselytizing. This is something of a paradox; although wide spread access to information on meditation would be beneficial for our society, meditators have never been big proselytizers. Gary Snyder describes the reticence of Buddhists: "We might light a stick of incense and open a window. If someone smells the incense, follows its scent to the window and inquires about the source, we'll be glad to answer their questions." Serious meditation involves hard work, dedication and readiness to confront one's injuries, fears and pain. Excessive proselytizing is really a waste of time because no one will take up meditation unless he or she has become ripe for it by seeing through life's more superficial enticements.

If some group goes in for obsessive proselytizing, it is more likely for its leader's or its collective ego aggrandizement, rather than to really benefit anyone. A healthy practice group should be all but invisible; it is just a collection of people who practice together. It is no more important than any of the people involved.

It is very helpful to find a group to sit with, but still, this is just a setting for work that ultimately must be done alone. The unmediated wrestling with the unknown, if it is deep, is finally a solo match. Sitting is sort of like dying, it is between the individual and the universe. Be cautious of groups that offer easy and comforting answers, rather than encouraging you to experience the real depths of your being.

> There are two kinds of religions. One gives you easy answers and charges a lot. The other gives more questions and is usually inexpensive.
>
> —Gary Snyder

This raises the question of money. In the Buddhist tradition, teachings have always been free. Of course, these days groups have mortgages and land payments, so this tradition is often stretched to account for the realities of practicing Buddhism in the West. Still, observing various practices over the last thirty years, I've noted again and again that the best teachings are usually the cheapest – and that the best retreat centers make an attempt to keep the retreat fees as affordable as possible.

In Herbert Benson's book "The Relaxation Response," he reports on experiments in which one group of subjects meditated using 'one' as a mantra and a second group meditated using mantras purchased from a popular meditation school, supposedly each mantra custom designed for the unique vibration of the individual meditator. The subjects of both groups were wired to measure brain waves, blood pressure and other bodily functions that have been shown to respond in meditation. The results for the two groups of meditators were identical—i.e. you don't need to pay expensive initiation fees to anyone for custom made mantras.

Unfortunately, religious organizations often get corrupted; all of the trespasses that I've described above are rampant. If people want you to join something, it often means that they want to try to control you in some way or get your money. As an alternative please consider joining your own religion.

> Variation is the sign of life. I pray that they may multiply so at last there will be as many sects as human beings, and each one will have his own individual method of thought in religion....Divine reality is infinite, and infinite are the ways to realize it.
>
> —Ramakrishna

Why allow anyone to file you away with their prejudices and pre-conceived categories? Personally I prefer to make up my own categories and keep them open and mysterious. Depending on my mood, some days I'm a Don't Worrier. Other times I may be a Now-ist. On other days I may prefer to be a Barksist or a Love Melter. Of course, if I'm in a mischievous mood, then I'm a monk of the Lingerie Zen Sect, a Don't-go-Straighter or a Buffonian. If I say I'm a Jew, a Catholic or a Buddhist, someone may think they know all about me, but being a Flippist keeps them guessing and may open a few doors to the unknown. If I claim to be a Non-Dualist, it is actually not just a label but a meaningful statement about my practice and experience. It puts something out there that people can relate to and opens doors rather than closes them.

DON'T KNOW MIND

The Bodhidharma was the first master to bring Buddhist meditation to China; he laid the foundations for the later development of Zen. The Emperor, hearing that an eminent monk had arrived from India and was living in the mountains, summoned the Bodhidharma to the capitol for an interview.

> Emperor: "I have endowed many temples and monasteries, what is the merit?"
> Bodhidharma: "Absolutely no merit."
> Emperor: "What is the Buddha's Way."
> Bodhidharma: "Vast emptiness, nothing is holy."
> Emperor: "Who are you?"
> Bodhidharma: "I don't know."

After responding with these brief answers, the Bodhidharma left the flabbergasted Emperor and royal court and returned to his mountain retreat. In the interview, he set several precedents out of which Zen later evolved. First, the enigmatic and cryptical nature of his answers. The Bodhidharma's responses set the tone for innumerable encounters among later Zen masters. The Zen style is to not give an easy or predictable response so that someone thinks they have a final answer, but rather to challenge them to question at a deeper level.

Second, the Bodhidharma emerges as a totally independent, gruff and uncompromising character, as well as a prime upholder of a 'democracy of the spirit.' Although he did answer the summons to the capitol, the Emperor couldn't get much out of him. It seems the Emperor would have to shave his head and become a novitiate, just like anyone else, in order to receive any special consideration or detailed teachings. (And the Bodhidharma was well known for being especially hard on novitiates; the Emperor probably wouldn't have wanted his 'special consideration.')

Finally, and most important, is the statement "I don't know." Since the Bodhidharma enunciated this, "I don't know" has evolved to become a major theme of meditation. Some schools of Zen base their teachings just on doubting everything and experiencing the 'don't know mind.'

A hundred years after the Bodhidharma, when the fifth patriarch decided to give his dharma transmission to the lowly peasant kitchen helper, rather than the head monk, he told the astonished monastery, "Hui-Neng is the one student to whom I can give the robe and bowl [transmission] because he does not understand Buddhism." The monks still weren't ready for such radical teachings; the fifth patriarch had an incipient riot on his hands and the future sixth patriarch had to make a quick get-away in the middle of the night. As Zen evolved further over the next century, the wisdom inherent in the empty, not-knowing mind became more widely appreciated.

Several hundred years after Boddhidharma, Zen had come into full flower. There were an amazing number of deeply enlightened masters wandering around China and sitting in monasteries on various mountain tops. Joshu was one of the greatest of them. A monk asked Joshu, "Does a dog have Buddha nature?" Joshu answered, "Mu." Mu has become the most frequently used meditation koan in Zen. It means—-

—-ha. You expected an answer? It has absolutely NO meaning. There is no rational answer. When you are completely filled with mu, so that there is no room for anything else in your mind, then you are in a state of complete doubt.

The doubt spoken of here is not a half-way compromised doubt, but a radical complete questioning of all our assumptions. We don't merely ask if some miracle could have happened two thousand years ago – but, rather, we ask, "Does time exist?" We don't ask if psychic communication is possible, but we question the very existence of space and separation. Not just, "Can I know spiritual union?" but "Do I exist? Does the world exist? Can I know anything for certain?"

Please try this 'don't know' meditation. Let 'don't know' fill you up. With each breath let go of every certainty and let not-knowing penetrate deeper into your being—especially into the sense of self that thinks it is meditating. As the suspension of all certainty deepens, there is still an awareness, but it is not yours or anyone's; it is the awareness of the universe. The more completely you enter into "don't know," the more radiant the awareness becomes.

You don't really have to seek the 'don't know mind' too ardently. As practice ripens, it will seek you and become a natural part of your mentality. As one's meditation opens to the experience of broad and intimate spaciousness, one just naturally lets go of the mind's rigid certainties.

> Don't be hard,
> It's more fun—
> Let your solid ideas run.
> —Buffo Sutra Rossini

To many people raised on Western religions, which emphasize faith, this recurring 'doubt' tradition may seem unsettling, or completely incomprehensible. Actually complete doubt and complete faith both lead to the same experience. When you radically know nothing and doubt everything, an unshakable faith will emerge from the depths of your being—that you and the universe are united in blissful perfection. This may sound strange, but it is true.

> The believer is happy,
> the doubter is wise.
> —Greek proverb

The Greek may have been obsessed with an either/or mentality; but there is room in us to be both wise and happy. Why not be both a believer and a doubter?

Kant, the late eighteenth-century German philosopher, was a major turning point of western history. Right in the middle of the most rational phase of western history, its exact opposite appeared. Kant said that we can never know the 'thing in itself.' All of our perceptions are filtered through the subjective senses and brain, and we really have no idea what reality is. He showed that the temple of rationality was built on a very shaky foundation. It took a few more decades for Schopenhauer and Nietzsche to fully unravel the implications of Kant's philosophy. Ultimately it was devastating to Western rationalism and inevitably led us to Eastern mysticism, wherein we embraced the mystery of the unknown.

Developments in science also undermined the West's optimistic faith in the omnipotence of reason. In a famous statement, the U.S. commissioner of patents in 1899 predicted that the patent office would soon close because "everything that can be invented has been invented." The commissioner spoke a bit prematurely. Instruments were soon developed that were capable of probing deeply into the atom and outer space. The general intellectual climate soon changed radically, in quite the opposite direction than that predicted by the commissioner. Statements such as

> What we know is so tiny
> and what we don't know is so vast.
>
> or
>
> The more we know,
> the more we know we don't know.

are more in keeping with the tenor of our times.

A hundred years ago, a statement like Nisargadatta's below would have been absolute gibberish to most Europeans. Today Nisargadatta is a spiritual best-seller.

> What people call self-evident, that is, the experience they get through the senses, is far from self-evident.... You are taking so many things for granted. Begin to question. The most obvious things are the most doubtful. Ask yourself such questions as: "Was I really born?" "Am I really so-and-so?" "How do I know that I exist?" "Who are my parents?" "Have they created me, or have I created them?" "Must I believe all I am told about myself?" "Who am I, anyhow?" You have put so much energy into building a prison for yourself. Now spend as much on demolishing it.
>
> —Nisargadatta

These days, I'm always glad to see 'deconstruct reality' bumper stickers when I'm driving around town. There is no better catch-word for the spiritual path. The ultimate is often described as the mystery. We can never know anything for certain, and the universe may always surprise us. The visible evident world that is right in front of us may be less than the tip of an iceberg. The things we know and deal with may be a very limited part of the picture. When we become less certain that what is in front of us is so final and definitive, we start to accept that anything may be possible: Angels, other worlds, many worlds. Our whole universe may be no more than an atom bouncing around in some other dimension. The tip of my finger may contain infinities.

> An American Doctor asks Ramana Maharshi: "Does such a thing exist as a personal God?"
> Ramana Maharshi: "Yes."
> Dr. (with astonishment): "What! With eyes, nose, ears, etc."
> Ramana Maharshi: "Yes, if you have them, why should not God have them."
> Dr.: "When I read in the Kabbalah and the Puranas that God has these organs , I laugh."
> Ramana Maharshi: "Why don't you laugh at yourself for having them."

This dialogue completes a full circle. Centuries ago humans may have believed in a God in their own image. Modern people laugh at such a belief as a superstitious absurdity. But really the world is a mystery; anything and everything is possible. It's best to not know anything and to not dismiss any possibility out of hand.

Do you see Ramana Maharshi's catch?—"If you have them, why should not God have them." But do you really have eyes, nose, ears, etc.? If you limit yourself, you limit God and vice-versa. You are God and God is you.

R. H. Blythe, an eccentric and irascible Englishman, was one of the first western writers on Zen. Someone asked Blythe what he answered when asked if he believed in God. Blythe replied, "It all depends on who asks the question. If they do, then I don't. If they don't, then I do."

In subtle topics as religion, we may all be talking in different languages. We fool ourselves when we think we understand what anyone else means by words like 'God.' Wittgenstein said "words were invented so that we can lie to each other." If we think we can define, understand or easily communicate about concepts such as God, we effectually limit God and limit ourselves. It is best to know that reality is undefinable and rationally unknowable. When we know nothing, there are no limits on God or ourselves.

Basically every approach to meditation is a way to quiet our mind. The contemplation of the limits of our knowledge is one of the best ways to do this. When the mind acknowledges its limits, it is sort of stunned into quiescence. Then we are flooded with the experience of our true nature.

A professor visited a master to inquire about Zen. The master poured tea for the professor and kept on pouring till the tea overflowed the cup and saucer—spilling onto the table and the floor. The amazed professor exclaimed, "Stop, stop, what are you doing?" The Zen Master replied, "You are like this cup—overflowing with your opinions and judgments. To understand Zen you must first completely empty your mind." When we finally let-go of our opinions and certainties, truth will embrace us right here and now.

> I never attempt to describe or to circumscribe God in any way, through any notion whatsoever....I only know that I know absolutely nothing. I do not even attempt to think about God, much less speculate about the creation....Whenever any description of God is attempted, no matter how subtle, the result is a false sense of duality.
>
> —Ramakrishna

Practicing meditation is something like re-wiring our whole nervous system. As it gets rewired, deep meditation will just happen; there will be no need to do anything, try anything or know anything. No particular technique will be required; such efforts will just entangle us in striving, hope and fear. The same with knowing: ; a lot of ideas will just impede our imminent and immediate openness and letting go.

Of course, all sorts of efforts, techniques, approaches and ways of thinking about and describing meditation are helpful to initiate the rewiring. Yet, as the rewiring evolves, these methods have served their purpose and can be disregarded. They are all just expedient means and need not be considered inviolate, ultimate, the only or best way, sacred or essential.

At a certain point, everything I've written here will seem like a lot of nonsense to you—and to me too! One can think and write all we might want about meditation, but when we go back onto the cushion, the meditation will open in some entirely new way. Our attempts to set the ungraspable and evanescent nature of the experience into rational ideas will seem like a lot of gibberish. To tell you the truth, after thirty years of meditation, I don't know what I'm doing or how it happens. That's OK, it just happens. Our attempts to understand or explain it have almost nothing to do with it.

A Zen Master said, "Yesterday's enlightenment is today's mistake." Whatever ideas, wisdom or power we think that we have gained, whatever we think we know or understand,; it is a mistake if we try to understand or possess it as ours, rather than letting go of the 'I' again and again. A famous Zen koan asks, "How do you proceed farther when you are at the top of a hundred foot pole?" To go deeper, we always have to let go and take another leap into the unknown.

> Eastern fools saw life not as a puzzle to be solved but as a mystery to be lived.
>
> —Wes Niskar

> Your greatest moment
> will be when you discover
> that you've been wrong
> all your life,
> and you'll
> have to realize this
> over and over.

MANY WAYS, NO WAY

A monk asked Baso, "What is Buddha?"
Baso said, "This very mind is Buddha."
Later another monk asked Baso, "What is Buddha?"
Baso replied: "Not mind, not Buddha."

This sort of dialogue is a Zen specialty. Buddha, not-Buddha, Mind, not-Mind—it does not matter what you call it, because you cannot call it anything. If you give it a name you may think you really know something that can be put into words. It can't be.

This whole book may read like one of these stories; the totally rationally-minded reader may find it to be a slippery mass of contradictions. I may be accused of 108 transgressions of logic and every variety of solipsism. The truth is that the meditation experience is beyond any technique or description—when you attempt one, such infractions are inevitable.

The first flowering of Zen which occurred during the Tang Dynasty (600-900 C.E.) in China was one of the golden ages of meditation. The dialogues of the Tang masters are still fascinating reading today. However, one rarely finds instructions on meditative techniques in the discourses of these masters. Some scholars have mistakenly drawn the conclusion that the Tang Zen masters did not really go in for much meditation. Nothing could be further from the truth. Actually 'Zen' is a Japanese transliteration derived from the Sanskrit word 'Dhyana,' which means— meditation. The Zen school literally means the Buddhist sect whose members have gone meditation crazy: i.e.—the heavy-duty meditators.

BUT the great Tang masters knew that meditation was beyond all techniques. They knew that descriptions of doing it this way or that way was for beginners; one could not really teach someone how to meditate. They could only inspire them, and challenge them to do it for themselves.

A few years ago someone climbed into the mountains of Central China. Deep in the mountains he found one of the few remaining hermit masters and asked him how he taught dharma. Master Te-Ch'eng replied:

> I teach all sorts of odds and ends. You name it. Whatever seems to fit. A little of this, a little of that. This is what practice is all about. You can't practice just one kind of dharma. That's a mistake. The Dharma isn't one sided. You have to practice Zen. If you don't you'll never break through delusions. And you've got to practice the precepts. If you don't, your life will be a mess. And you've got to practice pure land. If you don't you'll never get any help from the Buddha. You have to practice all dharmas.

The approach I've taken in this book has been something like this—the everything but the kitchen sink style. The enigmatic Tang dynasty masters were great in their day, but this is the 20th century—people want explanations. So I've enumerated many techniques and ways to describe meditation; we can use all of them. But they lead to beyond all techniques—to no technique. This is where real meditation begins.

I'm reminded of the old Hindu story of the blind men and the elephant. One blind man feels the trunk and says that the elephant is like a snake. Another feels the leg and says it's like a tree trunk. The third feels the tail, it's like a rope. Trying to understand meditation is something like this. It's different for each person. Even to one person, it can change day by day or minute by minute. We are always entering through a slightly different door and seeing a new facet of the beautiful mind-jewel. The words and metaphors with which we attempt to understand or explain it are all afterthoughts to the actual experience.

In every chapter I have basically said the same thing, just from slightly varying points of view. If we fill ourselves with enough of these points of view, we will paint our mind into a corner and tie it down with rope—there will be no escape. In whatever direction the ego turns, it is confronted with its extinction. Wherever the mind turns it experiences that it is not separate but is an indivisible part of the ocean of consciousness.

Yasutani Roshi said that entering the spiritual path was akin to engaging in a war. We must realize that we are not skirmishing with some rag-tag irregulars; the ego is no pushover, it is a crack SS panzer division—insidious, tenacious and resourceful. We need every possible weapon—artillery, tanks, infantry, air power.

The many approaches to meditation that I've described in these pages have all worked for me. I can't tell you what is best and will work for you; please experiment and try some, a few or all of them. The most important thing is just to sit: you will begin to hear your inner guide and your own unique path will unfold.

Here is how Rumi, the great 13th century Sufi poet, says it. In a famous poem he puts these words into God's mouth as God is speaking to Moses:

I have given each being a separate and unique
way of seeing and knowing and saying that knowledge.
What seems wrong to you is right for him.
What is poison to one is honey to someone else.
Purity and impurity, sloth and diligence in worship,
these mean nothing to me. I am apart from all that.
Ways of worshipping are not to be ranked
as better or worse than one another.
Hindus do Hindu things,
The Dravidian Muslims in India do what they do.
It's all praise, and it's all right.
It's not me that's glorified in acts of worship.
It's the worshipers! I don't hear the words they say.
I look inside at the humility.
That broken-open lowliness is the reality, not the language!
Forget phraseology. I want burning, burning.
Be friends with your burning.
Burn up your thinking and your forms of expression!
Moses, those who pay attention
to ways of behaving and speaking are one sort.
Lovers who burn are another.

In other words, no particular technique matters nearly as much as our perseverance, our dedication, our loosening around our attachments and the depths of our longing to experience reality. People at first think that some new style of meditation is going to miraculously put them in some 'high' state. With some maturity, they give up such spiritual day-dreams.

If one lives one's life in an honest, unattached, open-hearted and courageous way, going towards, rather than away from, pain and difficulties, meditation will be vast and intimate, regardless of any technique. However, if one leads a completely self-centered life, no technique will be of much value. Meditation will only create exhaustion and will be useless — other than possibly prompting one to adopt a more generous life style.

Someone recently came to the Don't Worry Zendo selling a line of teas. After a sales spiel she assured me that the teas are also an excellent aid for meditation and can almost guarantee me a deep and peaceful practice. I told her that in that case it was very important that I not buy them. I was only interested in meditation reflecting my life and relationships.

Contrary to much popular opinion, meditation was not at the top of the Buddha's list. His first pronouncement, the four noble truths, said, in essence, that attachments cause suffering. Somewhere down the list of his next teachings, the eightfold path, he brought in meditation. After writing and enticing you to buy this long tract on meditation, I am far from wishing to say that meditation is not an extremely precious tool. It has been a great blessing of my life. Unfortunately, many people who take up meditation do not relate it to the rest of their lives. They use it to isolate themselves, rather than deepen their connection to their world. In this chapter of summation and tying up loose ends, I want to re-emphasize what has been a recurrent theme throughout this book: in a life lived with an open heart, meditation will unfold with great ease and blessings. Great effort or concern with various techniques will hardly be necessary. At best, sitting is just making ourselves available for the inevitable embrace of oneness

Every practice eventually opens up vast energy within us, and uses itself up. Each one leads to the realization that right here and now this very mind is perfect bliss, creating all things in harmony and oneness. When one first takes up meditation, a definite practice is extremely helpful. We need the focus, intention and guidance. And then, practice leads to non-practice. It is not necessary, or even possible to know, do or reach for anything. Just stop doing.

Sometimes, however, one does wish for some words to describe 'non-practice' and the descriptions often sound something like a practice. You could call these 'practiceless practices.' They are somewhere on the border—the last and most ineffable, ungraspable and indescribable 'non-techniques' that more definite techniques lead to. They are the last outposts on the edge of —love, oblivion, God, oneness — that might sound like a doing something. The non-practices are all really just one, but can be described variously. Since they have largely been the subject of this book, a brief review is in order.

Silence. First, we become aware of the tyranny of our chronically cluttered mind. Then we might experience some moments of silence. In those moments our separate-self delusion disappears and our real unlimited self, which is always present, but usually hidden by the thought barrage, shines and includes all things.

Doubt/not knowing. Everything we think we know—our bodies, the world, time, space—are actually a subjective fixation, due to patterns of energy striking through our particular senses and cerebral cortex. We radically investigate and discount everything that is not absolutely certain. We sit in the embrace of what remains.

Faith in this moment. We seep our whole being with the affirmation that we don't need to wait for or do anything. This moment is perfect. There is no way because there is no where to go.

Inquiry. Everything we think we are or have—body, feelings, language—is a gift from a vaster, deeper matrix of allowing. Infinite coincidences in the past and present have created the setting in which we think we are doing something. The more we investigate the question 'Who am I,' the more we discover that the separate self is an elusive and disappearing character.

Choiceless awareness/Zenassana. Just be with what is, don't try to push any thought/feeling away. The small I concerns will naturally exhaust themselves.

Surrender. As grace embraces us, we know that what our heart really wants is beyond our powers. We can relax our strenuous efforts at meditation and just sit.

Metta. Feeling the presence and wishing to share the blessing of the moment with others.

It is often possible to jump start to no-practice at the inception of one's meditation career. This 'no way' is actually the most direct way. Any technique or practice inherently involves you in the idea that "you" need to do something to get somewhere. No-way practice actually de-programs us from this delusion.

At the Don't Worry Zendo we have two 'pith instructions' that we often read after sittings. They say it all best.

Stay open and quiet that is all.
What you seek is so near you
that there is no place for a way
—Nisargadatta

Do not look for God,
look for the one looking for God.
But why look at all?
God is not lost,
God is right here,
closer than your own breath.
—Rumi

One of the first books that I ever read on eastern religion was the 60's classic, Erich Fromm's *Zen and Psychoanalysis*. Fromm pointed out that the eastern mind accepts A and B, while the westerner's logical instincts are to see things in life as A or B. You could call this the rational mind's OR disease. I don't think that there has ever been one idea that has been more central to my life. I recommend the A & B mentality in life, meditation and, especially, in reading this book. Otherwise, as I said earlier, you might just see it as a mass of contradictions. Applying this personally, my practice is both A,B,C & D: no practice and none of the above. Many times when I first sit down or if the mind is wandering or lazy, I'll return to some practice for a while: breath, 'this,' feeling of space, asking who the 'me' is. Usually, with some grace, the practice gets used up in practiceless practice and no-practice. There is no contradiction. Then I just sit.

I recently saw a brochure for a Buddhist center offering a course entitled, 'Mastering meditation.' In the brochure was an urgent appeal for funds with a dire warning that unless they were forthcoming the 'place is going to go broke.' I was not at all surprised. Since we begin our meditation career 99% tilted towards the delusion of doing something, it is best to rebalance this delusion by stressing the complementary opposite. A more helpful and perhaps lucrative brochure might have been headlined 'Mastered by meditation.' The truth is, it will only happen through grace and surrender. Besides, trying to master meditation is an excellent prescription for a nervous breakdown.

Soen-Nakagawa Roshi said, "To practice Zen, you must think the unthinkable." Thinking the unthinkable is not something that can be described or taught in six easy steps. It will happen when all of your being is fully engaged in a wild wrestling match with the whole universe. Which is greater—you or the universe? Once 'non-practice' ripens, it does not matter what you think you are doing or trying to do. When you have gone beyond all methods, when you don't know what you are doing or who you are—then, you are no longer doing meditation, but meditation is doing you. The whole universe is meditating through you.

Here is Rainer Maria Rilke's description of losing the wrestling match with the universe:

> What we conquer are the small things,
> and the victory makes us small.
> The eternal and limitless
> will not be bent by us.
> There is the angel who appears
> to the wrestlers in the Old Testament...
> Whoever this angel overpowered
> (and she often declined the fight,)
> grew strong and erect

> and great out of that harsh hand.
> Winning does not tempt him.
> He grows through being deeply defeated
> by ever greater being.

Nisargadatta, makes the same point with fewer but less poetic words:

> When overpowered by the wide expanse which is without beginning, end or middle, there is the realization of non-dual bliss.

The 'wide expanse' is always right here for it is the very nature of consciousness; we are already and always it. Our mind is not separate and enclosed, but is this very space that includes everything that comes and goes. As we learn this over and over, the wrestling match turns into a joyous and easy surrender.

PART SIX
LOVEGAMES & DHARMAPLAY

WALKING MEDITATION

Walking is used in a number of ways in meditation practice. Many traditions use it as a break to stretch the legs between sitting periods. The Zen style is to walk around the Zendo in a single file. Vipassana meditators take a small area and walk back and forth individually. Don't Worriers often take a casual stroll in the garden. Any sitting practice can be continued during walking meditation. If someone is feeling especially restless, walking meditation can be an excellent alternative to sitting and will often help to calm and center them.

There is also 'out in the world' walking meditation: leaving the meditation hall behind and practicing walking as a meditation to appreciate the beauty of the world that we are a part of. You could call this the 'Thich Nhat Hanh' style of walking meditation.

Thich Nhat Hanh has been one of the most influential and highly respected Asian teachers to come to the West in the last few decades. He is a Vietnamese master who lives in France. He visits America regularly and teaches many hugely attended retreats. Popularizing walking meditation has been one of his greatest influences. At first people who went to his retreats were surprised that they did as much or more walking than they did sitting. By now the walking craze has spread to many other meditation centers.

When you've cultivated walking meditation, it can be an invaluable ally in your life. There have been innumerable times when I've felt tense, exhausted or upset about something and I've said to myself, "I'll go for a walk, just for a few blocks." By then I'm refreshed with increased energy. A few more blocks and I feel great and just want to keep on walking. I've left my weariness and distress behind.

The important thing is to keep the mind from running rampant in its habitual past, future and planning modes—i.e., to keep your mink right here, step…by step…by step. Thich Nhat Hanh gives excellent walking meditation instructions in his wonderful book, "The Long Road Turns to Joy." Here is a brief summary.

First find a rhythm that coordinates the natural pace of your breathing and steps. This gives the mind something to focus on and keeps it present. The rhythm you adopt will depend on the terrain, your physical condition and if you have to get somewhere. (This is not entirely disallowed—if there is a time limit and definite destination, you can up the pace and still have wonderful walking meditation.) It can be in-breath—left foot, out-breath—right foot: in- breath—left foot, out-breath—right foot. Or in-breath—left, right, out-breath—left, right: in-breath—left right, out-breath—left, right. Or in, out—left, in, out—right: in, out—left, in, out—right, etc.

After a while the strict attention to the coordination of breath and steps can be loosened. The most important thing is to remain aware of the in-breath and out-breath. If you forget the breath, your mind will almost inevitably wander off. Going back to it will keep you present in the moment. Fortunately, after a while, staying with the breath becomes habitual.

It is also important to allow your body to relax. After a while you will feel that you have something like a baby's body: loose, soft and supple. It is easy to spot a walking meditator; the arms are the giveaway. They hang so loosely that you can almost see tension dissipating away. Also, the walker's low center of gravity seems to be almost rooted in the earth. Great old Chinese Tai-Chi masters usually have this soft and grounded baby's body. An excellent way to learn walking meditation is to locate such a master, hang out at their school, follow the master around and imitate how he or she walks. My strongest memory of Soen Roshi is not anything he said, but just the way he walked. This is indescribable, but he seemed to be part of the earth—perfectly poised, at peace and absolutely not going anywhere.

To remind you to stay right here in this moment, you can also coordinate a mantra with your breath and steps. Thich Nhat Hanh suggests a number of them, here are a few:

> Just this moment, wonderful moment.
> Just this moment, perfect moment.
> Just this moment, only moment.

Of course, as you advance in walking meditation, you will find yourself making up your own mantras.

"A walk in the rain forest is a walk into the mind of God." These are the words with which Birute Galdikas, the orangutan lady of Borneo, often greets visitors to her forest station. But really the rain forest is everywhere—in Manhattan, the Sierras, a seashore or country road. There is one key to entering the 'Mind of God;' wherever you are, you have to know and experience that you are not going anywhere. Rather than getting somewhere as fast as possible, you have to get to nowhere as slow as possible. Unfortunately, I have found that this is usually very difficult or impossible for most Americans to do. They are going somewhere and they're in a rush to get there. But if you are busy going somewhere, then you are not really anywhere.

Among my non-initiated friends I am considered to be one of the world's truly slow walkers; after one or two outings, most of them will never walk with me again. Good riddance says the confirmed and stubborn slow-motion walking meditator.

John Muir said that even walking two hundred yards an hour was going way too fast. Gary Snyder stretches the point farther; he claims that all walking is too fast; it's better to get down on hands and knees and crawl. Then you might slow down enough to really see what's going on. At this point you are ready for the 'Buddhist Olympics'—in each race the last person across the finish line wins. To begin to take it all in, one has to severely slow down.

Walking meditation is a wonderful way to open the door to the numinous world. A friend of mine says that when walking she "falls apart in a cloud of love." I like that a lot, but it won't happen if you're set on arriving somewhere. Also, if you see someone walking with their head hanging down, they are usually lost in their thoughts. To really be present, it is helpful to smile and have the eyes open and turned towards the horizon.

Shinzen's saying is a good walking mantra:

> Turn to the left side, paradise of the left side,
> Turn to the right side, paradise of the right side.

or the Navaho prayer:

Beauty walking with me,
Beauty before me,
Beauty behind me,
Beauty besides me.
Beauty walking with me.

Now that we are near the end of this book, I can tell you the real truth. It isn't that meditation is worthless, let's just say that it's second best. As I've reiterated more than a few times on these pages, its not so difficult to learn to experience what we really are: that our true being is the all-permeating love source. And there is nothing wrong with the meditation cushion; BUT it's much more fun to experience the love source out in our big, fascinating and beautiful world.

Really, when we learn to walk with open eyes and heart, with each step, with each turn of our heads, we enter and are blessed by a new paradise—beautiful and alive and intimate with our heart. When we experience the more subtle levels of walking meditation, we are no longer this body moving through the world; we are the vast space of creation itself, the mystery that contains the myriad things, all transforming at every step.

BACKWARDS WALKING

For most people the limited little-body/self idea dies hard. Fortunately, there is one ally, backwards walking, that can quickly short-circuit our ingrained going-somewhere mentality and render the deeper subtleties easily accessible.

In the usual forward-facing mode, the future and where we are going are out-in-front and separate from us, visibly beckoning. It is only natural to always be psychologically leaning ahead of ourselves, in anticipation of where we are going and thus, being in a rush to get there. With backwards walking our whole emotional tone transforms. When we are always leaving, rather than arriving, it is much easier to get into the non-separation mentality. We are not going anywhere, but are in a dance with everything.

Here are a few of the advantages of backwards walking.

Surprise. Backwards walking is an excellent exercise for living totally in the moment. The unexpected object can most easily grab your attention and allow us to drop our usual self-centered ruminations. With each step, we never know what is awaiting us. Because there is no preparation for anything, one has no choice but to give one's self completely to everything.

Surprise has been the perpetual Zen specialty. The old masters were always waiting for just the right moment. A perfectly timed nose pull or door slam can sometimes precipitate an enlightenment experience. Of course with backwards walking everything surprises you full blown. It is true that every once in a while you may walk into something. To avoid spinal injuries, inveterate backward walkers often wear a padded backpack as a bumper.

Slow down. Backwards walking is the only way to get many people to slow down. If they backwards walk with the usual rushing, they'll only end up in a nervous fit. The body and nervous system just have to relax. The truth is that we are not going anywhere at all. However far or fast we go, we are actually always and only right here. the first step is the body, then the mind might follow along and slow down. We'll finally take it all in; stop at the oleander and watch the lady bug crawling up the papyrus stem.

Saying good-bye. The last moment is when we really see things; the last bite is the most delicious; we truly love our departing friend. With backwards walking every moment is the last moment. The truth is that we are always saying good-bye to everything. Walking backwards, waving good-bye rather than hello, we naturally become aware of this usually repressed truth. We enter a more poignant and gentle world. Our life becomes a love-filled letting go and farewell. When we don't think, 'Oh it will always be there,' then we really look at and appreciate things. It won't always be there, this is the first and last time.

Faith. As with meditation, or any other challenge, backwards walking may bring up insecurity and fear. When we allow ourselves to feel, investigate and defuse our defenses, we become more permeable, porous and malleable to the universe. Each step is an act of faith.

Guidance. At fifty and beyond, one begins to look back at life and see the patterns. We know somehow that it all fits, that we've always been led by some mysterious guidance. With backwards walking, since we're always looking back at where we've been, something similar happens. We come to know that we've been led all along.

Interbeing.

> The unenlightened person thinks that they are in the world,
> the enlightened knows that the world is in them.
>
> —Nisargadatta

Forward or backwards, this is my favorite walking koan. With each step we begin to know that our true self is this mysterious energy that allows all things to exist. When we slowdown everything is moving at different speeds in multi-dimensional, multi-layered depths. Putting one foot in front of the other, the whole world moves. It is obvious that we are creating the world; it takes its birth within our vast being.

For communion, backwards walking can't be beat. You're not just another walker out on the street, but the neighborhood's backwards walker. Other walkers won't just pass you by without a greeting. Everyone will know you, and you'll know everyone. You will undeniably be distinct in the neighborhood. Around my house, the slow motion walking was bad enough, but now I'm the backwards walker. You might want to dream up some excuse so that the neighbors won't think that you are nuts: a rare knee joint disease or some neurological disorder that necessitates backwards walking. I can only assure you that although I haven't converted the neighbors, they do eventually get used to it. Hopefully with time, the benefits will become more widely known and accepted and we won't need excuses.

And more people than you might think will understand what you are up to. I was out backwards walking on a recent afternoon when two Thai or Vietnamese little old ladies passed me by. They looked at me quizzically and asked in a thick accent, "Why you walking that way?" I stammered something like, "I like it better, go slower, look at things more, not in a rush.'" A big smile lit up both of their faces as they exclaimed in unison, "OH Buddha!"

I sometimes think people should mostly do backwards walking, at least for a few years, to re-balance the foreword walking delusive conditioning that made us think that we are actually going somewhere.

THE LINGERIE ZEN SECT

People often find it strange that I own a lingerie store and am also a student and teacher of meditation. They sometimes inquire whether these dual careers are not the cause of great conflicts and inner turmoil in my life. I am always quick to assure them of the exact opposite effect. Over the years I have learned to not be embarrassed by my trade and even proud of it.

At first this was far from the case. When I took over Playmates I was in my Vipassana phase. Typically, a retreat ends with a sharing circle. You finally get to meet the people whom you have grown to feel close to through sitting quietly with them for ten days. Everyone tells who they are, what they do, etc. The Vipassana crowd is generally quite distinguished: teachers, artists, writers, psychologists. I always wanted to climb out of the closest window before revealing myself as a brassiere and panty salesman. When my turn came I would try to evade the subject: talk about the weather, the last retreat, a few irrelevant jokes and hope no one would notice.

But eventually they always did. Inevitably someone would ask, well I never got just what you do back there in Hollywood. Word would spread like wildfire. And what do you know, rather than being ostracized, I was suddenly a celebrity. Everyone wants to trade with me: art, counseling, books for lingerie. They will all visit me and go shopping when they pass through LA. Come and see them wherever they are. And what, I'm not carrying? Bring a few panties along next time.

I've always found the same reality out in the dharma world as in my store: sexual preoccupation. From the novice sweeping the Zendo steps to the Rinpoche, from the Roshi to the cooks, this subject is usually never too far from anyone's mind. So, for 99.9% of us mortals it will do absolutely no good to try to avoid or evade it. Rather we should embrace it. And, I've got to admit, the best place to do this is in a lingerie store.

Over the past two and a half millennia, as Buddhism has spread across borders, it has typically merged with the indigenous cultures to form new schools. In Tibet it incorporated the native Bon Shamanism and the unique forms of Tibetan Buddhism emerged; in China a blending of Buddhism and Taoism produced Chan and in Japan a synthesis with Shinto produced Zen. As a student of meditation, for many years I have been contemplating what new forms will emerge in the West—a Christian Buddhism?, a psychological Buddhism?, an entrepreneurial, capitalistic Buddhism?

Twenty years ago, I inherited Playmates of Hollywood, 'the world's largest lingerie store.' I got my first hints of another possible form the new Western Buddhism might take when I attended meetings of the 'Lingerie Club,' a Southern California organization of lingerie store owners and manufacturers. Expecting a rather seedy crowd, I was amazed to discover that lingerie people are grossly misapprehended. Most of the side conversations were about going on retreats, the temples and churches that people attended, types of prayers and meditations, etc. I started asking myself if there was some connection between lingerie and meditation. Is it possible that spending one's days in a lingerie store naturally softens us, opens us to be receptive to the feminine side, to intimacy with the mother? Is sex actually the dominant religion in the West that Buddhism is going to have to accommodate and incorporate?

Since a lingerie store had, so to speak, fallen into my lap, these seemed to be questions worth pursuing. I opened a meditation hall above the store where several nights a week we have meditation practice. Before I knew it, the Lingerie Zen Sect was born. Since I am the founder, sole priest, theoretician and propagator, a detailed exposition of the principles and practices of the Lingerie Zen Sect would seem appropriate here.

It's partially a question of arousing energy: tell me a better way than to come in with your sweetheart and try on a few teddies, and then go through the bra and panty racks. Of course, the most basic practice for turning the sexual energy towards divine union is prolonged and meditative intercourse, hugging, etc. But if you're single or indisposed for whatever reasons, the Lingerie Zen approach is very effective—hang out in a lingerie store and the sexual energy is naturally aroused. Then, when you go upstairs to meditate, that energy will transform and strengthen your practice.

Some people have the mistaken idea that one should absolutely endeavor to avoid sexual thoughts and fantasies while meditating. Nothing could be farther from the truth. Actually, a few sexual fantasies can be very helpful in deepening your practice. If they are running rampant in your brain, there is probably not much you can do about it anyway. Just persevere in your meditation; the particular obsessive thoughts will eventually pass away while the energy that came with them remains and intensifies the meditation. I can say from personal experience that if you happen to be in the lingerie business this is certainly true. For the seasoned meditating lingerie store owner, to tell you the truth, it sometimes seems a that a few sexual thoughts are the doorway to a radiant and all encompassing meditation.

Usually when we try to focus we find our minds are scattered all over the place. At the Playmates Zendo we've already awoken from the usual totally unconscious scattered mind and narrowed our awareness to one area. From this starting point it's not so difficult to dissolve the separate mind into the formless universal mind.

I invite you to take a comparison test. Go to a 'straight' meditation hall and then come to the Playmates lingerie meditation hall (above the store on Wednsday evenings)*. In one of them you'll find half the meditators falling asleep while in the other, everyone is wide awake. Need I tell you which is which? The question is, why have meditators ignored lingerie stores for the last 2,000 years? I don't know, maybe it's a conspiracy of the sleepy heads. But, at last, the Lingerie Sect has released the sexual energy to be used for enlightenment. Of course, a few monks and nuns have been doing a little hanky-panky in the back room over the millenniums. And pederasty has been rampant in some traditions. But by and large, the tantric power of sex has been largely ignored, or marginalized, until the advent of the Lingerie Movement.

Before sessions, all meditators get a fifteen percent discount. This might not seem like much, but these days when you add all the expenses of a business— payroll, rent, insurance, energy— you're lucky if there's a five percent profit left. With a fifteen percent discount you could say that Lingerie Zen pretty much pays meditators.

---

* As of this printing meditation above Playmates is suspended, but is held in a Santa Monica Lingerie store on Wednsday evenings. Check www.dontworryzendo.com for address and any further schedule modifications.

When I inherited the store from my dad, he had a policy of giving a discount to all strippers. Of course, since about half of our customers are strippers, it took me over a year to get out of debt. If great numbers of meditators start coming it could threaten the business again. But since I'm determined to continue the experiment of Lingerie Zen—I'll have to take that chance.

A pet peeve of mine is the public's continuing misperception and vilification of lingerie store owners. I look like a nice guy, so when I'm in my store, people don't usually believe I own it. They expect some sleezoid, gangster type with a cigar and pin stripe suit. I have to show them my business card and get employees to verify that I'm me. This reflects that America still hasn't outgrown her Puritan roots; in the depths of our psyche, we still think of sex as sinful and evil. When we finally recognize sex as Goddess's greatest gift to humankind, as the front door and high road to experience our divine nature, then lingerie store owners will finally be recognized as the priests and priestesses of the coming millennium.

Between lingerie browsing and going upstairs to meditate, we have a period for discussing the spiritual path and practice. I wouldn't want to say that people have been wasting their time in ashrams and desert monasteries for millennia, but there is certainly no better place to hold these 'dharma' discussions than in a lingerie store. I will explain why.

There are endless metaphors used to attempt to describe the rapturous experience of absorption as the separate identity/ego dissolves. Among the most common are speaking of regression to the innocent child, and even earlier to the love and sustenance of the mother's breast, and still earlier to the peaceful, boundaryless world of the womb. Wandering the precincts of a lingerie store/temple can afford us a an easy access to these experiences.

Gathering within "L.A.'s best brassiere department" (L.A. Weekly), it is only natural to contemplate that with each breath the Goddess sustains us. We are taking precious sips at the Universal Mother's bosom—the whole world seems warm, nubby, grainy, soft and familiar. Sitting in the immense brassiere department, this state simply overwhelms us. And as soon as we are ready to plunge even deeper—we head for the panty racks.

Here, we become as a little baby who knows nothing and is seeing the world for the first time. The world is filled with luminescence and wonder; we are in the Goddess's all-embracing, warm and comforting womb. Everything seems to be a part of ourselves and everywhere we are at the sacred altar of the Goddess.

The Hindus describe this experience as the rising of the Goddess Kundalini up the backbone. In truth, the human backbone is the love clitoris of the Goddess. It is in constant orgasmic union with mind/consciousness and the created world of form. This may sound far fetched, but it is not as difficult to experience as you might think. And somehow, wandering the aisles of gold and silver sequin g-strings, the Goddess-womb's infinite light seems all the more immanent.

But we still go deeper to prepare ourselves for the evening's meditation; we head to the negligee department. Here we finally come face to face with the essence of lingerie, of the Goddess, and of our life —MYSTERY. In spiritual practices we ask, what are we doing here? What is this world? Are we really here, or is this all some being's dream? Wandering among endless racks and aisles of flowing night gowns and robes, teddies, cover-ups, peignoir-sets and negligees, our hearts are propelled into ever subtler realms of revelation and mystery.

People often ask me if a new order is being created at Playmates. I don't know how to determine this, but a new sect of monks and nuns will usually have its own particular habits and robes. And, in fact, at Playmates we have developed the devotional brassiere, a device which rapidly accelerates the revelation of the adept's particular devotional affinities. Basically we have produced a complete line of ikon bras with the appropriate incantations and meditations for each. You wear a different bra each week. One week you might wear a Shiva bra. Shiva represents your ego's death that necessarily precedes your rebirth in pure spirit. If these sorts of revelations occur while wearing a Shiva bra, then you know you are a Shaivite. Paint the stripes across your forehead and wear your bra proudly.

Wearing a Hanuman bra you contemplate lightness, mirth and the comic absurdity of our idea of a separate self. You grieve at the endless pain this causes and yet are able to embrace it. In a Ganesha bra you contemplate gratitude for life as an overflowing fountain of fullness and blessing; In a Jesus bra—love, sacrifice and compassion; in

Lakshmi—the mother of sustenance; in Buddha—the peace of understanding of interdependence, and on and on. After a while it will be clear which bra is right for you: in one or another you'll drown in waves of bliss-energy. That deity is calling you.

Maybe we should produce a line of devotional jocks for the men, but at this point in the evolution of Lingerie Zen, a man just sits between two women in the appropriate bras. Are you a Ram devotee? Sit between two women wearing Ram bras—the proof is in what works, and it does. You'll know if Ram is writing R A M on your forehead. Also, no one is stopping anyone from cross-dressing—if the gent is so inclined.

Of course we don't want to monopolize this important discovery to Hollywood Blvd. If you live far from the Playmates Zendo, just send us your size and preference. We'd like to see devotional bras in meditation halls across the land. $108 gets you your bra and appropriate meditational instructions and prayers. This may seem expensive but wait until you receive your bra: they are highly decorated, hand-painted and costly to produce—tassels, rhinestones, crystals, the works. Believe me, at $108 I'm not getting rich on them.

After a while, you'll probably want to start wearing your devotional bra out. They're little wearable, walking altars. Everywhere you go people will stop and want to light incense in front of you. You will be blessed and, in turn, you will bless. Can you conceive of the change in the tone of social intercourse in our country if half of us wore devotional brassieres? At last, we would become a nation of compassion, generosity and love. *

The question of desire lies at the heart of our dilemma. The world of separation in time and form is a dream created by our desires. And yet our true being is the fulfillment of our deepest desire. This desire will inevitably prevail, but when we are in their grips, our passing desires seem far from trivial. We just have to sort them out. To accelerate this process, sitting with them is far better than avoiding them. A lingerie store is certainly the best place to do this.

Here is a test I offer to anyone. Enter your typical Zendo: a room full of people straining at the gut to hold back the usual cascade of their

* To order your bra see www.dontworryzendo.com

disruptive thoughts. Let out a loud, "Bras and panties for sale." I guarantee you, if the sitting is restored at all, it will take at least two hours before the pandemonium settles. The question is, what are these people doing in a dark hall? Why aren't they meditating in a lingerie store?

The Lingerie Zen Sect can also solve the problem of rapacious male Dharma teachers. It seems that even the most respected Dharma teachers, given some power, respect, and the incumbent opportunities, just can't resist the temptations of sexual dalliances with their students. The frequency of teachers getting involved in improprieties with their students is notorious. What to do about this has become a major quandary for the emerging Western Dharma community.

A few of the most radical feminists have called for a complete ban on all male teachers. They claim that to counter-balance the last millennia of mostly all male teachers, for at least the next few centuries, all dharma teachers should be female. To tell you the truth, if you look at the sordid record, this doesn't seem like such a bad idea.

There is, however, an obvious alternative to such drastic measures: internship in a sleazy lingerie store like Playmates. Let them work it out in a more appropriate setting. If your sangha is troubled by a teacher who can't keep his hands off the goods, send him to Playmates for a year or two duty as a stockboy. He'll be returned chastised and pure—or such an incorrigible derelict that you'll know never to let him back in the door.

The truth is that one can only use up one's sexual obsessions by embracing and living through them, not by avoiding them. When that Karma is finished, the world will let you know in no uncertain terms. Being a lingerie store owner, and my personal obsessions having reached mega-proportions, this was true in my case. As a supplier of erotic dancers, I always had to keep up with the latest stripping fashions (or so I told myself) and, I got hooked on strip joints. After a few years I stopped frequenting these places, but still, I wondered, is the thrill gone or is there still a lingering itch of lechery?

A few years ago I was passing through Vegas, home of America's most famous strip clubs. I figured I'd go and see if the clubs still held anything for me. When I entered the club I was immediately attracted to one woman. After talking a while, I told her that I teach meditation. She started to cry and told me that she had been praying to God to send her someone to teach her to meditate. I knew that my strip club days were over. We had a nice time meditating together and I don't think I need to go back to any strip clubs.

I have no desire to limit Lingerie Zen to Playmates. If you're around L.A., we welcome you. If you live in Georgia or New Jersey I urge you—go to your local lingerie store, light a stick of incense and ask if they'd mind if you sat in and meditated. You might be pleasantly surprised with a new friend. One store/meditation hall is enough for me, but I would love to see Lingerie Zendos spread across America.

If you already practice meditation at some center, be it Hindu, Zen, Vipassana, Tibetan or whatever, please talk to the other meditators, board of directors and/or the abbot. Suggest that you would like to keep a rack of lingerie in a corner of the meditation room, or a few negligees displayed on the walls for a trial period. I can promise you that after a few weeks they'll want two or three racks. Being dedicated to seeing the Lingerie Movement spread throughout America, I am willing to supply the lingerie and racks at wholesale prices to all meditation centers. Please contact me at Playmates, Hollywood, CA.

Only the Goddess knows what's next here at Playmates. Lingerie Zen is still in its infancy; we are always expanding our experimentation in the two fields of our expertise—lingerie and meditation. Broader vistas and deeper realizations ever loom on the horizon. In a few years I hope to look back and have a good laugh at the primitive state of today's Lingerie Zen. The field is wide open. Anyone who wants to participate in these vital developments—just come up to Hollywood Blvd. on meditation nights. I'll see you there.

DIALECTICS OF DELUSION

Life is a dream.
If you find weird enough situations,
they will wake you up

Every extreme gives birth to its opposite. This is the basic premise of both Eastern and post-Hegelian Western philosophy. Many of the practices of Eastern meditators depend upon this dialectical nature of all phenomena. Monks are sent out into the jungle to meditate; fear of wild animals eventually exhausts itself in a state of fearlessness. Surrounded by death in graveyards, the initiate more readily accesses a deathless awareness. Amid piles of dead bodies in charnel grounds, he/she is propelled beyond the I-am-the-body delusion.

Contemporary Western societies have evolved far beyond the East in our manifestations of ignorance and materialism. Immersing ourselves in these depths of delusion might just open up new vistas of Enlightenment. Unfortunately, Western meditators have not yet begun to utilize the many new opportunities for awakening that this situation has created. I would like here to present just a few possibilities.

You could call this practice enhanced tantra. Tantra is recognizing the seemingly difficult situations of our life as opportunities for awakening. Enhanced tantra is recognizing our culture as inseparable from ourselves and seeking out its realms of delusion and ignorance as reminders to awaken.

LAS VEGAS CASINO MEDITATION

For anyone with the slightest aspirations towards awakening, Las Vegas may be the most fearsome sight in America. The casinos are unprecedented in American and possibly in the world's history: limitless masses of people sedating their brains in hypnotic trances of unconsciousness. As an experiment to determine if exposure to maximum ignorance may be the best reminder to awaken us to its opposite, I have dedicated a day to walking meditation through the Las Vegas' casinos.

Today casinos are being built everywhere. When we consider this Vegasization of America, the significance of this experiment is immensely magnified. If successful, it raises the possibility that the casinos of America could be converted into walking meditation salons. Oceans of ignorance would rapidly transform into mass enlightenments of unprecedented magnitude.

The above lines were the original opening paragraphs of this section. After writing them, looking for a few observations, lines of poetry and a quick wrap-up, I flew to Vegas. My preconceptions came tumbling down. All had changed; I could barely find the Vegas of my memory. Vegas has transformed itself into the entertainment capitol of the world. The endless rows of bored, mind-numbed people mechanically pulling at the slot machines are now overwhelmed by even vaster herds migrating from one theme park casino to another. And almost everyone appears to be having a wonderful time.

Since I had booked the flight and a room, rather than beat a quick retreat to the airport, I decided to stay for the weekend. This was a fortunate move as it gradually dawned upon me that the lessons to be gleaned from Vegas go far beyond mere casino walking. I soon realized that the casinos provide the most opportune environment conceivable, not just for some walking meditation, but for a whole week-long meditation intensive. The Mafia and casino owners have unwittingly created settings for potential enlightenments that could go far beyond mere Zen Monasteries and Advaitic Ashrams.

First a little review. With some diligence, anyone can experience the benefits of meditation that I have been describing throughout this book. Lacking one ingredient, however, the experiences will be a passing show rather than an integral and ever deepening component of one's life. The Hindus call this factor vairagya, which translates into something like world-weariness, detachment or futility.

There is some inevitable pain, sorrow, unsatisfactoriness within all of the activities of our life. They never deliver the complete and lasting happiness that we hope they will. Usually this realization ripens with the maturity of passing years. Meditation greatly accelerates this process. It allows us to realize that there is some matrix/source within which everything happens, that is equal to or even more important than all the activity. It is not that the things of this world are not real, but that there is a vaster and deeper reality that gives birth to everything. As this realization deepens, we go through our lives with some detachment from the passing show. And we experience indescribable peace knowing that we and everything exist within the source.

Eastern mystics call the show, the world of appearances and form, Maya. Maya is an illusionist and magician, conjurer and hypnotist; it is always trying to seduce us with the promise of delicious and all-satisfying rewards—if we accept it as the one and only reality and source of happiness. The subterfuge is dressed-up in increasingly more beautiful clothes and subtle disguises. The bottom line, however, is that Maya offers us something like a Faustian pact with the Devil. If we give everything to Maya, it will eventually ruin us.

Does all of this seem familiar? Like Maya, Vegas hides its true nature behind ever subtler and more insidious disguises. "Gambling" has now become "gaming." And it is only a sideline in the new Vegas, which mostly exists to provide you with luxury, elegance, fun, art and a world of make believe. You can even bring the kids!

The casinos are no longer just casinos; they are now more like huge theme cities, mind-boggling in their vastness. With a few steps one can go from the world of Gay 20's Paris to Renaissance Italy. Cross through another set of doors and you are in the Burmese jungles, Pre-dynastic Egypt or Imperial Rome. Over a bridge and you enter into a medieval castle or Caribbean pirates' village. Each casino is an immense, complete and self-contained illusion universe.

Has Las Vegas become our culture's supreme symbol and metaphor for Maya? Like Maya, the casinos are actually designed to put their victims into some sort of trance state. This is done through sensory overload and physical fatigue which finally produces a state of mental and nervous exhaustion. The light show on the strip begins the barrage. Once inside, the slot machines' incessant racket continues the assault on the nervous system. In the evenings, everyone goes to see the shows, which these days are mostly all magic acts: Siegfried and Roy, O, Mysteriere, EFX, Spellbound, Showgirls of Magic, etc. Subtly, the mind is being detached from its rational moorings. All the casinos have one-way people movers; they will assist your entrance, but not your exit.

Before long your senses are numb and you are barely dragging around your exhausted body.

The logical functioning mind finally collapses; it is subsumed in a free-flowing, letting-go energy which most people, not knowing any better, channel through their wallets. This state is actually a near-neighbor to the opened and expanded consciousness that meditation produces. If one subjects oneself to all the stimuli, but with dharmic aspirations, consciousness will be propelled in the latter and more wholesome direction. This would easily happen if an alternative energy outlet was offered. Say a giant meditation hall, a point of stillness, sitting in the center of each casino—something like the giant black hole that scientists now believe inhabits the center of each galaxy. Needless to say, this alternative is not offered to the masses of hapless victims. In the midst of the tumult, the dharma-wise person must somehow provide this alternate channel for him/her self.

Mindful casino meditation will especially accelerate anyone's development of the qualities of detachment and world-weariness. After a while, everything enters some sort of time warp kaleidoscope. Whole universes seem to float by as in a dream. Every variety of person, great art, scenes from nature, eras of history and culture—the whole totality of the human experience flows past one's eyes. In Vegas, fortunately, no matter how things are arrayed, the veil is still thin. It is no secret that everything is hollow and transparent. People know they are in the land of magical illusion, deception and delusion. They really want enlightenment and just don't quite realize that this is why they have traveled to the middle of the desert. If one visits Vegas with just a modicum of spiritual aspiration then the realization of the detached state of vairagya, which often takes lifetimes, can easily happen in a day.

By now there are casino's depicting almost every era and region of human history. As far as I can see, there is one last great casino waiting to be built. Why doesn't someone finally recognize Vegas for what it is and build a casino on the world's religious themes? Hindu temples along the Ganges with sadhus spinning roulette wheels; monumental Buddhas carved into cliffs above the silk route, with slot machines built into the toes; The Vatican and great Gothic cathedrals—place the wafers on the pass or come line; Zen gardens complete with poker dealing monks—rather than raking the gravel, they're raking in the dough.

> Work like you don't need the money.
> Love like you've never been hurt.
> Dance like no one is watching.
> —Anonymous

The line, 'love like you've never been hurt,' deserves endless repeating. It is my life's mantra, the essence of any real spiritual practice and the real gambling that our heart is yearning for. Our past injuries and fear tells us no, don't take a chance, you'll only be hurt again. The real gamble that we all yearn for is, every day with every encounter, to take a chance and open our hearts to love and connection.

Spiritual practice eventually gives us the resilience to gamble for love, again and again, no matter how many countless times we think that we have lost. For most or many of us, the injury is so deep and pervasive, our emotional contraction so pervasive, that the life gamble that we really want is buried and forgotten deep in our unconscious. Somewhere though, deep inside of us we still crave the forgotten gamble. We get addicted to the money gamble because it resonates from the forgotten gamble that we really yearn for. As long as we want to gamble, we may as well go all the way.

> Gamble everything for love,
> if you're a true human being.
> If not, leave this gathering.
> Half-heartedness doesn't reach into majesty.
> You set out to find God,
> but then you keep stopping
> for long periods at mean-spirited roadhouses.
> Don't wait any longer.
> Dive in the ocean,
> leave and let the sea be you.
> Silent, absent, walking an empty road,
> all praise.
> —Rumi

THE I-AM-THE-BODY DELUSION

> The only difference between you and me is that you want what you don't have and don't want what you have. With me it's so simple, I want what I have and don't want what I don't have.
>
> —Nisargadatta

The best method of dispelling the I-am-the-body obsession is to linger in places where it is the strongest. I've been especially fond of my neighborhood gym and the cosmetics departments of large department stores—both cathedrals of I-am-the-body intoxication. Then through Playmates' customers I found an even more powerful place to dispel the I-am-the-body delusion: the plastic surgeon's office. First, an aside to explain how I personally came across this deepest "not wanting what you have" realm.

The press has often dubbed my former business, Playmates of Hollywood, the 'silicone capitol of the world.' Many people claim that Playmates' alternate pseudonym 'the silicone mountains' will one day be a more widely known phrase than 'the silicon valley.' Many strip clubs subsidize their dancers' bosom augmentations. Since a club's dancers will all go to the same doctor, they often resemble some sort of marine-like precision bosom drill team: a hundred dancers in a row, not a fraction of an inch bosom deviance. A friend of mine has the only natural bosom at a big Orange County club. She makes more money than any of the club's other dancers. The men give her $20's at a shot—to get out of the way. She claims the men down there all think she is deformed.

I have volunteered on several occasions when customers have needed someone to drive them to their plastic surgeon's appointments. I urge you to offer to accompany someone to their office visit. Spend an afternoon in the waiting room, watching the bodies come and go. If you sit with mindful aspirations towards awakening, you will emerge deeply liberated from the I-am-the-the-body delusion.

One afternoon I was on the couch between two women: one going in for the usual bosom enlargement, the other for a reduction. Another time it was two noses sitting next to each other. I started to feel like I was in some sort of body garage or spare parts exchange. These days, after boob jobs, most people are there for liptosuction. Since they are going to leave their excess fat, maybe they will be in the mood to drop a few other things off as well. At my next visit I am going to distribute a few pages of the Third Zen Patriarch around the waiting room:

> Let go of longing and aversion,
> and everything will be perfectly clear.
> Cling to a hairbreadth of distinction
> and heaven and earth are set apart.
> If you want to realize the truth,
> just drop your opinions of for or against.

RIDING THE RTD

I pride myself as being one of Los Angeles' few auto-owning bus riders. When I don't have multiple errands, I take the bus. I don't often mention this in polite company. In a city that is known for its environmental oblivion and privacy obsession, conserving fossil fuel and communing through bus riding are not topics that often arise at the typical cocktail party.

I do have to admit that the RTD riding practice requires a certain bravery of soul. The last few decades have seen a definite unraveling of consciousness on the busses. Twenty years ago a typical bus might have carried one or two passengers who seemed mentally disturbed and/or potentially dangerous. Today's busses have devolved to the point that they often seem like traveling mental wards. L.A. has finally arrived at a full blown N.Y. subway situation: total fear and alienation, everyone in their own world, afraid to look at or talk to anyone else. Fortunately, I have found a skillful means with which I can board any RTD bus and, by the time I depart, a bus communion will have formed. The usual tension will have dissipated and the bus will be a veritable traveling party of friendly openness.

Native Americans burn Sage and waft the smoke to wish each other blessings and to purify an environment. This can be done with a whole bus. I am fortunate to have a nice backyard in which I grow a few sage plants. Before setting out for a bus ride, I pick a bouquet and take it along. Freshly picked sage has a strong fragrance that will quickly permeate an enclosed space, no burning is required. All you need to do is just sit there, hold your bouquet and smile. The Sage itself loosens peoples' inhibitions and separation. It won't take long before all the people, at least in your part of the bus, are talking to each other and inquiring about the Sage. The whispers grow to a murmur and a buzz.

"What is this plant that smells so good?"
"It fills the whole bus."
"It smells like incense."

Tell people that it was the incense of the local Native Americans. They would burn it or leave it in a basket and the aroma would fill their hogans for months. Then give a few branches to one or two people. Other people will ask you for some. Give away what- ever you have. Before long the whole bus will be passing it around. By the time you leave it, the bus is converted into some sort of sage drunken bar or, even better, a rolling altar

Waiting for the RTD
at Wilshire and Fairfax,
the little corner of the heart
where time meets space.
In this damn night city
people are afraid to talk to each other.
I need change but figure its useless
and can't break through.
Finally someone gets a whiff
and just gives me
the thirty-five cents.

Riding the RTD at First and Hill.
Dignified little Japanese lady
in an orchid jacket and white sun bonnet,
very precise, but maybe a retired geisha,
gets on and sits next to me.
I would have traveled across galaxies
to meet this lady,

but was only coming from First and Grand.
Even while still seated next to me
she begins her Sage arrangement.

I suppose I could have my life together.
I could drive,
But I take the 217 to work in the morning.
I like to be with the broken down
busses and people.
"Late again?" "Are they running?"
"What's going on?"
Sometimes the grumbling
unites people.
Sage is far superior.

Not much contact on the RTD.
All the people I've prayed for
but afraid to talk to.
What can I do for LA?
Break the isolation.
Practice a give-away day—
Sage and aromatic herbs
on the RTD.
Your bouquet won't arrive
intact.
Neither your heart.

So please, plant a sage garden and try it. Without this ally, defusing the fear on an RTD bus may be an impossible task. With it, it practically happens by itself. Can you imagine how the consciousness of this metropolis, and others, would transform if just five percent of bus riders carried sage bouquets?

TALK SHOCK

Spend an evening with a compulsive talker, preferably one who discourses on subject in which you have absolutely no interest. This can be a quick catapult into the deepest samadhis. Meditation is basically a self talk shock. Gradually you may get weary of your internal dialogue and just stop listening. The difficulty, of course, is that we are most interested in our own dialogue. The process is vastly accelerated if you are exposed to the deadly combination of a relentless monologue in which you have absolutely no interest. You have no choice but a quick exit to the silent depths of the mind.

You might think this is rude, but I promise you the compulsive will never be aware of the kindness they are affording you. I have availed myself of the talk shock samadhi catapult on numerous occasions. Just sit there smiling. The compulsive will be interminably oblivious that their verbal barrage is only hitting the surface of a vast ocean of consciousness, that they are helping you to enter.

The Talk-a-thon is the ultimate talk shock experience. This is when you are seated in the middle of a group of two or more compulsive talkers. I recommend taking any possible measures to contrive such a situation; you may be blessed with complete enlightenment in one evening. The best possibilities are at weddings or bar Mitzvahs. Before the event, inquire concerning the seating arrangements; if there is a table with several compulsives, request a seat at that table. The incredulous hostess will only be too glad to seat you between the infamous Aunt Gladys and cousin Esther. She was despairing of who she could seat there anyway. You will learn the art of turning an impending hell into a veritable heaven.

DRIVING MEDITATIONS

Someone once asked Suzuki Roshi to put all of Buddhism into a few words. Without hesitation he replied "Everything changes." Usually we spend our lives resisting the impermanence of all phenomena. The great masters say that Enlightenment consists only of observing, accepting and finally celebrating it. Then with each breath and step, our lives are born into a new and beautiful world.

We live with such an irresistible momentum of movement and communication today, that it often seems impossible to slow down. Some people claim that we are so out of synch with the rhythms of the planet and nature that the conditions of really deep enlightenment no longer even exist. We can have some taste of it, but knowing the complete stillness of the great old Tang masters or Advaitan Sages may no longer be possible for us.

There is always, however, the possibility that these transformed conditions can be used dialectically. Looking at it from this point of view, the best meditation might be out in the world where the inescapable truth of transience is relentlessly drilled into our head until we must escape to the polar opposite.

How can we measure the ripeness of our sitting practice? When we can non-react to someone's anger. We are given a chance to contemplate that their rage is due to ignorance and that without luck or fortunate karma, you could as easily be them and they you. With repeated practice, we can learn to let any situation pass with a a few deep breaths. The question is, how to find situations where we will you have numerous and repeated opportunities to practice responding to anger and abuse with feelings of compassion and oneness?

The best way I've found is driving the streets of L.A., especially around Beverly Hills and West L.A.—at the speed limit. Not to single out any particular personality type, but it does help to try to get in front of a convertible Mercedes, driven by a Hollywood agent type person talking on a cellular, before you slow down to the speed limit. And you can easily test your progress with this practice. When you can smile at clenched fists, 'the finger,' verbal abuse, incessant horn honking tirades and bluffed rear-end ramming charges, then you are beyond the need of any other spiritual practices.

But what if you are a non-driver? As is usually the case, the universe provides an alternative and possibly even more powerful practice. Get a job as a meter maid. (In L.A. they often walk or are on bicycles.) I'm certain that the future Roshis of the world will be drawn from the pool of meter maids—once they understand their employment's potential and utilize it as such.

MYSTICS' ALL-TIME HIT PARADE

If our eyes are open we will find dharmic truth in all of the circumstances of our lives. There are, however, certain circumstances that most clearly mirror and easily remind us of the deepest truth of our hearts. These special times and places comprise the metaphors that mystics of all traditions have used repeatedly in their attempts to describe the nature of spiritual truth. They are something like a mystic's all-time hit parade: the settings and activities which best describe spiritual reality and in which that spiritual reality can be most easily experienced. They have been the outer symbols for inner truth that mystics have referred to over and over throughout millennia.

A major benefit of any spiritual pilgrimage is that we usually bring our opened awareness home with us. The change of perspective reminds us to appreciate our ordinary mind and circumstances as being extraordinary; what we thought of as our drab and boring surroundings are actually as fascinating and awe-inspiring as wherever we've been. The hit parade may be God's gift to remind us that number one is actually in front of us right now.

THE OCEAN

Over the years, mystics of all schools endlessly describe reality as an ocean—a love ocean, awareness ocean, bliss ocean, etc. In truth, we are always playing at the edge of this ocean. We get excited at the water ocean because it is the closest that the material realm comes to approximating the vast and limitless quality of our true nature. It reminds us, perhaps at an unconscious level, that we are equally immense.

On my days off, more often than not I find myself heading towards Santa Monica or Venice; I wander the boardwalk or sit down somewhere on the beach. By the water all things seem to resonate with the universe's unlimited energy; everyone and everything—kids, birds, waves, clouds— are animated with an extra charge of excitement and adventure.

The rest of creation may give us a delusion of stability and permanence. At the ocean the mask is off; everything is in endless transformation. Moment to moment before our eyes, smooth glass turns to frothy foam to thundering breakers. At some level of consciousness we know that this is the truth of our life as well.

Meditation and the surf have a similar effect. They are something like a scrub brush, endlessly peeling away at our outer layers. In both cases, the urge toward immersion is irresistible. The next one may always be the big breaker.

The ocean and the waves are the number one metaphor that every mystic worth their salt has used to describe spiritual truth. The waves, like our sense of self, may momentarily appear to be separate. Calm the winds of our rampant thoughts and we experience our true vast ocean/one awareness being.

This heart flood
has created a body
to go swimming,
That is all.

FRUIT PICKING

Mystics are also always using the metaphor of fruit picking to describe spiritual practice. In both cases, when it is ready you only need to give a gentle tap and the most delicious gem will fall right into your hands.

There is the story of the Zen initiate who asked the master how long it would take him to attain enlightenment. "Ten years." "No I am impatient and cannot wait that long, I will try extra hard." "In that case twenty years." "No, I will work day and night." "In that case thirty years." etc. In both the orchard and meditation hall, some patience and surrendering to a process that has its own schedule for ripening is required.

In the summer, I am often seized by a fruit picking frenzy. After I've worked the trees in my backyard, I take my picking stick on a walk through the Beverly Hills alleys (for easy pickings on overhanging trees) or head up to pick-it-yourself orchards outside of Ojai. The full buckets appear at various friends and relatives homes, the DWZ and at Playmates of Hollywood

The ripe fruit is a perfect expression of the nature of our mind: a luscious explosion of soft and juicy fullness hidden inside of a seemingly hard and arid exterior. In meditation we need only to quiet our minds in order to experience our true nature as vastly intimate and tender.

The supermarket fruit has lost its flavor and luster. Eating under a real tree, we are not removed from the full cycles of nature. The fruit that falls into our hand with the slightest touch is a little shining jewel; bursting with sunlight and wet with delicious sweetness, it is a reminder of our true self and will give us a smile and full heart, as well as a full belly.

FLOWER VIEWING

You are not far from nature's most obvious, sacred and perfect altar. Probably not just one, but thousands of such altars are within a few steps of your front door. The best meditation I've ever found is just studying the shrine at the heart of every flower. Each will readily show you the nature of your heart and mind.

On flower meditation walks, I carry a few magnifying lenses—a 2x, 4x and a 10x—to help me enter deep into the flower's heart altar. Magnification opens whole universes in even the most humble flower. Each magnification level reveals a new realm of beauty and smaller creatures partaking of it. Beyond a 10x, the flower transforms to a rush of vibrant energy.

Personally, I can't figure out why the streets are not filled with lens-carrying monks and nuns. In meditation we experience that we actually are a flower; our very being is a radiating source of intimate love, beauty, tenderness and gentle grace. Even more, the whole world is part of this flower; you could say that our heart and mind are the stamin and pistil. Looking deeply into a flower's inner sanctum is one of the best meditations to remind us of our self-nature.

Every rose wants to make us proclaim that it is the most beautiful thing we've ever seen. We resist the odious business of comparisons, but the truth is that our instincts are accurate. Every flower is the sweet darling of an evolutionary beauty contest and has evolved to win the bee's attentions over the neighboring flowers. Each seems that God is shining a sacred spotlight just on it.

Flower meditation may also deepen our feelings of gratitude. Every flower is in an immediate and silent communion with the four elements. We often forget that without sunlight, earth, water, air we also could not exist for a moment. With a flower it is too obvious—we are reminded of our own interbeing and inter-dependence with all of nature.

JEWELS

The Bodhi Tree bookstore in West Hollywood is surrounded by L.A.'s 'spiritual neighborhood.' There are a few cafes, tea stalls and Eastern art emporiums, but especially there are crystal and gem shops proliferating in almost every direction. L.A.'s adepts are not the first to obsess upon the gem as the expression of enlightened consciousness, mystics have been doing this since the first hermit emerged from his cave.

The jewel is a perfect expression for the awareness that is revealed through meditation. In both cases something precious beyond description is hidden at first but revealed when either the surrounding rock and dirt or excessive mental chatter is cleared away. Most of the adjectives used to describe a beautiful gem apply equally well to the self-nature of awakened awareness; many-faceted, lustrous, brilliant, subtle, mysterious, ungraspable, beyond either hard or soft, hot or cool. In meditation, one experiences that one's own awareness is an ever transforming gem; it is always revealing subtler luster, new facets and doorways for deeper absorption.

OFF THE BEATEN PATH

I recently drove up to N. California to pay a last visit to an old dharma friend and teacher who was dying of cancer. When it was finally time to depart for L.A., his last words to me were, "Take Highway 394." In case the reader is not familiar with California, Highway 394 cannot be found on any map, because it does not exist; Chuck was offering me the perennial mystics' exhortation—to go wild.

Undoubtedly, here I can make no prescription; everyone has to find their own unique ways of going off the beaten path. However, the book must go on, so I share one of my favorites—which is to take the phrase quite literally. In the past few years I have become an addict to slow driving meditation on the back roads of Western America. Past fifty one begins to contemplate the perfect setting of one's demise: maybe at the place of one's greatest happiness. I want to die on a back road, looking up at a starry sky from the bed of my pick-up truck. Till then, I try to get someone to do the slow driving while I sit in the bed, embraced by passing beauty.

Every culture has its preferred beauty sharing communions: Japanese tea ceremonies under the cherry blossoms, French side-walk cafes, Russian winter sled rides, etc. Back roads pick-up truck touring parties is a natural for America. This book will have served its purpose if it does nothing more than present the reader with that possibility. I'm sure its time will come.

Since I commute between a Northern and a Southern California home, people are always asking me things like, "Can you make the trip in eight hours." They're often a little surprised when I answer something like, "Only thirty-six hours this time."

Find the dirt road passes on county maps.
Twenty MPH on back roads
through almond orchards and family dairies.
'Pavement ends,' in
pot holes and dust clouds
through potato and cotton fields.
An adventure
driving to L.A.
on the back roads.

Westley, Patterson, Dos Palos are
just names from the Interstate.
On the back roads,
I'm an honorary citizen.
Need to clean the windshield again,
an excuse to stop at every little town.

Rusted Klee boxcars
on a RR siding.
Barns from a Manet pallet.
Brancusi silos, cathedral silos, organ pipe silos.
Farmhouses on loan from the Met.
Everything is art comes right before
everything is God.

Giotto orchards,
Dark mother mystery orchards.
A wave that you'll never forget.
All the people you should have gotten to know
and must have been old friends from somewhere.

Old barns.
Red, green, yellow.
Thank God
for faded paint.

It's never really satisfying in L.A.,
but along the back road
passing through Mendota
a Taco Bell
is a complete experience.

Tomato harvest season.
Panoche road between Gustine and Mendota.
The loaded semis lined up on the roads
in front of the processing plants
waiting to disgorge their tomatoes.
Before its ketchup, V-8 or marinara,
stewing tomatoes aroma essence
enwreathing the countryside for miles.
Fries or burgers seem so impure.
Let mc just sit here
and breath deep
by the road.

Lower San Juaquin valley slipping by.
Broken down barns and chicken coups,
rusty tractors sinking into abandoned fields.
Even on the back roads
things are moving too fast.
This highway is the edge of longing.
At least I can contemplate
the things I could fall in love with.

Old barn, windmill,
Row of autumn poplars,
Field of tan alfalfa stubble.
From any direction
it's a pretty picture.
I stop to write poem.

Why go 80 and see nothing
when at 40 you can make love
with every old shanty town.
When you go slow
things are abandoned.
You might even try it yourself.

TWELVE THOUSAND FEET

Using the phrase 'getting high' as an expression for expanded consciousness may be a remnant from the drug culture days or may reflect the popularity of Kundalini Yoga, which describes meditation as energy rising up the spinal column. As deep meditation obliterates any idea of high or low, on one level this is a rather gross description; everything is just being—beyond any direction or dimension. On the other hand, there is something to it and the best way that I've found to get high is to just—get high.

I have an additional summer rite besides doing the back roads: wandering high up into some mountains. At about 12,000 feet, one passes through a mystical doorway. Suddenly one is as on another planet;

a beautiful vista spreads out in every direction. Every tiny clump of grass is an exquisite bouquet. Every rock or pebble part of Divinely arranged rock gardens.

At twelve thousand feet,
in wildflower fields
I grow tipsy.
Columbines and Penstemons
are more than good friends.
Waving in the wind,
reaching for the sun,
in their silence and patience
I find my true mind.
I talk to a Daisy,
it answers back
and I write silly poems.

At twelve thousand feet,
an unknown purple flower bouquet.
I graze my cheek on it,
share it with blue-winged moths
and mountain lady bugs,
shiver in the wind with it
and bundle it up
so I can kiss it all at once.
We just met
and I don't know it's name.
Some day
I'd like to try it like that
with a person.

At twelve thousand feet,
fields of purple shooting-stars
waving gaily in the breeze.
A fitting audience for a stream
coming off the slopes of Mt. Haekel.

You deserve a Wordsworth poem,
all you get is an Attie.

At twelve thousand feet,
I get dizzy.
I wander around
with five or six mentalities
and a bump of freedom.
Too weak to do anything
but sit still
and vow to love more.

MIDDLE OF THE NIGHT

When I go to sleep in the evening, I die and when I awaken in the morning I am reborn.

—Gandhi

Almost all mystical traditions observe the middle of the night as the preferred time to commune with the divine. Sufis do the dervish spin; Zen monks hold full moon meditations by their rock gardens; Hindus call to Shiva by the banks of the Ganges. Anabaptists believed that Jesus would return between midnight and two AM, so they had to be awake to await him. Westerners undoubtedly will evolve their own unique ways of observing all-night vigils. My personal preference is vending machine courtyards.

My favorite is an outdoor courtyard on the UCLA campus. Through the night they sit in a circle, humming, purring and whispering in some sort of primal chorus. Effusing a subliminal glow, with the proper supplication they dispense warmth and nourishment to the solitary sojourner. I sometimes feel the Celtic spirits called back and hovering near. Admiring Druids, praising the monolith arrangements as they once did at Stonhenge, invite the night wanderer to join in their meditation. (I wonder if in some past life I tended stone temples in Ancient Greece. Perhaps I haunt this place because it bears the closest resemblance I can find today to the old temples.)

If you don't live near UCLA and your local campus does not have an outdoor monolithic vending circle, try walking meditation in an all night supermarket. Suchness in a pyramid of Spam or Tide boxes; this is the discovery of the pop artists. Somehow, when it is just you and the night, the aisle of Pepsi cartons will shine all the brighter.

CUTE PEOPLE

Besides the above inspiring circumstances, there are also certain classes of people that are on the Mystics All Time Hit Parade. This is the compliment for such dialectical teachers as the talk-shockers, rude waiters etc. found in the previous chapter. Number one on every list is saints, enlightened masters, gurus, etc. In almost every spiritual guide ever written, no matter what the tradition, this is at the top of the list. Everyone who has ever written anything on spirituality has said that keeping the company of enlightened, spiritually advanced people is the sine qua non of spiritual life—as important or more important than meditation, precepts, good works.

There is one other class of people, however, whose company is equally beneficial to keep—cute people. Cuteness manifests in people whose existence is still half in the formless world: little children and old people—one coming from it the other going into it. Nature has made them cute so that the people who are more grounded in the material world will want to take care of them. Fortunately it's a two-way deal; if you hang out with cute people they will pull you to the formless world with them. In some states of elevated consciousness, you know that everything has half of its existence in the formless world; what the cute people make explicit you see everywhere—the whole world is cute.

AN ODE TO CUTENESS

At a fountain plaza in the center of Munich
I take my seat all day
watch the city get wet and splattered.
As things pass in the spray—they're cute.
Cigarette holding goatees,
garbage collector professor,

hard-on boys,
chicken ladies with fragile bones,
European gentlemen so dignified cute—
especially because they don't know it.

I don't know why cuteness was created,
a sub—variety of love and equally miraculous.
Any group of nuns walking across the plaza,
the way small dogs struggle to keep up,
people who don't want to have a good time,
people having a good time—
all the same in the splattering spray.

The tough guys in cool shades,
sullen, watching the girls,
part of her beauty and they don't know it.
I can't help it—they're cute.

Three and four year olds,
just not aware of that little body,
tip-toeing through hollow air.
At five or six they go to the edge
and may jump right in.
By twelve they push and throw each other
or threaten to.

Yes, we're all God's children
or at least step-children, grand-children, nieces or cousins,
related in some way in the spray.
Three year olds have a way
of sneaking up on things.
They'll settle first for just a look,
then a run around the fountain.
They make me wonder,
'What if the world
wasn't inhabited
by cute people?'

All these little jokes
are just excuses
to laugh at the big joke,
this one enormous heart
devouring the universe.
As things disappear—they're cute.

This solitary traveler feels like someone
who's snuck in and peeking at the world.
Days keeping alone to this smiling heart.
I want to talk to everyone
but hardly say a word—
just latch on to passing backbones.
I am in love with the human backbone
and the masks that God puts on it.
By this fountain in central Munich—
they're all cute.

If this book becomes a best seller and I get rich, I'm going to buy a little acreage somewhere adjacent to the Pacific Ocean. There I will dedicate the Mystics All-Time Hit Parade Gardens. Everything will be there. A beach with meditation verandahs. Fruit orchards and flower gardens: picking poles and viewing lenses provided. A gem and crystal pavilion. Tree pathways with devious direction signs and vanishing trails; people will get lost in overgrown jungles and wild thickets. The gardens will be open all hours; people will be especially welcomed at sunrise, sunset and for midnight communions amid monolithic arrangements of vending machines. Cuteness badges will be awarded to all visitors. And of course, there'll be a little stand with negligees—at discount prices.

COSMIC JOKE/COSMIC SMILE

When you get torn apart,
The mirth will bubble through.
We don't know what rolls we're playing,
So just enjoy the show
And let the universe tickle you.

One evening, after attending a performance of The Marriage of Figero, I wrote this poem and started thinking about opera, the cosmic Joke and meditation. The great comic operas of Mozart, Rossini, Donizetti are the most absurdly silly and anarchistic art ever created. The first act usually climaxes in a scene in which all of the main characters jointly declare themselves to be on the verge of insanity. Building up to this ensemble, everyone has been in disguises and involved in various intrigues and counter-plots. As the act progresses, the schemes backfire and the stage steadily descends into total chaos.

In the ensemble, the characters all sing that they no longer know who they are, what they are doing and, if their plans continue to unravel, the confusion will drive them completely insane. The strange fact, however, is that none of these characters mind losing their self-identity. Actually, they all seem to be drunkenly happy. These scenes are filled with some of the most infectiously joyous music ever written

Here, opera shares the stage with meditation. When we abandon all of our given certainties, we find our consciousness drowned in something that could be described as universal mirth. The after-effects of both meditation and comic opera are also nearly identical. For a few days after seeing one of the great comic operas, I'm just incapable of taking anything too seriously. I invariably feel like I'm stuck in something like a Laurel and Hardy movie, involved in little jokes and playful subterfuges with everyone I meet. And it's infectious; people don't mind, they're happy to have fun with you.

Meditators describe a similar 'afterglow.' After an intense meditation retreat, the world seems lit-up and filled with wonder, mystery and humor. In both cases, after a few days one's consciousness returns to normal, whatever that is. (Hopefully, for veteran meditators there is no 'back to;' that opened state of awareness becomes the 'normal.')

As one's meditation ripens, the 'Cosmic Joke' looms ever more enormous and inescapable. There are countless ways to express it: this world is just a dream shadow of reality; this very mind is the answer to all of our questions; although everything is given to us, we all go around thinking that we are doing something; we're an ocean of happiness searching the world for a drop of happiness. However one wishes to attempt to describe it, when the absurd truth of our existence dawns on us, we inevitably break out into an enormous fit of laughter.

Most humor plays with the collapse of appropriate behavior in our social roles. From the Chaplin tramp's viscous survival tactics, Laurel and Hardy's oblivious ineptitude, Marx Brothers' flagrant social anarchy, Uncle Miltie's cross-dressing, the outsider's attack on the proprieties of mainstream society has been the perennial staple. Woody Allen is the contemporary master: Jews, Wasps, Mafiosos, low-lifes, neo-hippy drop-outs, revolutionaries, urbanites, the past and future—all mixing, bruising and breaking each others rules and expectations. As a solidified chunk of one's social expectations and mental world collapses, a fit of laughter fills the void. Meditation is identical but continues to the most unexpected experience of all. When we realize that we are devoting our lives to someone who doesn't exist, the biggest joke is just—ourselves.

Since America is the planet's premier multiethnic society, it is not hard to see why our greatest export is entertainment and humor. In no other country are there such opportunities to experience people from divergent social milieus and cultures testing the limits of each others' social rules. Not surprisingly, these days another great export is dharma. Both meditation and humor tell us that we are free. We don't have to feel, think or do what we thought we had to. Fortunately, in both great humor and real dharma, the deep embrace of freedom is tempered and balanced by a compassionate heart.

A little leap of freedom in the pit of our being. A moment of the absurd. A release from some rule of bondage imposed by society or our self-image. Watching our momentary fear turn to delight when we are surprised by the totally unexpected. Right on down the line, the same phrases apply to both meditation and laughter. Our laughter is at the mercies of a good comedian or the incongruities of situations.

From the meditators vantage, the converse is true; the best way to get in the mood to meditate is to laugh. As we begin to know the spacious empty nature of our true self, there is still a momentum of ego delusion that, perhaps for lifetimes, we watch unwind—I am the person who needs this, is afraid of that, hoping, planning this , etc. and on and on. At first we might just smile at the parade. As understanding deepens, our smile might break into fits of laughter.

The new sect of Comic Opera Zen is at the leading edge in current efforts to integrate laughter and meditation. Consider the effects of attending a single performance of one of the great comic operas: at least two or three days in a light-hearted and fun-crazed daze. What would be the effect of attending two or three days straight of night and day non-stop comic opera performances? Of course, given the high costs and scarcity of opera performances, nobody knaows; up to now it has been impossible for any human being to obtain this experience. . With DVDs and wide screen TV, we no longer need to speculate but can finally subject ourselves to this experience. Will the effects be a permanent and irreversible laughing/enlightenment seizure? Will a week-end comic opera intensive achieve results that might have taken twenty or thirty years in a Zen monastery? Will this be the end of meditation halls as we have known them?

Admittedly this in taking a giant leap into unknown territory. We can't be absolutely certain where we will land. Although I believe it is ninety-nine percent certain that it will be in Universal Enlightenment, I have to admit that there is a one percent possibility that we will land in an uncharted mental landscape, in what some people might call a mental ward. Whatever the risks, the possible gains far outweigh them, so I have decided in the near future to organize the first comic opera intensive. I am looking for a few brave souls to explore this frontier with me. Please contact me if you wish to participate.

THE COSMIC SMILE

The cosmic smile is a corollary of the cosmic Joke. Where two becomes one the whole universe is smiling. The two is ourselves and the things that we think are separate from us. When we disappear into things, a smile is inevitable. And it is not so difficult to do. With some contemplation we're amazed that we've missed the most obvious fact; every person and experience of our life is creating us and allowing us this very minute. Once we get the hang of it, we are mystified that our life here is not a smiling party.

Right here and now is smiling; the street you live on, the Chinese Elm in the yard, the table and flower in front of you—everything is smiling. The question is, right here and now what are you? You cannot help but smile when you realize that right here and now has nothing to do with the separate you. That flower or Chinese Elm wants to give you its smile. You only have to drop your separation game for a moment.

SMILING PILGRIMAGES

Adobe shack gompa
overlooking Katmandu.
Two nuns serve tea-bag coffee.
Glad I don't speak the language.
Deep love happiness
wipes out
you and them,
just a stupid smile

I learned this in an early morning Kerala walk.
I couldn't find anyone
who wouldn't share it with me.
So I travel around the world,
head down lover going nowhere.
I get lost every day
and smile my way out of it.

Hardwar, Rishikish, Benares,
wandering holy cities
where I can't speak the language.
Raising hands to heaven
and the heart.
A gesture, a smile
and all is said.

Find kibitzers everywhere—
at Eat-a-Pita falafel stand,
chess players at Plummer Park,
Farmers Market morning coffee—
speaking Persian, Yiddish, Thai
or Russian.
Pilgrim to anywhere I can't understand the language,
I smile and postulate an axiom,
'We're all sharing the cosmic joke.'

As we learn to experience our non-separation from things, we usually find that our world is a reflection and extension of ourselves. Our inner smile can light up our whole world.

DON'T GO STRAIGHT DAY

I have a friend who claims that she suffers from chronic seriousness. Here and there she has tried the various remedies prescribed in this book, but she claims to need an even stronger dose of levity leavening in her life. As a last resort and strongest medicine for her serious malady, I've recommended that she practice a monthly Don't Go Straight Day.

A Don't Go Straight day is divided into five exercise periods and a grand finale.

Exercise period #1, string multiple negatives. This is a disease of the intermediate meditator. When one first realizes that nothing has an intrinsic, independent reality, every assertion has to be qualified by a disclaimer. "I'm going to get a cup of coffee" becomes "There is no person that does not know that there is no place to not go to." Of course this is great fun among friends at the Zendo, but might cause some confusion at the local coffee bar. It is sort of a half-way point; rather than get stuck in it one should proceed on to:

Exercise #2, appreciate pervasive paradox. This leads to many well known Buddhist jokes.

> "How's your son? I heard that he just lost his job."
> "It's OK, he went to a month long meditation retreat."
> "I'm glad he's not just sitting around doing nothing."

At the Dalai Lama's birthday party, monks watch the Dalai Lama open an empty box. They are proud and delighted as he exclaims, "Wow, Nothing! Just what I always wanted."

A Don't Go Straight Day, however, does not stop at a lot of dimwitted jokes but proceeds on to:

Exercise #3—pervasive ceremonies. You see and worship everything as cosmically symbolic. Tucking in the bed unites the world of form and formless. You brush your teeth and the mind mirror is bright. Buttering the toast—one mind shine. Burnt toast—all things impermanent. Sprinkling salt on a hard boiled egg you are confirming the oneness of grace and the formless field of benefaction. Your morning cup of coffee can be worshipped empty as well as full. A mysterious little smile may lead people to suspect that every action and statement portends more than meets the casual eye. They are right. The day continues and you move on to:

Exercise #4, announce everything. If done with awareness, every little action is sacred and worthy of the grandest announcement. Why short change things? Pervasive ceremonies and announcements can also be combined into one exercise: just announce every ceremony. You can also escalate and announce preparation ceremonies for every event and ceremony. "Now turning off the light switch" becomes "Prepare for turning off the light switch ceremony" becomes "Light of awareness turning off transient electrical wattage preparation ceremony." Of course, if one keeps expanding this sort of thing, turning off the light might take half a day, so, it is important to keep moving on to:

Exercise #5, see the world as song and dance, movie set, march, display, parade. Yourself too. When we are truly present, the ordinary becomes extraordinary and numinous. Taking a walk to the corner store can provide all the adventures and fascination of crossing the Andes or floating down the Amazon. The truth radiates wherever we go; every ashtray, restaurant tabletop, bookshelf, or toilet.

The five preliminary exercises finally culminate and climax in the total deconstruction of reality in all social discourse. They have been a warm-up to get us into this one mood—an adamant and absolute refusal to be serious. The paradox of everything both being and non-being leads to a complete breakdown of the usual mundane transactions of our life. They are either ruthlessly disregarded or transfigured with a transcendental purpose.

At last the world is your zendo. You refuse to take anything at face value. Wherever you are is just an excuse for awareness, nothing else matters. You are waiting for a bus that is never coming, so you can miss it a hundred times. The things that people spend their lives getting worked up over are immaterial; the world of things is an absolute joke. You see the reality that is shining through all the usual delusions of coming or going, early or late.

You can never predict what will happen during the course of a Don't Go Straight Day. My serious friend, mentioned at the beginning of this section, changed her name from Johanna to Ishkie. I don't know what it means, perhaps that's the point. But Ishkie does have sort of a cosmic cushion resonance about it. And who can take her too seriously when she introduces herself as Ishkie. Perhaps renaming should have its own exercise period.

As the DGSD deepens, you may feel that the world— wherever you go and whatever you look at—somehow is created by an essence of mystery, beauty and good-humor that pervades and gives birth to all things. Sometimes people have their first Don't Go Straight breakthrough at a long meditation intensive. This was my case. Here is a poem that I wrote when I had my realization.

The sixth day is my fun day.
I become a crock bug,
 read comics on the john,
 hang out with the bad guys
 who break the rules and have no decorum.
I do Charlie Chaplin imitations,
 bee walks and cat walks,
 and go too slow or too fast.
I hide behind the cubbies
 and steal cookies.
 Things are only good for fun or beauty.
I've had my fill of beauty,
On the sixth day—
 I go for fun.

A likely, though unnecessary precaution: Don't Go Straighters do run the risk of getting kicked out of overly serious meditation centers. They don't usually mind. Another precaution: with enough Don't Go Straight days under your belt, you may awaken one morning and find that you've become a Fun Monk (or Nun).

ODE OF THE FUN MONK

Today you be a
 Fun Monk—
Have a funkissitation
 at a kissafuntession.
Funicate & funtificate.
Use frumfuny words &
Frumfuny names:
 Frumpy Funpee,
 Curly Funearly.
Be a snoofy goofy
 &

See the world as a sideshow.
Today's Sunfun Day,
        you be in the middle—
        having some fun!

WIDE OPEN DHARMA

When we look for the one word that most nearly expresses the state of deep meditation, more often than not we end up with 'openness.' Meditation is being open to everything that is going on right now: saying yes to the passing car, to the person shuffling next to us, to whatever thoughts or feelings we are experiencing. When we say yes, not only with our thoughts, but with our muscles, our nervous system and our feelings, we become something like a vast open window, not holding on to anything and letting all things flow through us. We experience something that is often described as vastness or spaciousness; our bodies and consciousness are made of a light and expansiveness that includes everything. And we find that this spacious open yes is not so difficult to experience. When we simply quiet our minds we realize that it is always present and wants to penetrate ever deeper into our being and dissolves our separation delusion.

Sometimes, sitting ourselves down in a physical setting of a vast and open vista easily elicits a resonating response in our awareness. Seeking out such settings with an intent towards awareness, one barely needs to think of a deliberate activity such as the word meditation might imply; a spontaneous, in-the-moment openness just happens.

Some Tibetan sects have a practice that they call the "sky-mind-ground vast-space meditation." The initiate seats himself on a high ground with an unobstructed view of a wide-open sky and a vast landscape. It is most advantageous to do this practice on a day of dramatic weather. Viewing the panorama, the questions that are most central to the spiritual quest spontaneously arise. Contemplating fleeting and elusive elements as sky, clouds, rain and ever-shifting light, our usually unexamined assumption that our perceptions correspond to some objective material reality quickly implodes. It becomes obvious that our limited perceptions and point of view create a strictly subjective version that bears but only the slightest shadow resemblance of to what is actually "out there." In a sort of mental humiliation, the mind resigns and the usual separation of things collapses. We spontaneously experience the oneness of sky, ground, space and our very mind.

In a very significant way, the poorest Indian villager is wealthier than the average American millionaire. Traveling across India by train or bus, one of the first things that one notices, whether in villages, towns or cities, is that nearly every house has an attached stairway leading up to the roof. For watching the sunrise or sunset, sleeping under the stars, the Indian has easy and deliberate access to the most ideal meditation platform.

I especially like to go to places where the wide open vista is filled with features of immense proportions, reminding us of the insignificance of our little selves and of our interdependence with all of the things that create our world. The classic theme of Chinese painting has always been the tiny human swallowed in the vastness of nature. One of my favorite places is a little wooden platform under the shadow of the Brooklyn Bridge. The Manhattan skyline or endless ranges of a Chinese landscape — anything that re-balances the usually distorted perceptions of our individual self-importance will do.

CAFÉ-SITTING MEDITATION

If you don't have a roof access or a view of Manhattan, that is OK. Any place with an unimpeded view of an open setting will do. Cafes are among my favorite places to meditate. At the Don't Worry Zendo's monthly all-day meditations, in the afternoon we sometimes do walking meditation down the side streets to Fairfax Ave. and spread out at the garden tables of the Eat-a-Pita falafel stand. It is here that we've experimented with and experienced significant breakthroughs in the realm of cafe sitting meditation.

Please, sometime get together with a group of dharma friends and try it. Don't be too cavalier though, this is not just random cafe idling. One needs to be mindful of some deliberate precautions and intentional practices. Spread out at separate tables around the fringes of a cafe. Try to keep in eye contact with each other. Order only drinks, so you're not too distracted. Try not to be too conspicuous, but through eye contact, smiling and sometimes standing or spreading your arms wide, remind and bring each other to the moment.

Here are the basics of cafe practice:

Cafe Metta. Practice group lovingkindness. Extend and share a silent and secret love web. Visualize that everyone who passes through the cafe is actually passing through the one-heart awareness. Then extend the metta to each person already seated in the cafe. A koan of sorts often arises. Are you creating a love field or experiencing a love field that already exists, though no one may have been aware of it?

Be eaten. It is important to enter the cafe with an already sated appetite. If one forgets food, but is present for awareness, cafe sitting will render the transformative experience easily accessible.

Prasad. Designate someone to order one dish and pass it around. When each person takes some, think of it as communal prasad (sanctified food).

Interbeing—You are the café. The mystic's challenge is to trade in the body-love delusion for the love-body truth. When this happens, we experience that our real body is not this little bag of flesh and bones, but includes all of our surroundings and is made of love.

At certain moments, if attended to mindfully, a consciousness door opens and a leap of awareness is possible. The moment when the appetite is fully satiated is an opportunity to jump from the little body to the big body. When we finish sharing prasad, our feelings might deepen to include the fullness and well-being of all things.

HUNGRY FOR LOVE

It's not the food,
It's the atmosphere that I like—
greasy diners,
middle of the night neon-lit stands.
I'm often not that hungry—
but I like to join everyone
in the communion of home fried potatoes
at early morning cafes.

And when McDonald's grease
is the incense that permeates
an empty evening's downtown,
how can I not join in the worship

with other refugees from the city's loneliness?
I may be full,
but I like to look
in someone's refrigerator
and let them know I was there
with a bite of friendship.

And my old lady neighbor baker,
when they're right out of the oven
I've got to be able to tell her
how delicious and chewy the bagels are.

I'll end up fat.
There is something invisible,
I don't know how to eat it—
my mouth
my arms
my nose—
I really want to eat with my heart.
The belly is a sad excuse.
It's all I have.

MINDFUL LOITERING

People usually live their life in a rush; they are busy and going somewhere. Meditation is often separate from this life; in a darkened room with altar and incense, they take a little time out from the busy world to do some practice or offer some prayer. They make the mistake of thinking that Enlightenment is something big or separate, so they miss it at every moment of their lives. The challenge, fun and beauty of dharma is to live our lives so that Enlightenment is not in that separate room but our whole world, in every insignificant thing and step of the way. When we are intimate with the cup on the table, the tufts of grass growing through the pavement cracks, the row of newspaper vending machines, the fire hydrant—enlightenment will be right now.

For some strange reason there are still anti-loitering laws in effect through out much of America. This may be the last vestige of our

Puritan work ethic heritage and is a national tragedy of the highest order. Loitering is probably the healthiest activity we can engage in, but somehow we often need to find an excuse for just hanging around. If your wallet cannot afford afternoons of cafe sitting meditation, that is no problem. Parks are an equally viable alternative setting for wide-open meditation.

Park benches make the best Zendo.
Far superior to black cushions and blank walls.
This is what the heart looks like.
There are people passing through,
flocks of pigeons,
nannies with strollers,
old men sharing stories in the autumn air,
kids playing jump rope
and on their way to school,
Oak and Maple leaves raining on everyone.
I don't know if I want to die of happiness
or sadness
or just fade away.
I look up.
everyone is gone.
Time to move on
to the next park.
Find my heart again.

I'm the lazy poet
who needs to fall in love
in order to write anything.
It's a crazy world—
there's too much beauty
or not enough.
Either way,
the pain seems inescapable.

GRACE

Beginning meditators often take themselves and their practice very seriously. There is a definite meditator doing a definite practice. With time, things are not so clear cut. We increasingly feel that the universe is conspiring to help our meditation. We are not so much doing it as just opening to allow the forces of nature to work through us. The same forces that grow the trees or move the clouds are opening, guiding and filling our meditation.

When something fantastic happens in our life, we know that we cannot and did not do it—it is a gift from beyond us. This is where religious feeling originates. During orgasm may be when most people first get religious and exclaim "Oh God, Oh God!" In most of our lives we are preoccupied with what we are going to do and can do. During orgasm we momentarily forget such things and just open in gratitude to the gift of pleasure that comes from beyond our capabilities.

If we love something enough, no matter what it is, we usually stop and thank some power greater than ourselves. I like the scene in Patton where George C. Scott stops by the side of the road and proclaims with fervent emotion, "I love war! God help me I do love it so. I love it more than my life." This may be a soldier's Grace.

The meditator's Grace can't be described, though the whole of this book has been my feeble attempt. As the feeling of the heart opens and becomes intimate, we know that it has nothing to do with the little us, yet it is what we are. As our practice becomes filled with Grace, we realize that trying to make this happen would be no different than trying to make the sun rise, the sky be blue or a tree just be.

Dharma is something like re-balancing our lives between the 'can-do' and 'cannot- do.' When we allow ourselves to become aware of the cannot-do which allows the can-do that we are obsessed with, Grace begins to flow in our meditations and lives. It is the greatest and most inconceivable cannot-do of all. We know it is totally and absolutely a gift from something outside of and greater than our little selves.

> For the moment you get into the quest for the self and begin to go deeper, the real self is waiting there to receive you, and then

> whatever is to be done is done by something else and you, as an individual, have no hand in it....At first it is impossible for you to be without effort. When you go deeper, it is impossible for you to make any effort....If you go one tenth of the way, the inner guru will come nine tenths of the way to met you.
>
> —Ramana Maharshi

Here we encounter the ancient paradox of effort and grace. We must take the one first step; this is the effort. It is absolutely essential. For the one step we take towards reality, it will take ten steps towards us: to come and meet and carry us home. Really, just putting some time aside and sitting is all one needs to do, and maybe about all one can do. With this much effort, the inner teacher begins the process of opening, unfoldment and enfoldment.

> There is butter in milk, but one must patiently churn the milk to release it. There is oil in mustard seed, but one must gather the seeds and place them under great pressure to extract this nourishing and delicious substance. Immense fish live in the depths of a large lake, but to glimpse them you must throw spiced bait into the water. Although Divine Grace is omnipresent, to receive this Grace takes more effort and skill than churning butter, pressing oil or catching carp.
>
> —Ramakrishna

Well, maybe it takes three or four steps. Aitken Roshi says, "Meditation is just wearing out the brain so it will finally give up." As it starts to give up, grace will flow.

Grace is the disappearing act into the universe's gift of love that one often first experiences in sitting. An understanding that all phenomenon are part of this gift becomes irresistible and all-consuming. At first the channel of our life is like a stream whose banks are high cliffs. For the seasoned meditator the banks become shallower. Finally the stream overflows onto the vast flood plains of all of our surroundings.

Paul Reps, an early Western Zen poet, was walking on a Northern California beach and was amazed to see a Japanese Zen monk meditating on the sands. (This was in the 1950's when such an encounter was still a great rarity.) Reps went up to the monk and asked him, "What is Zen?" The monk immediately replied, "Zen is love."

I have an old neo-hippy friend who's name was once 'Love is Everywhere.' It would always be nice to encounter him coming down the road because I could call out, "Hey, Love is Everywhere—." Times have changed and lately he's known as Clearwater. But I think I'm going to revert to calling him Love is Everywhere, because this is actually the deepest truth of our heart and our lives. It is the deepest truth that we can learn to experience in meditation as well.

1650, 1950, 2150—it will always be the same. Love is Everywhere. As a final attempt to say it all in one word—this misused and often abused one is still the closest: Love. Maybe I should have headed each chapter 'Non-Duality is Love,' 'Emptiness is Love,' 'Self-Inquiry is Love.' I've reached the end of the book and I still wonder if I've been blatant enough. Everything else was just footnotes and preparations—do I need a LOVE chapter to say the main thing? Maybe a few poems will do.

THE LOVE ZOO

Valentine's Day,
morning tea at the
Farmers Market.
Some skywriter spreading
big hearts above L.A.
I'm scribbling poems on Darjeeling
tea bag packet.

The connection is always here,
just a question of finding people to celebrate it with.
Maybe I'm the fool,
and everyone is celebrating.
Why do I have to make things so explicit?

Groups of French or German tourists
wandering through the market,
cameras at ready,
eyeing the morning's regulars.
We're all in each other's zoo,
casing and sizing each other up;
"How can I fall in love?"

Word games—
How many words will get you
into someone's heart?
Find the shortest route.

THE LOVE MOTHERS

Afternoon tea at Fred Segal's
Malibu cafe and playground.
Oh God, keep me from trying to say it.
A day when things seem to be floating,
dogs running around free,
strangers bussing each other dishes,
seagulls kettling high and
pigeons flocking through the swaying eucalyptus.
Kids on swings and slides,
babies in strollers and love-mothers everywhere.
African, Latin and All-American mothers,
Jewish mothers and little old grand-mothers too.

Babies are for more
than just perpetuating the species.
We forget
but they remind us.
Every baby is a whole universe,
and we too
outside the edges of out beings,
are love,
    are love,
        are love.

THE LOVE THOUGHTS

When the heart is open
          you won't mind the thoughts.
They'll have to follow along
          and can't get too far away,
become stupid and useless
          love thoughts

          like

when the mind is still
what does the heart know—
only love.

          or

When the heart opens
it becomes the heart
of the whole universe.

          or

All the things of your life
are in love with each other,
just stay out of their way.

          or

This is real,
This is love,
This is your very self.

ACKNOWLEDGEMENTS

The author wishes to thank the following authors and publishers for permission to quote from their works.

Yoel Hoffmann, *Japanese Death Poems*, Charles Tuttle Co., 1986.

I Am That: Talks with Sri Nisargadatta Maharaj, trans. Maurice Fryman, edit. by Sudhakar S. Dikshit, Acorn Press, 1982.

Rainer Maria Rilke, *Book of Hours and Love Poems to God*, trans. Anita Barrows and Joanna Macy, Riverhead Books, 1996.

The Essential Rumi, trans. Coleman Barks, Harper San Francisco, 1995

ABOUT THE AUTHOR

Michael Attie has been a student of Zen, and Vipassana Buddhism and Advaita Vedanta for over 40 years. In the sixties and seventies he joined the Western pilgrimage to Asia, residing in Japanese Zen monasteries and Indian Ashrams. In 1973 the revered Indian Guru, Neem Karoli Baba told him to teach Dharma in the West. Ever Since then he has been pursuing his Guru's instructions through a variety of mediums, always emphasizing the recurrent theme that one need look no farther than the current circumstances of one's life for spiritual inspiration.

After Michael returned to America and inherited Playmates of Hollywood, he performed *The Lingerie Zen Review* to packed houses to celebrate his dual life as meditator and panty salesman. A few years later Michael performed the *The Zen Opera Show* around California, celebrating opera-mania as a shortcut to spiritual enlightenment. His new performance piece, *Buddha to Broadway*, demonstrates that one needn't learn Tibetan or Sanskrit to study dharma. It is all there--in Gershwin, Berlin, Porter and Johnny Mercer. Michael is currently filming *Dog Realization*, a documentary on 'Canine Tantra;' through loving our dogs, we can learn to love the whole universe.

Michael founded and owns DharmaBanners, a company that designs and markets prayer flags in English, of all the world's spiritual traditions. He also plays the accordion with the PujaToons, specializing in Musette, Tango, Klezmer and American Swing tunes. Michael currently resides in Los Angeles, where he founded and teaches Dharma at the Don't Worry Zendo.

Michael has authored two books of poetry, *This Smiling Heart* and *The Love Beggars*. The poems are reflections on a life lived with humor, playfulness, and an open heart.

For more information on Michael's schedule &/or to order books, please click onto www:dontworryzendo.com